Daily Mail

SAVINGS &
INVESTMENTS GUIDE

D0264151

JANE VASS

P
PROFILE BOOKS

For Francis Vass

First published in Great Britain in 2005 by
Profile Books Ltd
3A Exmouth House
Pine Street
Exmouth Market
London ECIR OJH
www.profilebooks.com

Typeset in Plantin by MacGuru Ltd
info@macguru.org.uk

Printed and bound in Great Britain by
Clays, Bungay, Suffolk

A CIP catalogue record for this book is available from the British Library.

ISBN 1 86197 738 7

Contents

Acknowledgements

I would like to thank Tony Hazell and his team at *Money Mail*, Nicholas Conyers of Pearson Jones, Imogen Clout, and the many organisations that reviewed sections of the text. Special thanks are due to Gillian Cardy of Professional Partnerships who undertook the Herculean task of reviewing the whole manuscript.

Stephen Brough of Profile Books has, as always, been a tremendous master of ceremonies and I am very grateful for his help, and for that of Penny Williams, Jonathan Harley, Ian Paten and Diana LeCore.

However, all errors remain my own, and I welcome comments, via the publisher.

Jane Vass

Note

Everyone's personal circumstances are different and the rules and regulations affecting savings and investments frequently change. If by chance a mistake or omission has occurred I am sorry that neither I, nor the *Daily Mail*, nor the publishers can take responsibility for any loss or problem you suffer as a result. But if you have any suggestions about how the content of the guide can be improved, please write to me, care of the publisher, Profile Books, 3A Exmouth House, Pine Street, Exmouth Market, London ECIR OJH.

Introduction

Our savings have been under attack from all directions in recent years. The government takes more in tax, the stockmarket is only gradually recovering from several years of turmoil and some people have been sold totally inappropriate investments. Against this background we are being told that we must take more responsibility for our own financial welfare. We need to save more over the long term to ensure a comfortable retirement and more over the shorter term to provide for day-to-day essentials as well as for the 'luxuries' we now expect, such as holidays or a new car.

With such a wide range of products to choose from and continuing unease about the safety of investing, where do we start? Better financial education has to be the answer – not just in schools but throughout our adult lives. We must arm ourselves with sufficient knowledge and understanding so that when we are offered a new product we know the right questions to ask and can make sense of the small print. And when we have money to invest, we need to have a clear idea of the type of investment we require and the risks we are prepared to take.

This is where the *Daily Mail Savings & Investments Guide* comes in. Split into two parts, it explains saving strategies and looks in detail at all the products you are likely to come across.

As investors we are facing a period of immense change instigated by both government and the savings industry. In April 2006 the rules governing pensions will be overhauled, making them more flexible in many respects but at the same time removing one or two perks. One of the benefits is that many of the restrictions on saving into a pension will be removed, so as long as your earnings are large enough, there will simply be annual limits of £215,000 and a lifetime limit of £1.5 million. Another change will allow savers whose total pension savings are £15,000 or less to take the whole pension as a lump sum.

For those who prefer to save without risk, banks and building societies can offer terrific deals, often paying more than the Bank of England base rate. In the best of these, children have been able to earn double-digit returns for no risk on their regular savings. Pensioners, too, are benefiting from better deals on high-street savings accounts offered by several building societies following a *Money Mail* campaign.

On the other hand, the worst savings deals have become even worse. Many banks and building societies still pay less than 1% interest on high-street accounts. There has also been an increasing reliance on small print, catches and clauses. Top-paying accounts may restrict the number of withdrawals you're allowed to make or contain short-term bonuses which vanish after a few months.

This guide explains how to be on your guard when hunting out the best deals. As far as choice of products is concerned, savers have never had it so good. There are now niche products for people at each end of the risk spectrum. So if you want to boost your retirement income or find a no-risk savings account to get you started, or if you are a sophisticated investor and are prepared to risk your capital for a potentially higher reward, there are investments to suit. In addition, regulations governing investing are tighter than ever, offering more protection to consumers.

Our guide takes you through all of these investments, whether they are stockmarket-linked investment bonds, unit trusts or with-profits bonds. You'll find sections explaining risk and how to put the basic building blocks of your savings into place. There are also pointers on where to get help and clear explanations of the different products you can use in your particular situation. And 'jargon alerts' put the more complicated terms into plain English.

To help you further, Part 2 contains detailed explanations of the main types of savings products. In addition, you'll find useful tables showing the level of return you can expect from your savings and how inflation can eat into your money. So whether you are confused about how Individual Savings Accounts (ISAs) work or you want to know how much tax is charged on a particular investment, you will find it here.

I very much hope you enjoy reading the *Daily Mail Savings & Investments Guide*, and I am sure you will find it an indispensable tool when it comes to planning your own family finances.

Tony Hazell
Editor, *Money Mail*
July 2005

How this book can help you

Some people in the savings industry think that investments are like a car – customers don't need to know what is under the bonnet, they just need to know that it works. Don't believe it. So many problems – from endowment mortgages to with-profits bonds – have arisen because people simply didn't realise what they were getting into, and nobody made it clear to them.

Now, more than ever, you need to understand what is happening to your money. We are increasingly expected to fend for ourselves. These days, if you get a new job, you may have to pay more into your employer's pension scheme. If your child is one of the 44% who go on to college or university, you are more likely to have to support them. If your offspring then want to buy a home, house price inflation means that they are more likely to need some help from you. There is also a great deal of wringing of hands in government circles about what is called the savings gap – the estimated £27 billion difference between what the great British public need to save to provide for a comfortable retirement, and what they are actually saving. We can expect to hear much more about the need to save.

So what is putting people off? These are some typical comments:

'I just haven't got round to it.'
If this rings a bell with you, you've just taken the first step by buying this book. Be comforted by the fact that the first step may be the most difficult: research has found that people who start saving usually keep saving.

'It's not worth saving. I won't be any better off than those who don't bother to save and just rely on state benefits.'
Yes, if your income is low and you haven't got much put by already. But not saving is a risky strategy – the rules could change. And the means-tested pension credit, which tops up state pensions and is thought to be putting people off saving, now gives most people some reward for saving. (See page 243.)

'I can rely on my house.'
There are growing numbers of schemes that allow you to raise cash on your property. But recent research has suggested that few people will be able to

raise enough money to do anything more than top up their income – even assuming that their property never falls in value.

'It's all too complicated.'
True. All too often, investment is presented as some sort of black art, and if you are into that sort of thing there is plenty of scope for complexity. But for most people it needn't – and shouldn't – be so tricky.

What you really need to save safely

Know-how
You don't need a degree in rocket science. You do need some know-how and you might need some tools, in the form of investment schemes and savings accounts. But it's important to remember that you might not actually need to buy anything. Just sorting out what you've already got may be all that is needed.

The first part of this book will take you through the know-how, broken down into four steps:

- review
- plan
- choose
- review again

Review
Look at what you are trying to achieve, your current finances and what sorts of risk you are prepared to take.

Chapter 1 will help you decide on your savings goals and how much money you have to put away. This will determine how long you can put your money away for and what types of investment are suitable. But you may not actually need to buy anything – you may find that reducing your debt is the best way for you to save.

Chapter 2 explains the different sorts of risk, the regulators that may be able to protect you, and how you can protect yourself. Risk includes not just whether you feel able to invest in the stockmarket, where the value of your money could rise or fall, but also things like the effect of inflation.

Plan

Think about what types of saving and investing might suit you, and how you can put together all your financial assets into a sensible framework, including your existing investments. Chapter 3 describes the building blocks. Chapter 4 explains the tax rules and how you can use them to your advantage. And if you think you'll need advice, Chapter 5 covers choosing an adviser, and how to get the best out of them.

Choose

Remember that you may not need to buy a savings plan or investment scheme at all. But if you do, Chapter 6 will help you decide which account or fund to go with. Chapter 7 explains what sort of investment to use for various purposes, such as providing income or saving for your children.

Review again

Many people choose an investment and then forget about it. Don't fall into this trap – review your plans regularly. But keep it simple, otherwise your good intentions could come to nothing. Chapter 8 suggests some ways of staying on top of things, and has checklists to help you keep your records tidy.

Tools

Once you have the know-how, you can consider the tools. In Part 2 we look 'under the bonnet' of the main types of savings and investment available. These are listed in alphabetical order, from annuities to unit trusts. For each type of investment we explain how it works, the good and bad points, the risk factors, the tax treatment, how much it costs, how to buy and what alternatives there are.

Lastly, the Fact file has contact details for all the organisations named in the book and other useful information.

Throughout this book, look out for 'Trade secrets', giving useful tips, and 'Jargon alerts', explaining some of the jargon you might come across.

Jargon alert

Saving or investing?

Saving generally describes a home for your money where you get back at least the amount you put in (your capital). Investment usually suggests that you could get back less than you put in. But don't get hung up on it. The terms are often used interchangeably.

Trade secret

Beware the 'flavour of the month'

The herd instinct is strong in financial services, and once someone has what seems to be a cunning plan, others pile in. But what may be a good idea for some people is dangerous for others. This has led to problems such as the mis-selling of endowment mortgages, split capital investment trusts and with-profit bonds. Another problem is that private investors often find out too late about the really good deals – the risk is that you buy at the top of the market, just as people 'in the know' are getting out.

Visit our website for updates
that may affect this book:
www.janevass.net/investment

Part 1

The know-how

1

....

Know yourself

'Know yourself' was a favourite saying of the ancient Greeks and it's a good starting point for managing your money. It is also the professionals' first step: if you go to a financial adviser, they will usually work through what they call a 'fact find' with you, collecting information about your needs and your existing investments.

In practice, of course, many financial decisions are taken under pressure: for example, when moving house, deciding what to do with money given to your new baby or trying to use up your tax allowances as the end of the tax year approaches. However, even these decisions become easier if you have a framework to set them in. You can also avoid some expensive mistakes with a bit of forethought. So, in your quest for self-knowledge, first ask yourself:

- What are my goals in life and what money will I need to meet them?
- What have I already got?

Carry out a stock-take of your financial assets and liabilities. Don't forget to include money you owe and any insurance policies that protect your home and family.

> Trade secret

Define your 'savings style'
The financial industry's marketing gurus tend to categorise people under headings such as 'careful shoppers' and 'family spenders' and then use these categories to target their advertising. A realistic assessment of your own strengths and weaknesses may help you, too – and not just as a way of recognising and resisting the tricks of financial ads.

> ## Trade secret

Adapt your planning to your lifestyle

There is no point coming up with a perfect savings plan that you abandon after a couple of months because it doesn't fit in with your lifestyle. For example, if money in your bank account trickles away on inessentials, consider setting up a regular standing order into a savings account. If regular saving is not easy for you – because you're self-employed, say – internet accounts which allow you to transfer money easily between accounts are helpful. And unless you have the time and inclination to monitor your savings and investments, or the money to pay someone else to do it, keep things simple.

Setting your goals

The single most common reason people give for not saving more is 'there always seems to be something more immediate to spend my money on'. Many people don't really save for anything specific, they just put money aside. But it is helpful to set some goals in order to avoid today's needs swallowing up tomorrow's income.

Another reason for setting goals is that it will help you decide when you will need to cash in your investment. Some types of investment are best kept for a minimum period (such as stocks and shares and life insurance), so setting some time horizons will help you narrow down the range of suitable homes for your money. Chapter 3 will give you further information.

Here are some examples of common savings goals:

- *Rainy-day savings.* Unless you have a good disposable income, it may take a bit of time to build up an adequate safety cushion. Consider some form of regular saving.
- *Saving for a major purchase.* For example, to replace your car. You need a clear timescale in mind so that you don't tie yourself up in a fixed-period savings scheme with penalties for early withdrawal.
- *Saving for a home.* If you are buying your first home, the larger your deposit the lower is the likely cost of a mortgage. If you are a homeowner with an endowment mortgage or other interest-only mortgage, you may need extra savings to be sure of being able to repay

the loan (see page 20).

■ *Children's education.* From 2006, students in higher education may have to pay tuition fees of up to £3,000 a year. These won't have to be paid until after the student leaves college, but you may want to pick up the bill to avoid your child starting adult life in debt.

■ *Finding a home for a child's own money.* The birth of a child often brings a succession of small cash gifts 'for the baby', and babies born after 31 August 2002 also receive a minimum £250 Child Trust Fund voucher from the state to be invested on the child's behalf (see page 150).

■ *Retirement.* Use the sections on state and private pensions in Part 2 to check how much pension you might get. Consider when you are likely to start withdrawing from the world of work, and how your savings plans might be affected if this were to happen five years earlier (or later) than expected. Also work out how much income you will need to draw from your savings in order to top up your pension.

■ *Preparing for long-term care.* If you need to go into a care home, you will usually have to pay the cost yourself, unless your income and assets are very low or unless you have been assessed as needing nursing care (and personal care in Scotland). Alternatively, there may come a time when an elderly relative has to move in with you, perhaps reducing your own ability to work or requiring home alterations.

You will need to review your goals regularly in the light of changing circumstances in your life and also external changes, such as a drop in house values. There is more about specific goals in Chapter 7.

Jargon alert

Growth or income?

You may be asked if you are investing for income or growth. If you do not need to draw an income from your savings now, and your aim is to preserve your existing savings for future use, you are a growth investor. This doesn't mean that growth investors should choose only schemes that pay no income, or that income investors should confine themselves to income-producing investments. Growth investors can reinvest income, and people seeking income may be able to cash in part of a growth investment at intervals.

Taking stock

Few people start with a clean slate, so first carry out a stock-take of all your savings and investments, your pensions, insurance policies, your mortgage and other money owed. This will help you decide on your savings goals (see Example 1.1 on page 12) and where your priorities should lie.

Completing Tables 1.1 and 1.2 on pages 10 and 11 will provide you with a summary of all your financial assets and debts. However, you also need a record of each of your savings accounts or investments. Chapter 8 has a checklist that you can fill in and keep.

Think about your family

If you are living with someone, it makes sense to take stock jointly. Also think about the impact if either of you were no longer around. Would those left behind be able to cope financially?

You need to check which of the following types of life insurance would pay out for your family:

■ *'Death in service' cover from your job.* This might be, say, four times your salary. Check with your company's personnel department.
■ *Life insurance with your mortgage.* If you have an endowment mortgage, you should already have enough cover; if you have any other type of mortgage, you may have a special mortgage protection insurance policy to cover it.
■ *A separate protection-type life insurance policy.* A whole life policy covers you for the whole of your life; a term insurance or family income benefit policy pays out only if you die within a set term.

A prolonged period of illness or unemployment could also have serious consequences. You may have the following types of insurance cover to protect you:

■ *Critical illness insurance,* which pays a lump sum if you are diagnosed with various types of serious illness, such as cancer or a stroke.
■ *Income protection insurance* (sometimes known as permanent health insurance), which pays out a regular income if you cannot work.
■ *Payment protection insurance,* which covers loan or mortgage payments

for one or two years if you are unable to work because of accident, sickness or, sometimes, unemployment. This is often sold as part of the cost of a loan.

Note that hospital cash plans and private medical insurance do not count. These only pay out to cover specific health costs and won't replace your income. An accidental death benefit policy is often tacked on to other financial products (such as credit cards) and may pay out only small sums, in limited circumstances.

Jargon alert

Life insurance

It's often difficult to be sure what sort of life insurance policy you've got:

■ Protection-only life insurance policies pay out only if you die; illness or unemployment policies pay out only if something happens that is covered by the policy (for example, critical illness policies cover you against a specific list of serious illnesses).
■ Other policies are savings-type. Your money is invested for you, so they should pay out at some point (how much depends on how well the investment does). These are covered on page 196.

Some protection policies (such as some whole life policies) invest some of your money, rather than using it all to provide cover. This means your policy may have a cash-in value if you do not claim on it. But do not count on this: it may be very small. If a surrender value is shown somewhere on your documentation, part of your policy is invested in this way. If in doubt, ask the insurance company.

Completing the tables

If you have a partner you can either complete the tables jointly or complete one each. But if you are filling them in separately, remember to include only half of any joint income or investments.

First use Table 1.1 on page 10 to work out how much spare income you have, or how much extra you need. Enter the annual amount of income you are receiving under 'income now' in the 'Money coming in' section of the table. Also enter any income from pensions, state benefits, savings and investments, or other sources. Add up the figures in the column and enter the result in the 'Total income' row.

If most of your income is received after tax, just enter the amount you actually receive. However, if your tax is paid separately (for example, because you are self-employed or a higher-rate taxpayer) you should enter it as an outgoing.

Next you need to enter any outgoings, such as mortgage and loan repayments under 'Money going out'. Work out your regular spending on things like household bills, transport and clothing and enter it under 'other outgoings'. (More detailed budget calculators are available on several websites, including that of the Financial Services Authority.) Deduct your total outgoings from your total income to find out how much spare cash you have.

Now you can move on to Table 1.2 and your assets and liabilities. Enter in the 'value now' column the amount you would get if you sold or cashed in your financial assets tomorrow. Some things can't be sold immediately: for example, pensions and long-term insurance policies are designed to run for a set period. (Some insurance policies can be cashed in early but this is rarely a good idea.) Leave the 'value now' boxes for these things empty.

Your main liability is likely to be your mortgage. Enter the amount outstanding under 'owed now' (you should already have entered the repayments in Table 1.1). Your annual mortgage statement should tell you how much you still owe, and if you have an endowment mortgage you should have received a forecast of its possible value from the insurance company (see page 20).

Deduct your debts from the value of your assets to find out how much you are worth at present.

Looking ahead

So far you have established your overall financial position today. You can also use the 'value later' columns to work out where you might be at some point in the future. Retirement is an obvious point, but you could also use it for shorter periods such as when your children leave school. It is also a good idea for couples to use it to check how much they would have if one partner died or was disabled.

Some pension schemes provide combined pension forecasts that cover both your state pension and your private pension. Otherwise, you can get a forecast of your state pension from the government's Pension Service (see the Fact file). If you have a private pension, you should get regular statements from your pension company or employer's personnel department (see Chapter 8 if you have lost touch with the company). You may be entitled to both a pension and a lump sum, as well as death benefits if you die before retirement.

Don't forget that by retirement you might have paid off debts like your mortgage, so the 'cost later' for this might need to be changed to zero.

When thinking about your future position, you hope that your assets will appreciate in value. However, inflation will probably reduce the spending power of your money (this is covered in Chapter 2). Most pension schemes now provide a projection of your future pension in today's prices. So it's simplest, when using the table, to work entirely in today's values, without adjusting things like the expected value of your home.

Are you covered?

Lastly, check the amount of insurance you have. Any loan or mortgage documentation should say whether you have any related insurance that would meet your loan repayments if you were to die or have to stop work. But you may also have free-standing policies or some linked to your job (ask your personnel department), so make a note of the cover you have for each type of loan or for your income generally in the 'insured' column.

Enter any insurance that just meets the repayments on a loan, or pays you an income, in the 'insured' column in Table 1.1. Any insurance that pays off the loan altogether, or pays you a lump sum, should go in Table 1.2. There is more about insurance to protect you and your family on page 14.

Table 1.1: Money coming in and going out

Money coming in	Insured?	Income now	Income later
Earnings/business profits			
Other income (e.g. state benefits, tax credits, rental income)			
State pension			
Employer's pension			
Other pensions			
Interest on savings			
Dividends from investments			
Total income			

Money going out	Insured?	Annual cost now	Annual cost later
Mortgage payments			
Loans/hire purchase			
Credit & store cards			
Tax (if paid separately)			
Other outgoings (e.g. household costs, insurance and pension, transport, food, clothing, leisure)			
Total outgoings			
Deduct outgoings from income to find your spare income (or income shortfall)			

Table 1.2: How much are you worth?

Assets	Insured?	Value now	Value later
Your home			
Other property & possessions			
Mortgage endowment policy			
Pension lump sum			
Savings accounts & National Savings			
British Government stocks & other bonds			
Investments (e.g. unit trusts, shares, savings-type life insurance)			
Total assets			

Debts	Insured?	Owed now	Owed later
Mortgages			
Loans/hire purchase			
Credit & store cards			
Total debts			
Deduct debts from assets to find your total wealth (or debts)			

Example 1.1: **Financial stock-taking**

Anya has recently returned to work full-time. She and her husband Errol want to put some money aside to help their daughter through college in about five years' time, and to meet the shortfall on their endowment mortgage which is due to mature shortly before they retire. They also have to find £1,500 in a year's time to pay off a car loan.

Their joint income is just over £30,000 after tax (their tax is taken off their pay so they do not need to account for this separately), and after deducting their outgoings they find that they should be able to save about £240 a month. They have insurance to cover their mortgage and loan payments if they cannot work or if they die, and Errol has some life and health insurance from his job. But they would feel happier with a bit more cash in the bank to cover emergencies.

They use the 'later on' columns to work out their retirement income. By then they hope to have paid off their mortgage, so their outgoings will fall, but even so they will be short of income. Errol expects a small pension from his job, but Anya has none.

Next, Anya and Errol check their assets and debts. In the 'value now' column they enter the full value of their home (£120,000), and the £60,000 mortgage under 'debts'. Because it is an endowment mortgage they don't pay off any of the loan until the end of the term, so £60,000 also belongs in the 'value later' column. However, their endowment policy is projected to pay out £45,000, which they enter as an asset in the 'value later' column. So far their only savings are £1,500 in the building society and £750 in various shares. If they die, the endowment policy would repay the mortgage; Errol has some life insurance from his job, but Anya has none.

The stock-take helps Anya and Errol decide that in the coming year they should build up their building society account to pay off the car loan and increase their emergency savings. Anya should also shop around for some cheap life insurance. This won't leave much spare cash this year but next year they will have a further £150 a month once the car loan is paid off. At that stage, as well as building up savings to help their daughter, they could ask their lender about making extra capital repayments to help pay off their endowment mortgage shortfall. They should also consider some longer-term savings. Although they are reluctant to tie up their spare cash in pension contributions, they could think about a stocks and shares ISA.

Table 1.3: Anya and Errol's stock-take

Money coming in	Insured?	Income now	Income later
Earnings/business profits	✓ (Errol)	£30,000	0
Other income		£1,169	0
State pension		0	£8,278
Employer's pension		0	£3,339
Interest on savings		£45	£45
Dividends from investments		£10	£10
Total income		*£31,224*	*£11,672*

Money going out	Insured?	Annual cost now	Annual cost later
Mortgage payments	✓	£3,000	0
Loans/hire purchase	✓	£1,800	0
Credit & store cards	✓	£6,000	0
Other outgoings		£17,540	£12,340
Total outgoings		*£28,340*	*£12,340*
Spare income (or income shortfall)		£2,884	(£668)

Assets	Insured?	Value now	Value later
Your home	✓	£120,000	£120,000
Other property & possessions	✓	£20,000	£20,000
Mortgage endowment policy		0	£45,000
Pension lump sum		0	£10,000
Savings accounts & National Savings		£1,500	£1,500
Investments		£750	£750
Total assets		*£142,250*	*£197,250*

Debts	Insured?	Owed now	Owed later
Mortgages	✓	£60,000	£60,000
Loans/hire purchase	✓	£5,000	0
Credit & store cards	✓	0	0
Total debts		*£65,000*	*£60,000*
Total wealth (or debts)		£77,250	£137,250

Plugging the gaps

Once you have a good picture of your overall finances, you can decide where the gaps are and decide how to plug them. You need to:

- review your life and health insurance
- make sure you have enough rainy-day savings to see you through a few lean months
- deal with your debt
- decide how much you can afford to save, and for how long.

Life insurance cover
The diagnosis

How did the 'insured' column in your stock-taking chart look?

If there is nobody who would suffer financially if you died, you may not need life insurance, but everybody else will need some. As a rule of thumb, you should have at least enough life insurance to pay off all your debts, plus enough to replace your lost income until your children are no longer financially dependent.

Less insurance may be necessary if you currently pay out a lot on loans or mortgages that would be paid off by special insurance policies on death. But remember that your partner will need to cover costs such as extra childcare. Many money websites have life insurance calculators (including the *Daily Mail* 'thisismoney' website).

If your total assets are more than the inheritance tax threshold (£275,000 for deaths in the 2005–06 tax year), you may also want life insurance to meet the tax bill. This is particularly important if you and your partner are not married: anything you leave to your husband or wife is tax-free, but this does not apply to unmarried couples.

The prescription

- *For young families.* The cheapest, simplest and usually the most suitable types of insurance are either family income benefit or term insurance. You are covered for a set amount for a set number of years and get nothing back if you don't die within that time. Family income benefit insurance pays out a regular tax-free income, whereas term insurance pays out a tax-free lump sum. You can buy these types of insurance online, over the telephone, or through a financial adviser.

■ *If you really need lifetime cover.* Whole life insurance will pay out whenever you die, so it's usually more expensive. Another disadvantage is that the premiums may not be guaranteed to stay the same – they could rise at intervals.

■ *If you have a partner.* Look at your needs as a couple – a non-working partner is just as likely to need to be covered for the costs of childcare and so on. You can buy joint policies, which pay out when either one partner dies (a 'first life' policy) or only when both have died ('last death'). This may be cheaper, but less flexible, than separate policies.

■ *To cover funeral costs.* Special policies for older people available 'without medical' are particularly expensive and some have restrictions such as no payout on death within the first year. Instead, shop around for an ordinary whole life policy – preferably before your age makes the cost prohibitive – or build up savings in a separate account.

■ *To get the money straight to your family.* Ask the insurance company about having your policy written in trust. This means that the payout does not form part of your estate on death and is free of inheritance tax. Another advantage is that it can go straight to your beneficiaries without having to wait for probate.

■ *To cover an inheritance tax bill.* Either whole life or term insurance policies may be suitable – but you will need specialist advice (see Chapter 5). The policy must be written in trust, otherwise its value counts as part of your taxable estate.

Trade secret

Buying protection insurance

Keep it simple. It's vital to get a policy that you can afford to keep up. Concentrate on the types of cover you really need and which give you maximum flexibility as to how you spend the money (such as an income protection policy which you can use to meet a range of expenses, rather than loan insurance which will cover only one loan). And get lots of quotes – some companies will charge you twice as much as others for similar cover.

Cover for sickness and disability

The diagnosis

If you are off work sick your employer will pay you statutory sick pay for up to 28 weeks. After 28 weeks, or if you are not eligible (for example, if you are self-employed) you may qualify for incapacity benefit instead.

You can claim incapacity benefit only if you have paid enough National Insurance contributions. Otherwise, you will have to claim means-tested state benefits (such as income support). However, means-tested benefits are reduced if your savings and capital rise above a certain limit (£6,000 from April 2006), and you only get help with your mortgage interest after 39 weeks of claiming (unless the mortgage was taken out before October 1995).

Your employer may top up your sick pay for a limited period through its own sick pay scheme, but otherwise you are on your own. Unless your partner can support you, or you can live off your savings, or you are happy to rely on means-tested benefits, you need some form of private cover.

The prescription

- *To cover a loan.* Payment protection insurance sold with a loan only pays out enough to cover the loan repayments for a limited period (up to 24 months), and there's a waiting period before payouts begin. You don't have to buy the policy offered by your lender. Stand-alone policies may be better value, or consider an income protection policy.
- *To provide a regular income.* An income protection policy is your best bet. They pay out a proportion of your normal income every month for as long as necessary (up to retirement, say) and you can reduce the cost by choosing a longer waiting period (the amount of time between claiming and receiving the first payout). A waiting period of six months, say, would mean that the benefit starts when any statutory sick pay runs out. Watch out when buying: some policies have fixed premiums, whereas with others the premiums are reviewable, which means that they will rise during the life of the policy.
- *Don't depend on critical illness cover.* These policies pay out a lump sum if you are diagnosed with a serious illness, but only if the illness falls within a tightly defined list, such as some forms of cancer, heart attack and stroke. Stress, depression and backache – common causes

of inability to work – are not included. You can often buy critical illness cover as an add-on to a life insurance policy. As with income protection, the premiums may be either fixed or reviewable.

■ *To pay for long-term nursing care for yourself or an elderly relative.* You can buy long-term care insurance policies against the risk of needing care in future (called 'pre-funded' policies), but few companies offer them, and you risk tying up considerable amounts of money in premiums for cover you might not need. Instead, you need to build the costs of care into your overall retirement planning.

■ *With any policy, check the definitions.* For example, the definition of a critical illness. With an income protection policy, check if it will cover you if you cannot carry out your own occupation, or whether you have to be incapable of any occupation before you can claim. With a payment protection policy check the definition of unemployment (particularly if you are self-employed), or what cover you will get if you already have a medical condition.

Rainy-day savings

The diagnosis

How much did you have under 'savings accounts' in your financial stocktake? If the answer is not much, you may be vulnerable if you have a financial emergency such as major repairs on your car or losing your job. Even if you have insurance, there will probably be a delay before it pays out. A welcome event like a new baby can also put a strain on your finances.

You may be tempted to borrow your way out of trouble, and certainly credit cards can ease you over a lean patch. But you are only deferring the problem, you will need to pay off the borrowings at some point. If you owe just £500 on a typical credit card, and you pay only the minimum each month (say, 3% of the balance or £5 if greater), it will take you eight and a half years to clear your debt at a typical monthly interest rate of 1.2%. And that's assuming that you never borrow another penny on the card.

The prescription

Build up an emergency fund in an instant-access savings account. How much you need is a judgement that only you can make. Three or four times your monthly expenditure is a figure that is often quoted, but you may need a bigger cushion if you are not in a stable line of work or if you are self-employed. If you are self-employed, you also need to be careful to put enough aside to pay your twice-yearly tax bill.

Suitable accounts are available from most banks and building societies, or you could consider the National Savings & Investments easy access savings account. Think about:

- access – the money needs to be readily accessible, but there are many instant-access savings accounts that offer high rates. Newspapers (including *Money Mail*) regularly publish current interest rates
- keeping your emergency fund in a separate account from other savings, to reduce the temptation of dipping into it for non-essential spending
- having at least one joint account that your partner (if you have one) can draw on in the event of your death, to tide them over until your estate is settled.

Reducing your borrowing

The diagnosis

In the UK, the average debt per person is around £18,000. Table 1.2 on page 11 will help you work out your overall borrowings, and if you have disposable income, you should seriously consider reducing your debts first. If you find that your mortgage and loan repayments leave you with no disposable income, switching to a cheaper lender may leave you with cash to start building up some savings.

As well as making your lifestyle less vulnerable to unexpected shocks, such as redundancy or illness, paying off debt is a good way of saving money. Financial institutions make their profits by charging borrowers more interest than they pay to savers. For example, in April 2005 the best rate for a savings account was around 5% before tax, while a best-buy variable rate mortgage was around 5% after tax on your income. Generally, a mortgage is the cheapest form of borrowing – you might be paying an annual percentage rate of around 30% on a store card.

The prescription

- *Pay off your most expensive borrowing first* (unless there are penalties for early repayment). However, if you are falling into arrears, prioritise any loans where the lender could repossess your home (such as a mortgage).

■ *Move your remaining borrowings to a cheaper lender.* But take into account the costs of switching, including any early repayment fees or credit card balance transfer fees. Don't be dazzled by introductory offers: how long do they last and is there a good rate after the introductory period?

■ *Beware of consolidation loans,* where one lender offers to take on all your debts. There are two problems: they often use your home as security for the debt, and they may appear to be cheaper simply because you are repaying the debt over a longer period. So even if the monthly payment is lower, you may pay much more interest overall – and you risk losing your home if you can't keep up the payments.

■ *Consider a basic bank account.* These are accounts that do not allow you to overdraw by more than, say, £10. (See the Financial Services Authority leaflet *No bank account? Why it could pay you to have one.*)

■ *Get help early with problem debts.* If you are struggling to pay, free help is available from many money advice organisations, including National Debtline or the Consumer Credit Counselling Service (see the Fact file).

Trade secret

How to pay off your mortgage early

You may be able to reduce your mortgage with lump-sum payments, or even by over-paying on a regular basis. But check first that there is no penalty for repaying early. You also need to check when the repayment will be credited to the account. You will benefit immediately only if the interest is worked out on a daily basis.

Alternatively, you can get a special offset or current account mortgage. This combines a current or savings account with your mortgage, so that effectively you use your savings to reduce the size of the mortgage you pay interest on. The disadvantage is that they can be complex and often have a higher interest rate than a traditional mortgage. And some allow you to miss payments or borrow more, which could tempt you into increased borrowing.

Dealing with an endowment mortgage
The diagnosis

Until the 1990s, more than four out of five mortgages sold were endowment mortgages. Instead of paying off the loan as you go, you pay it off at the end with the proceeds of a special endowment life insurance policy that is invested largely in stocks and shares. After falls in interest rates and share prices, most mortgage endowment policies are likely to pay out too little to repay the mortgage. If you have an endowment mortgage, you should have had at least one letter from the insurance company telling you whether your policy is on target to repay the mortgage.

The prescription

Remember that even though they were sold together, the endowment policy and the mortgage are separate. You can keep your mortgage going without the policy, and vice versa. If there is a risk that your endowment policy won't pay off your mortgage, these are your main options for making up any shortfall:

- Convert part or all of your loan to a repayment mortgage.
- Repay part of the mortgage early, or overpay on your monthly repayments (see Trade secret on page 19).
- Start a separate savings plan or earmark an existing one to pay off the loan when it matures.
- A few endowment companies have guaranteed to meet some of the shortfall provided that investments grow at a minimum level, or sold policies with guarantees attached. However, check the terms of any guarantee. It may be limited, in which case you should make back-up plans as well.
- Claim for compensation to help meet the shortfall (see Trade secret opposite).

You may be able to vary the endowment policy, either to pay more in or to extend the term of the policy and the mortgage to give you more time to pay. But the tax rules for policies may make this difficult and you may incur extra charges.

Both the Financial Services Authority and *Which?* have useful factsheets.

You also need to decide what to do with your endowment policy if you are no longer depending on it to repay your mortgage. If you can afford to keep paying the premiums, it is purely a decision on how well the policy is likely to perform – and this will depend on the company.

Remember, if you surrender the policy (or, possibly, if you stop paying in) you will lose the life insurance it provides. (See page 14 for how to replace this.)

Trade secret

You can complain, but get your skates on

If you were inappropriately sold an endowment mortgage, you can complain to the person who sold it to you, and if they fail to deal satisfactorily with your complaint, you can complain to the Financial Ombudsman Service (in most cases). If you have a valid complaint and you lost out financially you may get some compensation.

However, you must complain within three years of first receiving a re-projection letter warning you that there is a high risk that the endowment won't pay off the mortgage. A few companies waive these limits, but most do not.

For more information ask the company that sold you the policy and see the leaflets available from the Financial Service Authority. Complaining is free, so beware of firms offering to handle complaints for a fee.

How much to save?

The diagnosis

Once you are satisfied that you and your family are secure in the event of misfortune and your borrowings are under control, you can start to narrow down the range of savings and investments that are suitable for you. But this will depend on the amount you are able to save and for how long.

The prescription

■ *If you want to end up with a set lump sum.* Regular saving is less painful, and reinvesting the income, rather than drawing it

Table 1.4: How savings of £100 a month might grow[a]

After year	No interest	After-tax interest rate				
		1%	2%	3%	4%	5%
1	1,200	1,207	1,213	1,220	1,226	1,233
2	2,400	2,425	2,450	2,476	2,501	2,527
3	3,600	3,656	3,712	3,769	3,827	3,885
4	4,800	4,899	5,000	5,102	5,206	5,312
5	6,000	6,154	6,313	6,474	6,640	6,810
6	7,200	7,422	7,652	7,888	8,132	8,383
7	8,400	8,703	9,018	9,344	9,683	10,035
8	9,600	9,997	10,411	10,844	11,297	11,769
9	10,800	11,303	11,832	12,389	12,975	13,590
10	12,000	12,623	13,282	13,980	14,719	15,502
11	13,200	13,955	14,761	15,619	16,534	17,510
12	14,400	15,301	16,269	17,307	18,422	19,618
13	15,600	16,661	17,807	19,046	20,385	21,831
14	16,800	18,034	19,376	20,837	22,426	24,155
15	18,000	19,421	20977	22,681	24,549	26,596
16	19,200	20,822	22,609	24,581	26,757	29,158
17	20,400	22,236	24,275	26,538	29,053	31,848
18	21,600	23,665	25,973	28,554	31,441	34,673
19	22,800	25,108	27,706	30,630	33,925	37,639
20	24,000	26,566	29,473	32,768	36,508	40,754

a Assuming interest is compounded once a year.

out, means that your money grows more quickly (this is called compounding; see Jargon alert opposite). Table 1.4 will help you work out how much you need to put aside each month, assuming various interest rates. Remember that you need to take account of tax and inflation. If you are a basic-rate taxpayer, a 5% return will be worth only 4% to you; and if inflation is running at 2.5%, the real rate of interest is 4% − 2.5% = 1.5% (there is more about inflation in Chapter 2). If you are planning to invest a single lump sum see Table 1 in the Fact file.

■ *If you want to use your savings to increase your income.* See Example 2.2 on page 30 and also the suggestions for income-producing investments in Chapter 7.

Table 1.4 shows you how your savings grow if you save £100 a month, but you can still use it if you want to save more or less – simply multiply or divide as necessary. For example, if you save £150 a month you will get 1.5 times the amounts shown.

Example 1.2: How much to save

Imagine that you have decided you need £10,000 to help your daughter through university. Table 1.4 shows that if you start saving £100 a month from her tenth birthday, you will meet your target by the time she is 18, even if the return on your money is only 1%. However, if you wait for another year before starting, you will reach your target only if your money grows by nearly 5% a year – a much taller order. And if you wait until she is 13, you will have to save about £150 a month (£6,640 × 1.5 = £9,960) to get near your target.

Jargon alert

Compound interest

Most savings accounts work out the interest on your savings on a daily basis, but they only add it to your balance once a year. Once the interest has been added to your balance, you start to earn interest on the interest. This is called compounding. If the annual interest rate is 5%, for example, you will earn £5 interest in a year on a £100 deposit. The next year, if the interest is compounded once a year, you get interest on £100 + £5 = £105.

As Table 1.4 shows, compounding is valuable, and it becomes more valuable the more times during the year that compounding takes place. Most bank and building society accounts used to compound twice a year, for example, but now once a year is the norm (see Jargon alert: Annual equivalent rate on page 270).

The next step

By now you should have a good idea of what you've already got, what your savings goals are, and how much cash you have available to meet them. The next step is to think about the sorts of risk you might face when investing, and how to control those risks. Chapter 2 will help you.

2

....

Know the risks

The word 'risk' is sprinkled through financial documents like confetti at a wedding. But risk covers a multitude of different concepts and can mean different things to different people.

A committee of MPs has recommended that a risk-rating system be developed to give investors a quick and easy guide. However, nobody has yet come up with a reliable industry-wide system – although various financial organisations will give you an indication of how they rate their investment funds, for example by marketing their funds as cautious or aggressive (higher-risk).

The problem is that there are many different types of risk: risk to your capital, risk to your income, the risk of inflation taking off (or falling) and so on. An investment might be low risk in some respects and high-risk in others. For example, there is usually no risk to your capital if you put it in the bank. However, money in the bank risks losing its purchasing power if interest rates are lower than inflation.

This chapter explains the different types of risk and what you can do about them. It also explains how savings and investments are regulated and what protection you have. There is more detail about risks for particular types of investment in Part 2.

But first, some warnings:

- You can't entirely pin down and eliminate risk. You have to trade off one kind of risk against another, and only you can decide what trade-offs you are prepared to make.
- The more complex the investment, the more questions you should ask about risk. One of the problems with endowment mortgages was that many people didn't realise that they were linked to the stockmarket (see page 214). Don't be afraid of asking what may seem like stupid questions – maybe the emperor really does have no clothes.

■ Don't let concerns about safety stop you saving altogether. Research suggests that you can be so obsessed with avoiding a loss that you actually take on more risk, for example by hanging on to a duff investment in the hope that it will come good. But if you want to sleep at night, it's what you are happy with that matters.

Jargon alert

Capital

Strictly speaking, your capital is your total financial resource. However, it is commonly used to describe the amount you originally invested in a particular scheme.

Is your capital at risk?

With a savings account, the risk to your capital is small – unless the company collapses, you should get back the amount you originally deposited. But you can't just leave your money in a bank account and forget about it. You have to make sure that the after-tax interest on it at least keeps up with inflation, or its purchasing power will fall.

With other investments, you do risk your capital. You may get back less than you invested, but if you accept this risk, you might get back more than you invested. This is often called the risk/reward trade-off.

Investments where you risk your capital include property, stocks and shares and any stockmarket-linked investment, including most life insurance policies, most pension policies, unit trusts, investment trusts, and some index-linked investments. They may fall in value because the stockmarket in general falls ('market risk') or because a particular company in which your money is invested runs into difficulties ('company failure risk'). In this book, this logo ❶ is used to show products where you risk your capital.

Protecting yourself

■ Only buy investments where you risk your capital if you can afford to leave your money there for a long time, say 5–10 years. Then, if you fail to sell at the right time and its value falls, you can hang on in the hope that it will rise again. But as Example 2.1 overleaf shows, you might have to wait for many years. If you invested £1,000 in the average UK all-companies unit trust in mid-1998 (point A) and failed to sell it at the height of the stockmarket boom in 2000, four years later it was still worth less than you paid for it.

■ Keep track of your investments by regularly checking their performance. You can then decide whether to cut your losses or hang on in the hope of an improvement. As Example 2.1 shows, if you had invested at point A, you could still have ended with an overall profit even after prices had started to fall, provided you had sold at point B.

■ If you have to cash in your investment at a set time, you could lose out if values drop just before the cash-in date. It's worth gradually cashing in as the date approaches, or moving to safer investments, to reduce the potential impact. (See also Jargon alert: Lifestyling on page 54.)

■ Don't put all your eggs in one basket. Spread your money around several different types of investment, and several different companies within each investment type. Investment funds such as unit trusts and insurance funds exist to make this easier for people with only small amounts to invest.

■ Guaranteed or protected investments may be tempting, but you must read the small print with a magnifying glass. See page 172 for what's available, but remember that a guarantee is only as good as the person behind it and 'protection' is usually limited.

Trade secret

Beware the top of the market

Small investors are notorious for buying investments just as the market peaks and for selling just as it is about to improve. It's not easy to tell when a peak or trough has been reached. One way to avoid this is to review your investments regularly and sell when you have made a reasonable profit, rather than hanging on in the hope that you can guess the timing of any downturn. This is sometimes called 'taking your profits'.

Example 2.1: **Long-term investing**[a]

Average UK all-companies unit trust, £

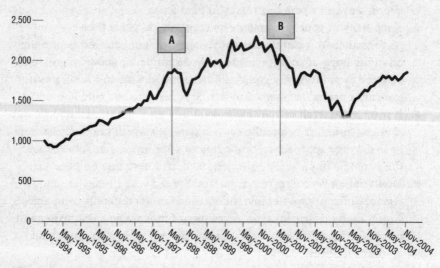

a Offer-bid prices, income reinvested.
Source: Standard & Poor's

Jargon alert

Market risk and performance risk

These are both ways of describing the risk that the value of your investment drops simply because of the type of asset in which you have invested (such as the stockmarket or property). You have no comeback if this happens unless the product was sold with some sort of guarantee (see page 172), or you were advised to buy it by an authorised financial adviser and it was not suitable for your needs (see page 35).

Jargon alert

Hedging your risk

This means reducing your risk of loss (in a bet, say) by also betting on the other side. In the financial world it can mean a wide range of strategies, such as 'shorting' (selling shares you do not own in the hope of buying them back more cheaply later on). You need expertise to do this successfully, and it is costly. Some investment funds specialise in using these strategies (see Jargon alert: Hedge funds on page 288), but a much more sensible tactic for small investors is simply to hedge your bets by spreading your money over a range of savings and investments.

Is your income at risk?

You may be prepared to lose capital if you can be sure of a good income in return. For example, an annuity is an investment where you pay over a lump sum in return for a fixed lifetime income (see page 129). And buying your own home is a sensible investment for many people partly because it saves you so much in rent (but see Jargon alert: Gearing on page 34).

If you put your money in a savings account, the main risks to your income are inflation and changes in interest rates (which are strongly affected by inflation). But if you are relying on drawing an income from investments where the value of your capital can fluctuate, there is an extra risk, as shown in Example 2.2 overleaf.

Protecting yourself

- An annuity is the most secure way of protecting your investment, although the cost of annuities has rocketed over recent years. (See page 116 for other income-producing investments.)
- If you are relying on income from your investments to maintain your living standards, work on the assumption that you will want to draw an increasing amount in order to compensation for inflation.
- Drawing an income from a stockmarket-linked investment? It's safest to draw just the dividends each year, or else a percentage of the value of the funds, rather than a fixed amount. That way you can be sure of not eating into your capital, as demonstrated in Example 2.2.

> Example 2.2: **Drawing an income from an investment**

James has £20,000 invested in insurance bonds from which he draws income of £1,000 a year. His bonds grow by 5% a year except in years 4, 5 and 6, when they fall by 5% a year. As the chart below shows, continuing to draw income of £1,000 eats into the value of the bonds, and even when their performance recovers in year 7 their value continues to dwindle. What's more, neither the income nor the value of the bonds is keeping up with inflation. If James wants to draw 2.5% extra each year to provide a growing income, he will actually run out of money in year 20.

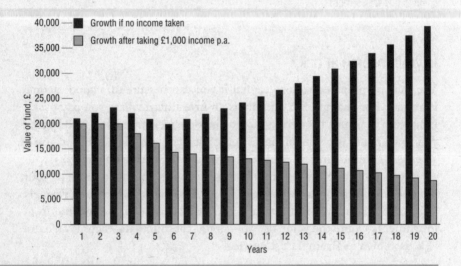

What if inflation rises?

Your real return from an investment will fall, and the value of each pound will depreciate. Example 2.3 shows how this works. Imagine that you rely on your savings to top up your income by £1,000 a year. Even with the current low inflation rate of around 2.5% a year, your £1,000 will buy only £884 worth of goods after five years. And it will reduce the purchasing power of your capital by a quarter in just 12 years – this is particularly significant if you have retired.

Note that annual statements for some private pensions now have to give you a forecast of your pension income after taking inflation into account (Table 2 in the Fact file shows how different rates of inflation can affect the purchasing power of your money). Products that are particularly affected by inflation include savings accounts, British Government stocks (except for the index-linked variety) and corporate bonds held to maturity.

> Example 2.3: **The effect of inflation at 2.5%**

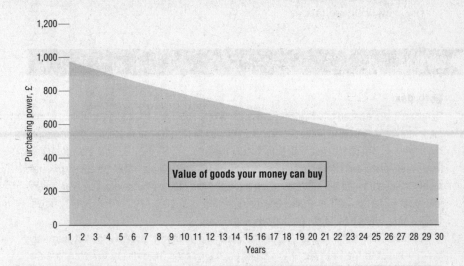

Protecting yourself
■ Always try to get an after-tax return on your money of more than the rate of inflation. If the interest rate after tax is 3% and inflation is 2.5%, say, the true rate of return is 0.5%.
■ If you want your capital to keep its purchasing power, you cannot spend all the income and growth you receive from it each year. To put it another way, with inflation at 2.5%, £1,000 needs to have grown to £1,025 by the end of the year just to stand still. If your total return is

only 3%, spending more than 3% − 2.5% = 0.5% will reduce the real value of your capital.

- Consider buying index-linked investments. These include index-linked National Savings Certificates (see page 223), index-linked British Government stock (page 139) and index-linked annuities (page 129).
- Stockmarket-linked investments are often recommended as a way of countering inflation, because company profits should rise in line with prices. But don't let this tempt you to buy a riskier product than you would otherwise consider.
- Only buy fixed-return investments if you think interest rates are unlikely to rise. If you opt for a fixed-rate investment, and rates then rise, you will lose out.

Jargon alert

Deflation

Deflation is a sustained fall in prices across the whole economy – not to be confused with a fall in the rate of inflation (where inflation continues to rise, but more slowly). Your money buys more as prices fall, but it also costs you more to pay off debt. People put off buying things until prices fall further, so stockmarkets are hit, and interest rates are cut as governments try to stimulate the economy. Low interest rates may worry savers, but even a very low or zero interest rate has a value because your money goes further. In deflationary times, fixed-interest investments are particularly attractive.

Deflation has continued to plague the Japanese economy since 1995, but currently is not a threat to the UK. Even if this changes, the lessons for ordinary investors are the usual common-sense ones: reduce your debts, shop around for the best interest rates, and steer clear of stockmarket investments unless you can accept the risk of falling share values.

What if interest rates rise or fall?

When rates fall, savers suffer and borrowers benefit; when rates rise, savers benefit and borrowers suffer. But there are other implications.

In particular, interest rate changes may make some types of investment more or less attractive. For example, when interest rates fall, share-based investments usually become more popular, partly because they offer the prospect of higher returns, but also because companies are likely to find borrowing cheaper. Fixed-return investments, like British Government stocks, also become more attractive and their cost rises to compensate. Rate changes may also affect house prices because the cost of a mortgage changes.

This doesn't mean that you need to become an economist to make sensible savings plans. But it does show that you need to review your investments regularly, and, if necessary, switch to a different type of investment.

One word of warning: don't expect to be able to beat the market by, for example, buying a fixed-return investment just before rates fall. Financial organisations are usually a step ahead of the game and take expected interest rate changes into account when setting their rates.

Protecting yourself

■ If rates change, paying off loans or reducing your mortgage may give you a better return than saving (see page 18 and also Jargon alert: Gearing on page 34).

■ If you are looking for a better income, when interest rates fall, beware of the temptation to put money into riskier investments than you would normally consider. (See Jargon alert: With-profits bonds on page 207 for a cautionary tale.)

■ Keep an eye on your investments to check the impact of interest rate changes. There is a tendency for banks and building societies to offer good rates initially but then rely on customer apathy to let them become less competitive when rates change. (See Trade secret on page 93 for more on savings accounts.)

■ If you are considering a fixed-interest account, you can reduce the risk of being stuck on a low fixed interest rate if rates rise by choosing a shorter notice period or term (two years, say, instead of five). Tying your money up for longer periods does not necessarily give you a much better rate.

Gearing

If you borrow to buy something, the greater is your potential return but also your potential loss. 'Gearing', as this is called, therefore magnifies your risk. The most common type of gearing is borrowing to buy a home (see page 147). However, gearing will also affect you if you buy an investment which is itself geared – for example, if you buy shares in a company with large borrowings.

What if the investment company fails?

Financial organisations such as banks, building societies, insurance companies, and investment advisers and managers can and occasionally do go bust. To reduce the risks, all such UK organisations must be authorised by the Financial Services Authority (FSA) before they can carry on most types of financial business.

The FSA checks that authorised firms are financially sound and supervises how they do business. It tries to stop firms going bust but does not guarantee to do so. The Financial Services Compensation Scheme provides limited compensation if an authorised firm cannot pay claims against it – either after it has stopped trading or because it is insolvent. (See the Fact file for contact details, and Part 2 of this book for how particular investments are regulated.)

Financial Services Compensation Scheme

The compensation available depends on the type of investment:

- *Life insurance and pensions* – the first £2,000 in full and then 90% of the value of the policy.
- *Savings accounts with a bank, building society or credit union* – full compensation for the first £2,000 of the amount in your account, and 90% of the next £33,000. Maximum compensation is £31,700.
- *Investments, investment managers and advisers* – the first £30,000 of a valid claim in full and 90% of the next £20,000. Maximum compensation is £48,000.

The scheme also covers mortgages and general insurance, such as house, travel and motor insurance. It does not cover company pension schemes (see page 230 for how these are protected).

Protecting yourself

■ Compensation is limited. If you are investing large amounts, be wary of putting it all with one firm.

■ The compensation scheme does not apply if you use a company or adviser operating without FSA authorisation (which is illegal). You can check whether or not a firm is authorised by using the FSA's Firm Check service (see the Fact file).

■ Nor does it apply if you buy from an overseas company, unless the firm is also authorised in the UK. It may be regulated by an overseas regulator with its own compensation scheme, but it is up to you to read the small print of any documentation to see what protection there is.

■ A few types of investment are not regulated by the FSA and are not covered by the compensation scheme. These include investments in property (such as buy-to-let properties and mortgages) and in physical objects such as fine wines, as well as company shares, including shares in investment trusts. (But if you buy these through a wrapper such as an ISA the wrapper will be covered, and the FSA does set down rules for information about shares in public companies.)

What if you have a problem or complaint?

You may have a problem with the way an investment or savings account has been handled, or feel that you have been poorly advised. If you cannot resolve the problem with the firm in question, the Financial Ombudsman Service (FOS) may be able to help.

The FOS is an independent body, set up by law to help settle individual disputes between consumers and financial firms. It can handle most complaints about most savings and investments, investment and fund management, and financial and investment advice, as well as bank and building society accounts and insurance. However, it does not cover complaints about the way an investment has performed.

There are also time limits: you need to refer your complaint to the FOS within six months of receiving a final response from the firm in question. Other time limits may also apply if you leave it too long to complain after you know (or should have known) that there is a problem.

Something else to watch out for is non-members. UK firms that are authorised by the FSA are covered, but see page 189 for investment trust companies and page 40 for non-UK firms. And complaints about employers' pensions and how personal pension schemes are run may be covered by the Pensions Ombudsman instead – the Pensions Advisory Service can direct you to the most appropriate scheme.

It costs nothing to go to the FOS. However, you must complain to the firm first. If you are still unhappy with their final response, you can then contact the FOS. If they uphold your complaint, they can order the firm to compensate you for any financial loss you have suffered, plus a limited amount for distress and inconvenience. The maximum award is £100,000. Any award is binding on the firm, but if you do not agree with a decision, you can still sue the firm in the courts if you want to.

For more information and useful tips see the FSA's leaflet *FSA Guide to making a complaint*. Contact details for the FSA and the FOS are in the Fact file.

Protecting yourself

- Good records can help resolve problems. As well as keeping all paperwork and emails, make a note of people you speak to at the firm in question, their names, the date and time, and what was covered. If a financial adviser asks you to complete a questionnaire about your financial circumstances, you should be given a copy if you request one.
- Check whether any firm you are dealing with is covered by a complaints-handling scheme such as an ombudsman. The paperwork describing the firm's services should give this information.
- Specialist complaints firms may offer to handle your complaint, either for a fee or for a cut of any compensation. This is not necessary: the Financial Ombudsman Service is designed to be a free, user-friendly way of complaining and you shouldn't need specialist help.

> Trade secret

You can challenge an unfair contract
You may feel that the standard terms and conditions of an investment or savings account are stacked against you – for example, if there is a disproportionately large penalty for cancelling a deal. If so, the company may be in breach of the snappily titled Unfair Terms in Consumer Contracts Regulations 1999. You can report the company to the FSA if you feel that a term is unfair. The FSA cannot force them to give you compensation, but it may be able to force them to change their contract. And you may have grounds for a complaint, first to the company and then (if necessary) to the Financial Ombudsman Service. For more about these regulations, see the FSA factsheet *Challenging unfair contract terms*.

What if a firm is conning people?

As described above, the FSA regulates most financial organisations. If you think that an organisation is acting unethically or illegally, or its advertising is misleading, you can report it to the FSA (contact the consumer helpline). The FSA cannot usually tell you what action it takes in response to your report. However, if the firm is eventually found to have broken FSA rules, the FSA can fine or ban it, or ask the courts to order it to compensate its customers.

The FSA is responsible for ensuring that all the firms it authorises are sound and properly run. It also regulates the way that most investments are sold and marketed. But it is not responsible for the way that bank and building society accounts are sold and marketed, or for banking practices generally. There is a voluntary Banking Code of practice in place to cover this, overseen by the Banking Code Standards Board (BCSB).

Virtually all banks and building societies, except a few of the smaller ones, subscribe to the Banking Code. Copies of the code should be available in members' branches. If you feel that the code has been breached, and you cannot resolve matters with the bank or building society, you can complain to the Financial Ombudsman Service.

However, there may not be much the FSA or the BCSB can do if you fall victim to a fraudster operating from overseas, particularly by telephone, internet or fax. The FSA website has a useful 'warnings and alerts' section covering current scams.

Protecting yourself

- Only deal with a firm that is authorised by the FSA. You can use the FSA's Firm Check service (see the Fact file) to check this. If the company is not authorised in the UK, take extra care (see page 40).
- Make your own checks on what you are told. If a salesperson tells you a particular return is guaranteed, does the documentation confirm this?
- Check that full contact details are given, including street names (not just post boxes) but remember that fraudsters often hide behind reputable-sounding offices which turn out to be just a front.
- Give yourself time to check things out. But if you regret your purchase after you've bought, you may be able to cancel it if you act quickly. Many investments must give you a cooling-off period.
- If you make a payment, make it to the firm, not the individual salesperson, and ensure you get a receipt.
- If you are sending personal information over the internet look for 'http' in the address bar and a closed padlock at the bottom of the window, indicating that the site is secure (although fraudsters have been known to use these too).
- Protect your financial details, so that nobody can impersonate you in order to obtain money, goods or services. See the Home Office website www.identitytheft.org.uk.
- Don't be tempted to let the salesperson 'help' you by filling out an application form for you – forgery is not unknown. Always ask to keep a copy.
- Don't be swayed by charm, bullying or plays on your sympathy, and be particularly careful if you are visited at home, especially if you are on your own.
- If you are caught out, don't be embarrassed to report it to the regulators. Even experienced investors can get caught out.

Trade secret

Scams – the danger signs

■ A very high rate of return. If something looks too good to be true, it probably is.

■ Being asked to keep something confidential or pressured for an instant response.

■ A phone call or email out of the blue from someone asking you to buy shares. Read the FSA leaflet *Share investment scams* first. In this country it's generally against the law to cold call you and try to sell you shares or similar investments.

■ 'Phishing' emails. These are fake emails from supposedly reputable organisations asking you for personal financial information that fraudsters can use to raid your accounts. Alternatively, they may direct you to fake websites. Don't send any such information without calling the organisation in question first.

■ Advisers who want you to hand over your money but do not first ask you questions about your own financial situation. Their advice is unlikely to be suitable.

■ A complicated scheme peddled by a charming and persuasive individual with an expensive lifestyle, unless that individual is prepared to spend time explaining the scheme fully and can provide full, clear documentation to back it up.

■ Suggestions that a scheme will save you tax in a slightly dodgy way. HM Revenue & Customs Is tightening up on tax avoidance.

■ Any unsolicited phone call, email or fax from overseas, unless the firm is authorised by the FSA (contact the Firm Check service).

Trade secret

Small investors are at the bottom of the information food chain

Don't risk your money on the basis of unsubstantiated information. The sad truth is that the less you have to save or invest, the less attractive you are to financial organisations (unless they can lend you money). This means that by the time investment research and investment tips have trickled down to you, they are probably either out of date or other, more favoured, investors will already have acted on them. And, if it really is the inside track, the odds are that both you and the person who told you could be in breach of insider trading rules. Fraudsters may also put out false information in order to manipulate share prices.

Jargon alert

Currency risk

This means that the value of your investments will be affected by changes in exchange rates. You can protect against currency risk – for example, futures contracts give you the right to buy something at a fixed price at some point in the future – but this is complex and costly, and unlikely to be worthwhile for small investors.

What if you are investing overseas?

It often makes sense to invest part of your money overseas as a way of spreading your risk. Indeed, part of your money may well be invested overseas without your being aware of it, if you have a general investment fund, such as an insurance company managed fund. Guaranteed stockmarket bonds may also be set up through overseas companies (see page 172).

If you have got money overseas, you will be exposed to currency risk (see Jargon alert). The other problem with investing overseas is that the protection you have if things go wrong varies and may be non-existent. You need to distinguish between:

- Foreign companies that are operating here through a UK branch which is authorised by the FSA. In this case you get the full protection of FSA regulation, including the compensation scheme and the Financial Ombudsman Service.
- Companies that are registered overseas and simply marketing their products here. They are allowed to do so without FSA authorisation in certain circumstances, but they will be outside the remit of the UK compensation scheme and the Financial Ombudsman Service.
- UK financial organisations offering 'offshore' accounts to UK residents through an overseas subsidiary. These subsidiaries are regulated by the financial regulators of the country in question, not the FSA, so you do not have the protection of the UK compensation scheme or the Financial Ombudsman Service. However, they have got a UK company standing behind them, and the paperwork will be in English.

Protecting yourself

■ If you are investing overseas, it is even more important to ensure that you have an adequate spread of different types of investment.

■ Read all documentation carefully to see where the company is registered. Try to check whether the company is regulated in its home country. If it is, try to find out as much as possible about how regulation, ombudsmen and compensation work there.

■ There is a European internet site called FIN-NET that can tell you whether there is an ombudsman scheme or equivalent in various European countries. There is a link to it on the UK Financial Ombudsman Service's website.

■ Most UK fund management companies offer UK-authorised overseas investment funds. Investing through these won't reduce the currency risk to which your money is exposed (although the fund manager will try to manage the risk), but it will mean that you are covered by UK financial regulation, including the UK compensation scheme and the Financial Ombudsman Service.

■ If you are investing abroad over the internet, you are particularly vulnerable to fraud. (See page 39 for the danger signs.)

Your personal risk factors

Not all threats to the safety of your money come from external sources. Changes in your circumstances could have a major impact on your saving and investing. If your income drops, you may have to stop paying in to a particular investment. You may also have to start drawing an income from your savings, so that they drop in value faster than anticipated.

A good financial adviser will spend some time asking you about your personal risk factors. Are you in good health? Are you the head of a large and needy family or a single person with a good job? What are your job prospects: if you lost this job, could you easily get another one?

Personality also comes into it. How much time and interest do you have to manage your investments? Do you often have to rein your spending or are you a saver by nature?

Protecting yourself

■ Keep some money in a readily accessible emergency account. (See Rainy-day savings on page 17.)

■ Your personal risk factors may change, so you should review your finances regularly, particularly if your income or capital falls.

■ If you have a partner, you might find it helpful to go through the financial stock-take in Chapter 1, to see whether you would be able to manage if you lost one income. If you have an annuity or pension, check what your dependants would get on your death.

■ Couples also need to consider whether it is better to own investments jointly or individually. Joint ownership has some advantages (see page 118), but it is not always easy to divide investments (such as joint insurance policies) if you split up.

■ Before you choose a particular investment, check whether there are penalties for withdrawing your money early or for stopping your contributions. Try to avoid investments with penalties unless there are compelling reasons for choosing them.

Jargon alert

Political risk

This is the risk that your investments might be affected by changes in government policy, such as a change in tax treatment. You also have to make decisions about saving for retirement without being sure what the state pension will be when you retire. There's not much you can do about this sort of risk, except to review your investment plans in the light of any such changes and be prepared to change tack if necessary.

Balancing the risks

Once you have considered the various types of risk, you have to make trade-offs between them. You cannot eliminate them all, although you should be able to use our 'protecting yourself' tips to reduce the potential impact. But you can balance the various risks, in line with your personal risk factors:

Figure 2.1 Balancing the risks

Keep more in savings	Shorter timescale? Less cash? High personal risk factors? ←	→ Longer timescale? More cash? Low personal risk factors?	Consider investments with a risk of capital loss

■ The shorter your savings timescale, the less likely it is that you will be able to recoup any capital loss.

■ The longer your savings timescale, the greater is the impact of inflation and possible low interest rates.

■ The less money you have to play around with, and the lower is your earning capacity, the more money you need to keep in cash.

■ If you have quite a bit of cash, or lots of earnings capacity, you can afford to risk some of your capital in share-based investments.

You can look at it as a risk seesaw, with investments where you risk your capital (for example, stockmarket-linked investment) at one end and savings accounts at the other. Your aim is to keep the seesaw level, by adjusting the amount you keep in each type, in line with your personal risk factors.

However, this is your overall risk profile. If you have enough money, you can mix and match investments with different types of risk. This is covered in Chapter 3.

3

....

Planning: the building blocks

There is no shortage of savings and investments schemes on offer. But you need to strip away all the packaging and think in terms of the underlying investment type – for example, whether you are being offered a savings account or a share-based investment. This is because the type of investment usually makes a bigger difference to your eventual return than the individual company.

If you bought a share-based investment in 1994 and kept it until 1999, for example, you could hardly have failed to make money. Example 3.1 shows that even poorly performing UK all-companies unit trusts outstripped inflation. But if you invested between 1999 and 2004, you would have been lucky to avoid losing money. Because of stockmarket falls, only the top-performing quarter of unit trusts kept up with inflation.

This chapter will help you decide how much money you need in each type of investment, taking into account how much risk you are prepared to take. Chapter 7 covers different investments for different purposes, and Chapter 6 looks at how to choose an investment company.

▶ Jargon alert

Collective, pooled and packaged investments

These are all names for investments where you put your money in a fund with other investors. They include unit trusts, investment trusts, life insurance and pension funds. There are two big advantages. First, you can buy into a fund with a few hundred pounds (less if you invest regularly), whereas if you had that amount to invest in shares, say, you'd probably be able to buy shares in only one company, and the cost of buying would eat up a big proportion of your investment. Second, you don't have to take the decisions. The fund manager decides which investments to buy, within the objectives of the fund.

Example 3.1: **Cash versus shares**[a]

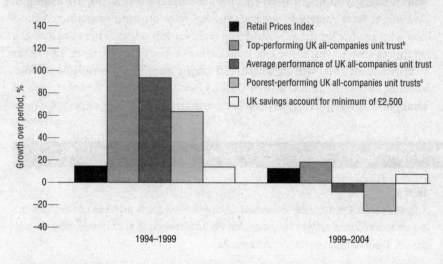

a Offer-bid prices, income reinvested.
b Average of top-quartile trusts.
c Average of bottom-quartile trusts.
Source: Standard & Poor's

The investment family tree

The underlying types of savings and investment are summarised in Figure 3.1 overleaf. Each type works differently and is affected to a varying extent by the different risk factors, for example inflation, interest rates and stock-market performance. So by putting your money in more than one type of investment you hope that if one type is performing badly, it will be balanced by another type that is performing well.

You can spread your risk further by investing in several different schemes within each type. But this can be impractical for investors without much money. So over the years financial organisations have set up investment funds that pool your money with that of other investors, allowing them to spread the risk across a range of investments. There are various types of investment funds – for example, life insurance funds, unit trust funds, and pension funds – but most of them work on the same principle.

On top of that, there is the product packaging – the legal structure within which you might hold various accounts or funds. So, for example, you might have money in several types of pension fund (a managed fund and with-profits fund, say) within the one pension policy. There are also tax wrappers within which you can hold various types of investment. The main wrapper is an ISA, within which you might have, for example, a savings account and some unit trusts or OEICs (see Jargon alert). Another type of wrapper is the self-invested personal pension or SIPP (see page 276).

Jargon alert

OEICs

This stands for Open Ended Investment Companies, a variant on a unit trust. OEICs are set up as companies rather than trusts, but from the investor's point of view they are very similar. There is more information on page 287.

Jargon alert

Asset allocation

Each of the types of investment in Figure 3.1 is known as an asset class. The process of spreading your money between the asset classes is sometimes called asset allocation, and the result is known as your asset mix.

What have you already got?

If you carried out the financial stock-take in Chapter 1, you may wonder how the investments in your stock-take relate to the types of underlying investment in Figure 3.1. Which category does a savings-type life insurance policy fit into, for example? It's not immediately obvious, and the reason is that in the past the UK savings industry has concentrated on selling you a life insurance policy, or a pension, or an ISA – in other words, on the packaging rather than the underlying type of investment.

Figure 3.1 The investment family tree

Enter the total amount you have in each category on the dotted lines.

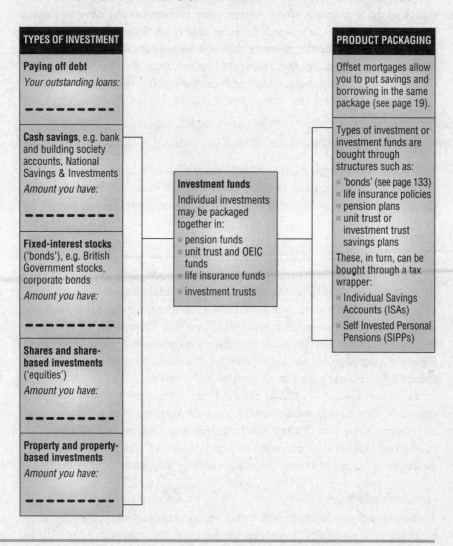

TYPES OF INVESTMENT

Paying off debt
Your outstanding loans:

Cash savings, e.g. bank and building society accounts, National Savings & Investments
Amount you have:

Fixed-interest stocks ('bonds'), e.g. British Government stocks, corporate bonds
Amount you have:

Shares and share-based investments ('equities')
Amount you have:

Property and property-based investments
Amount you have:

Investment funds
Individual investments may be packaged together in:
■ pension funds
■ unit trust and OEIC funds
■ life insurance funds
■ investment trusts

PRODUCT PACKAGING

Offset mortgages allow you to put savings and borrowing in the same package (see page 19).

Types of investment or investment funds are bought through structures such as:
■ 'bonds' (see page 133)
■ life insurance policies
■ pension plans
■ unit trust or investment trust savings plans

These, in turn, can be bought through a tax wrapper:
■ Individual Savings Accounts (ISAs)
■ Self Invested Personal Pensions (SIPPs)

However, if you peel away enough of the layers of packaging, you will usually find that your money is invested in one of the groupings. For example, an insurance policy may be invested in UK or overseas shares or in a managed fund where your money is split between cash, shares and property. It's worth keeping an eye on what sort of fund you have, because you could discover that you have more than you expect in share-based investments, for example. The literature sent by the company should explain how much is in equities, how much in bonds and how much in cash. Using the explanations below, try to write in the total amounts on the dotted lines.

Paying off debt

This is not really a type of investment, but it is included here to remind you that, as explained on page 18, paying off a loan will usually save you more money than you could get if you put the money in a savings account.

Cash savings

These include money in a bank or building society savings account, or in National Savings & Investments accounts and bonds (with the exception of the National Savings Guaranteed Equity Bond, which is linked to the value of shares). With these accounts, the risk of losing your capital is minimal and you benefit from regular interest. However, there is a risk that your money will depreciate in value because of inflation. As you can see from Figure 3.2 on page 50, the average savings account for a minimum invest-ment of £2,500 has barely kept up with inflation.

However, Figure 3.2 shows only average rates, and you can do better than this. The best accounts available easily keep up with inflation, even after taking basic-rate tax into account. But you need to keep an active eye on interest rates and be prepared to switch accounts if necessary. See page 92 for more information on choosing a savings account.

Fixed-interest stocks

These are effectively loans you make to an organisation, either the gov-ernment or a company. Loans to the UK government are called British Government stocks or gilts, and loans to a company are called corporate bonds. You get a regular fixed interest payment. But what makes them different from other loans is that you can trade them on the stockmarket. This means that you can either invest when the stock is first issued and hang on to it until it is repaid – the safer option – or take a chance and buy and sell it on the stockmarket at a price that depends on demand – which means that you may sell them for more or less than you paid. There's more about gilts on page 136, and corporate bonds on page 154.

As you can see from Figure 3.2, gilts and bonds usually track each other quite closely. However, gilts are very secure, and you can also buy index-linked versions that protect you against inflation. Investing in company stocks can produce a better return because you are exposed to the risk that the company may fail to pay you back, or that the price will fall because the company's credit rating becomes less favourable.

You can put money into gilts directly or through a gilts fund. But it is not easy for small investors to invest directly in corporate bonds without professional help, so it is more common to invest in these through a bond fund. Fixed-interest investments are often called bonds, but that term has been avoided here because so many other types of investment are also marketed as bonds (see the table on page 133).

Shares and share-based investments

As well as shares that are owned directly, this category also includes investment funds that are invested in shares, such as a UK equity unit trust, or a European growth investment trust. These investments are often called equities (see Jargon alert on page 262).

As Figure 3.2 shows, you can have an exciting ride with shares. If you buy and sell at the right time, you can make a big capital gain; but if you get it wrong, you can lose money. Companies and funds pay income in the form of dividends, but this income will vary. In addition, if you have invested in an overseas company or fund, you will be affected by changes in exchange rates.

These factors make share-based investing unsuitable if you cannot afford to risk a capital loss, or if you only want a short-term investment. However, if you are investing over the longer term, and already have money put by in safer investments such as savings accounts, share-based investment offers a chance of beating inflation and producing a capital gain. (For

Figure 3.2 How different types of investment have performed[a]

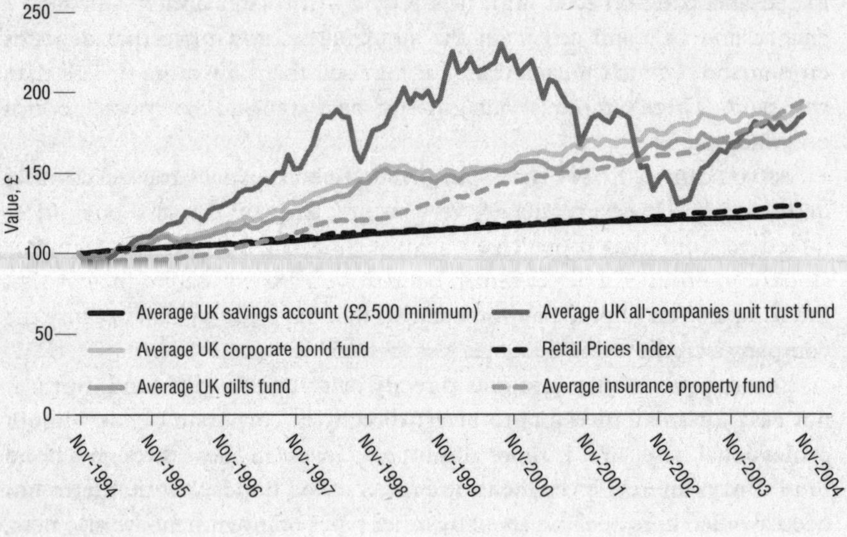
250
200
150
100
50
0
Value, £
Average UK savings account (£2,500 minimum)
Average UK corporate bond fund
Average UK gilts fund
Average UK all-companies unit trust fund
Retail Prices Index
Average insurance property fund
Nov-1994
Nov-1995
Nov-1996
Nov-1997
Nov-1998
Nov-1999
Nov-2000
Nov-2001
Nov-2002
Nov-2003
Nov-2004

a Offer-bid prices.
Source: Standard & Poor's

more information on investing in shares see page 279, for unit trusts see page 287 and for investment trusts see page 189.)

Property and property-based investment

Property, to professional investors, usually means commercial property such as shops and offices. As with share-based investment, you run the risk of a capital loss or gain, but you should also get an income. Investing in property is covered on page 259, but for a private investor usually the most practical way of doing this is to invest through a property fund.

Note that commercial and residential property values are affected by rather different factors. If you are tempted to invest in buy-to-let properties, proceed with care. You could end up with a lot of money tied up in residential property, when you include your own home, and you could lose a lot if the property market slumps. (See the example on page 147.)

Jargon alert

The risk/reward trade-off

Risk and reward are inextricably linked. If you want to get a better return than a cash-based investment, you have to be prepared to take more risk. The expected average gain from investing in shares is higher than from investing in, say, British Government stocks. But a larger number of investors in shares will actually lose money. You have to trade off the extra risk that you will be one of the unlucky ones against the chance that your shares will increase in value.

Trade secret

The future may not repeat the past

Treat graphs showing how well shares have done in the past with caution. Shares out-performed cash and fixed-interest securities in each of the decades of the twentieth century. However, you cannot assume that they will out-perform to the same extent in future. Economists point out that lower inflation and an ageing population are just two of the trends that may make shares perform less well in future.

How much in each type?

You can narrow the choice of investment by deciding how soon you are likely to want your money back. But first check Chapter 1 to make sure you have dealt with any gaps in your personal stock-take – for example, paying off debt, insuring your life, planning how to repay your mortgage, building up an emergency fund.

Money you might want back within five years

For this relatively short time period, an investment where you risk your capital isn't really appropriate. Cash-based savings are usually the most sensible option, so your first port of call should be a bank or building society, National Savings & Investments, or possibly a credit union if you are eligible to join one (see page 160). The table on page 266 provides a spotter's guide to the different types of bank and building society accounts; see also page 219 for National Savings.

However, if you already have some money in an instant-access account, and are prepared to tie your money up for a set period – such as one year or five years – in the hope of a better return, there are many different types of 'bond' available, with varying maturity dates. Beware, though: these may be cash-based savings accounts, fixed-interest securities, or share-based investments, and not all guarantee to return all the money you invested. Some are not appropriate investments for short-term saving. (See the table on page 133).

Money for later

If you have spare funds that you are not going to need within 5–10 years, you should widen your investment horizons to look at a broader range of investments. This is because cash-based investments are likely to lose their value over time because of inflation.

A common method of deciding how much to put in each type of investment is to use a risk pyramid – a typical example is shown in Figure 3.3 (but see the warning below). You need to know how much risk to your capital you are prepared to take, and this will depend on the amount available, your timescale and your personal risk factors. (See Figure 2.1 on page 43.)

The more money you have available, the longer it is before you need to spend it and the lower your personal risk factors, the more you can afford to put into the investments further up the pyramid. The potential growth of these investments is not limited, but neither is the risk of capital loss. As your timescale reduces – if, for example, you will soon need to cash in your investments – you should move further down the pyramid.

Warning

There are different models for deciding how much to invest in each type of investment, and lots of different versions of the risk pyramid, depending on how people view different investments and their relative risk. There is no correct answer. You can work only in terms of principles:

■ The sooner you need the money (for example, if you are planning your pension, the sooner your retirement), the less you should put in

Figure 3.3 The risk pyramid

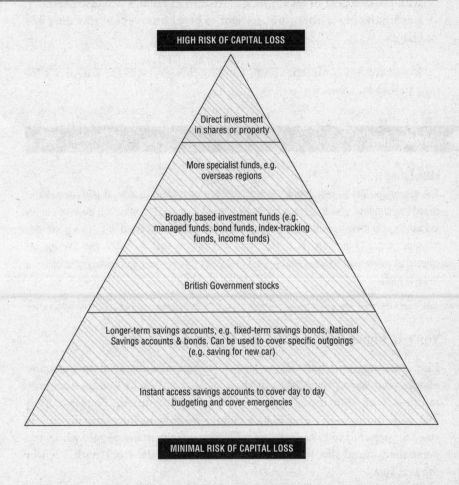

HIGH RISK OF CAPITAL LOSS

Direct investment in shares or property

More specialist funds, e.g. overseas regions

Broadly based investment funds (e.g. managed funds, bond funds, index-tracking funds, income funds)

British Government stocks

Longer-term savings accounts, e.g. fixed-term savings bonds, National Savings accounts & bonds. Can be used to cover specific outgoings (e.g. saving for new car)

Instant access savings accounts to cover day to day budgeting and cover emergencies

MINIMAL RISK OF CAPITAL LOSS

shares and the more in fixed-interest stocks and cash. This also means that you should review and probably change the balance of your investments as you age (see Jargon alert overleaf).

■ The less money you have, the less you should put in investments with the risk of capital loss.

■ Your own feelings about risk are important. If you are uncomfortable with the prospect of losing your hard-earned savings because the stockmarket falls, then you are right to be cautious about investing in shares.

If you are not confident about deciding this yourself, see Chapter 5 for how to find an adviser.

Jargon alert

Lifestyling

The nearer you get to retirement, the less risk you can afford to take. If you have share-based investments, you could lose out badly if the stockmarket is low when the time comes to cash in your investments to produce a retirement income. To avoid this, it's a good idea to move gradually from shares to less risky investments such as bonds and savings accounts as retirement approaches. A fund that does this for you automatically is called a lifestyle fund.

You can't have it all

Life insurance and fund management companies are keen to persuade people who have previously put their money purely in savings accounts to move some of their money into share-based investment. They point out that your money will never have a chance of growing substantially unless you are prepared to take some risk. Unfortunately, many people who were persuaded found themselves out of pocket when the stockmarket fell in the late 1990s.

To persuade savers back into the stockmarket, financial organisations have come up with all sorts of schemes to reduce the risks. These include new-style with-profit funds and protected and guaranteed funds and bonds. For full information about these see page 198 (for with-profits funds) and page 172 (for guaranteed and protected stockmarket bonds).

Be careful to check what you are getting in these dressed-up products, and don't assume that they are necessarily the answer. New-style with-profits funds cannot protect you against prolonged stockmarket falls, and they can still apply penalties that effectively lock in your money. And with guaranteed funds, you cannot usually get your money back early. Because the cost of providing the guarantees reduces the return, you could find that you have tied up your money for a return that is not much better than what you would get on a good building society account.

4

Planning to save tax

Everybody with savings and investments needs to take tax into account: a 5% interest rate is worth only 4% to you if you are a basic-rate taxpayer, and 3% if you pay higher-rate tax. So even if a tax-free investment has a lower headline rate than a taxable investment, it may put more money in your pocket.

There is information about how each type of investment is taxed in Part 2. This chapter explains:

- which investments are free of tax
- how much income tax is due on other savings and investments
- how the way the tax is collected affects your choice of investment
- whether you are likely to be affected by capital gains tax
- how your investments might affect your right to tax credits
- how to arrange your savings and investments to save tax.

Note that tax rules, rates of tax and tax-free thresholds may change each tax year (which runs from 6 April in one year to 5 April the next). This book is based on the rules and tax rates for the 2005–06 tax year. Any tax changes are covered in the *Daily Mail Tax Guide*, published in April each year.

Jargon alert

Tax-efficiency

Investments with tax advantages are often said to be tax-efficient. But although you should take tax into account, it is not the be-all and end-all of investment. Sometimes people have been persuaded to invest in tax-efficient schemes, such as insurance bonds, without appreciating the level of risk involved, and even when they were not taxpayers at all.

Tax-free investment income

You can save tax on money you put into a savings or investment scheme only if you invest in a pension plan, Venture Capital Trusts or Enterprise Investment Schemes. The tax rules for these are explained in Part 2. All your other investments have to be paid for out of your after-tax income. However, there is no tax to pay on the interest or dividends coming out of the following investments:

▪ Individual Savings Accounts (ISAs). Note that an ISA is a tax wrapper, not an investment in itself (see page 183).
▪ Savings certificates from National Savings & Investments (both fixed interest and index-linked versions – see page 222).
▪ Ulster Savings Certificates, if you normally live in Northern Ireland, and were living there when they were bought or repaid.
▪ Children's bonus bonds from National Savings & Investments (see page 224).
▪ Child Trust Fund accounts (see page 150).
▪ Premium bond prizes (see page 227).
▪ Venture Capital Trusts (see page 163).
▪ Tax-exempt friendly society life insurance polices (see page 169).
▪ Income from a family income benefit life insurance policy (see page 14).
▪ Special annuities to cover the immediate costs of long-term care, if paid direct to the care provider. Pre-funded long-term care policies are also tax-free if taken out before the need for care became apparent.
▪ Part of the income from non-pension annuities (ones you buy independently, not in connection with a pension – see page 129).
▪ If you are not ordinarily resident in the UK, British Government stock.

Life insurance policies (apart from some friendly society policies) are not tax-free, but you are unlikely to have to pay tax on the proceeds unless you are a higher-rate taxpayer. However, they do have an important tax disadvantage for some older people (see page 68).

How much income tax?

Any tax-free income, such as interest from an ISA, is ignored. Tax is then worked out on 'bands' of income, each taxed at a different rate. The first band – your personal allowance and, if relevant, the blind person's allowance – is tax-free. When it comes to deciding which tax rate applies to the rest of your taxable income, your income is taxed in this order:

1   *Earnings, pensions and business profits* (note that the state retirement pension counts as taxable income).
2   *Taxable interest* from bank and building society accounts, National Savings & Investments, credit unions, non-pension annuities, British Government stocks, corporate bonds, and unit trusts and OEICs that themselves invest in interest-paying investments (such as bond funds).
3   *Dividends* from shares, investment trusts, and unit trusts and OEICs invested in dividend-paying investments.
4   *Life insurance gains* (note that there are special rules for life insurance; see page 63).

The result is that any income from savings and investments that exceeds your tax-free allowances will be taxed at your highest rate of tax. Table 4.1 and Example 4.1 show how this works.

However, there is one important type of saving that will actually cut your tax bill: a pension. Even though the money you take out of your pension is taxable, the money you pay in is tax-free and doesn't have to be included in your taxable income (see pages 238 and 257).

▶ Example 4.1: **How much tax?**

Hannah has a pension of £8,500. Because she is over 65 she gets a personal allowance of £7,090 in the 2005–06 tax year. This means that the first £7,090 of her pension is tax-free. The remaining £1,410 is taxed at the starting rate of 10% (£141).

Hannah also has savings interest of £2,000. Her pension has used up £1,410 of her £2,090 starting-rate band, so £2,090 – £1,410 = £680 of her interest is also taxed at 10% (£68). But the remaining interest of £2,000 – £680 = £1,320 falls into the basic-rate band and is taxed at 20% (£264). The tax on her interest is £68 + £264 = £332.

Table 4.1: Income tax bands and tax rates for 2005–06

	Tax band	*Tax rate*
Personal allowance	First £4,895 of your taxable income (possibly more if aged 65-plus, see page 68), plus £1,610 if blind	Tax-free
Starting-rate band	Next £2,090 of your taxable income	No tax for life insurance because the fund has already paid tax 10% tax on all other income
Basic-rate band	Income between £2,091 and £32,400	22% tax on earnings, pensions or business profits 20% tax on interest 10% tax on dividends No tax for life insurance because the fund has already paid tax
Higher-rate band	Anything above £32,400	20% on some life insurance (see page 63) 32.5% on dividends 40% on all other income

Jargon alert

Non-taxpayer, basic-rate taxpayer

If your total income, ignoring tax-free income, is below the level of your personal allow-ances, you are said to be a non-taxpayer. A basic-rate taxpayer is someone whose top slice of taxable income falls within the basic-rate band, and whose top rate of tax is therefore the basic rate. On the same principle, you may also be called a starting-rate or higher-rate taxpayer.

How tax is collected

Tax is collected by HM Revenue & Customs (HMRC – a merger between the Inland Revenue and HM Customs & Excise).

A few types of investment income are paid out before tax, but other types have basic-rate tax taken off before you even get it. If you are a non-taxpayer or starting-rate taxpayer you should check whether you can reclaim the tax. This is possible with interest-paying investments, but not with life insurance or shares. Higher-rate taxpayers will have extra tax to pay in any case.

More tax to pay?

If you do have extra tax to pay, or receive taxable income paid out before tax, and do not get a tax return, you are legally required to tell your tax office by 5 October after the end of the tax year in which you received the income (the tax year ends on 5th April each year). Your tax office may send you a tax return, if the amount is substantial, but where possible they will adjust your tax code so that the tax is deducted from your earnings or pension. Your tax code is usually calculated on the basis of your savings income for the previous year, then adjusted for future years when your tax office knows exactly how much the income was.

Trade secret

You do not have to wait to reclaim tax

If you have paid too much tax on your investment income you do not have to wait until the end of the tax year to reclaim it. You can send in a tax reclaim form (R40, available from tax offices) as soon as you have received all your income for the year, or send in an interim claim. Note, though, that repayments of less than £50 are not normally made before the end of the tax year.

Interest paid out before tax

The following investments have the advantage of paying out income with no tax deducted, but if you are a taxpayer remember that tax will have to be paid eventually.

- Taxable accounts and bonds from National Savings & Investments, except for fixed-rate savings bonds (paid with tax taken off). Tax-free National Savings products are listed on page 229.
- Credit unions.
- British Government stocks acquired after 5 April 1998 (but you can opt to have the income paid with tax taken off if you prefer).
- Corporate bonds and building society permanent interest-bearing shares.
- Offshore accounts. This income is taxable in the UK, even if foreign tax has already been deducted (you can claim tax relief for the foreign tax). If you are tempted to keep quiet about overseas income, bear in mind that the UK tax authorities have information-sharing agreements with many countries.

Interest with tax taken off

The types of investment listed below pay income with 20% tax taken off. You have no further tax to pay if you are a basic-rate taxpayer, but if you are a higher-rate taxpayer you will have a further 20% tax to pay to bring the total tax up to 20% + 20% = 40%. You can reclaim part or all of this tax if you are a non-taxpayer or starting-rate taxpayer. A special benefit of bank and building society accounts is that non-taxpayers can register to have income paid before tax; and with British Government stocks you can choose to have the income paid out with or without tax.

- Bank and building society accounts.
- Non-pension annuities.
- Income from British Government stocks acquired before 6 April 1998 (but you can opt to have it paid before tax if you prefer).
- Fixed-rate savings bonds from National Savings & Investments.
- Interest distributions from unit trusts and OEICs that invest in interest-paying investments.

If you have tax to reclaim, contact your tax office or phone the special Taxback helpline (see the Fact file). You may be sent a tax reclaim form (R40) to complete, and if you regularly have to reclaim tax, you may be sent one automatically each year.

Trade secret

You can get interest paid out before tax

If your total income, including savings income, is too low for you to pay tax, you can get interest from a bank or building society paid without tax taken off. To do this, ask your bank or building society for form R85. (See page 274 for further information.)

Example 4.2: How the tax is collected

Hannah (from Example 4.1) is liable to pay tax of £332 on her savings interest. But tax of 20% has already been taken off all her interest before it was paid out to her (£2,000 × 20% = £400). She should contact her tax office to reclaim the extra £400 − £332 = £68.

Dividends have 10% tax taken off

Share dividends from UK companies and dividend distributions from UK unit trusts and OEICS are treated as if 10% tax has been paid before you receive the income. This is called a 'tax credit'. The taxable amount is the dividend you received, plus the tax credit, but you can set the tax credit against your tax bill. So if, for example, you receive a dividend of £90, the tax credit is £10: you are taxed on £90 + £10 = £100, but you can set the £10 tax credit against your tax bill.

You cannot reclaim the tax credit on share dividends, even if you are a non-taxpayer, or even if the shares are held in an ISA.

If you are a starting-rate or basic-rate taxpayer, you have no further tax to pay on your dividend. But if you are a higher-rate taxpayer, you will have a further 22.5% to pay, to bring the overall tax up to 32.5%. So on a dividend of £90, with its £10 tax credit (a taxable amount of £100), you pay further tax of £22.50: £32.50 in total.

Sometimes, instead of getting cash dividends, you may get dividends in the form of extra shares ('stock' or 'scrip' dividends). These are taxed in a similar way to other dividends. You are treated as having paid tax at 10% on these payouts, which can be set against your tax bill, but higher-rate taxpayers have further tax to pay.

Example 4.3: **Higher-rate tax on investments**

Henry, a company director, is a higher-rate taxpayer. He buys an ISA each year, but the income from ISAs is not taxable and does not have to be declared. However, he has also got some British Government stock, which pays out interest before tax, some taxable interest from a savings account not in an ISA, and some shares. The tax position is:

■ No tax has been deducted from the British Government stock. He will have 40% to pay.

■ 20% tax has been deducted from his savings account interest. He has a further 20% to pay.

■ Dividends from his shares come with a 10% tax credit. He has a further 22.5% tax to pay on these.

Henry declares the income in his tax return, but his tax office collects the tax by adjusting his tax code so that more tax is taken off his salary each month.

Life insurance

Special – and rather complicated – rules apply to life insurance policies. The life insurance fund in which your money is invested is taxed. When the money is paid out to you, you are treated as if you have already paid 'notional' tax of 20% of the amount received. This tax cannot be reclaimed even if you are not a taxpayer.

You have no further tax to pay if you are a starting-rate taxpayer or basic-rate taxpayer, or if you have a regular-premium policy, such as an endowment, that you keep for at least ten years (or for three-quarters of the term, if less). But you may have tax to pay if:

■ you have a single-premium insurance bond, or cash in a regular-premium policy early, *and*

■ you withdraw money from your policy, or sell the policy, *and*

■ either you are a higher-rate taxpayer or you are a basic-rate taxpayer and the gain from the policy pushes you into the higher-rate band.

There is more about how life insurance bonds are taxed on page 211, and endowment policies on page 217.

Trade secret

Side-effects of an insurance gain

Not many people realise that even if you don't have to pay tax on an insurance gain, there may still be unwelcome side effects. The gain may increase your tax bill if you are receiving an extra personal allowance because you are aged 65 or more (see page 68), or reduce any tax credits you may be receiving.

Do you have to worry about capital gains tax?

Capital gains tax is a tax on the capital sum produced when you dispose of an asset. The most common disposal arises when you sell something, but you also make a taxable disposal if, for example, you give something away (or sell it an artificially low price). Taxable assets include property, investments and, if worth over £6,000, possessions such as antiques.

Capital gains tax only applies to investments that offer you a chance of a capital gain. So it does not affect investments such as National Savings & Investments accounts and bonds where the only return comes in the form of interest. The following investments offer a chance of capital gain but are exempt from capital gains tax:

- investments held in an ISA
- National Savings Certificates
- Child Trust Fund accounts
- shares in a Venture Capital Trust or (with some conditions) an Enterprise Investment Scheme
- life insurance policies (unless you bought the policy second-hand)
- pension plans (assuming the scheme is tax-approved)
- British Government stock
- most types of corporate bond.

This leaves shares, unit trusts, OEICs and investment trusts not in an ISA as the main investments potentially liable to capital gains tax. You may also have tax to pay if you invest in property (apart from your main home, which is exempt). However, you only have to pay the tax if your total profits on disposing of all taxable assets in the tax year come to more than the annual tax-free amount – £8,500 in the tax year running from 6 April 2005 to 5 April 2006. And you can deduct from your profits:

■ the costs of buying the investment (or the market value at the time of acquisition if you were given or inherited it)
■ any losses you make – for example, if you sell some shares for less than you paid for them
■ taper relief – this relief means that the longer you keep an asset, the smaller the percentage of the gain that is taxable.

If you have made taxable gains, they are treated as your top slice of income and are taxable at 10%, 20% or 40%, depending on which tax band the gains fall within.

Example 4.4: Are you liable to capital gains tax?

Harry sold some shares that cost £5,000 six years ago and are now worth £8,000. His gain is £3,000 before taper relief. Because of taper relief, only 80% of his gain is taxable (£2,400), so he is well within his annual tax-free amount of £8,500 for the 2005–06 tax year. His remaining tax-free limit is £8,500 – £2,400 = £6,100.

However, Harry also has some other shares, on which he is showing a profit of £8,000 (after taper relief). Selling these in 2005–06 would take his gains over the tax-free limit, and since he is a higher-rate taxpayer, he would have to pay tax at 40% on the excess. He can avoid this tax altogether by waiting till the 2006–07 tax year (which starts on 6 April 2006) to sell, when any gain will fall within his 2006–07 tax-free amount.

How investments might affect your tax credits

If you are claiming Working Tax Credit or Child Tax Credit, the amount you get depends on your income – and this means your joint income, if you are married or living with someone. However, the first £300 of your joint total pension income, investment income, property income and foreign income is ignored.

Broadly, your investment income is defined in the same way for tax credits as for income tax. So it excludes income from any tax-free investments, but includes any taxable gain from a life insurance policy.

Arranging your investments to save tax

It cannot be said too often: do not base your investment decisions on tax considerations alone. But you should certainly take the following tax tips into account.

Consider tax-free investments

These are listed on page 57. A mini cash ISA, in particular, should be an automatic choice for virtually all taxpayers. You can usually get your money out of an ISA with minimal delay if necessary, so it is suitable for all funds except money you know you will want to put in and take out again regularly.

> Trade secret

Tax-free investments don't cut inheritance tax
Investments in ISAs or other tax-free schemes still count as part of your estate for inheritance tax purposes, and an ISA loses its tax-free status when the investments in it are transferred to a new owner on your death. The exception is National Savings Certificates: although these count for inheritance tax, they can be transferred to a new owner and still remain free of income tax and capital gains tax.

Avoid slipping into the next tax band

It is particularly important to consider tax-free investments if, like Hannah in Example 4.1, your income from investments is pushing you into a higher tax band. Hannah could avoid paying any tax at all by saving in a tax-free investment, such as a cash ISA. You should also look for tax-free investments if, like Angela in Example 4.5 (see page 69) you are losing age allowance.

Other ways of keeping in a lower tax band include:

■ *Deferring your income* so that you receive it in a new tax year, when you expect your income to be lower. Many investments pay income at a set date that you cannot change. But you can defer your state pension (see page 245), and if you have insurance bonds you can cash them in at times that suit you (the return from these bonds is taxed as income rather than capital gains). See Example 4.5 on page 69.

■ *Timing your sales of investments.* The same thing applies when disposing of investments that are potentially liable to capital gains tax: only sell enough each year to keep within the annual tax-free limit (£8,500 in the 2005–06 tax year).

■ *Investing for growth rather than income.* If you are anxious to avoid increasing your taxable income and are investing long-term, it is worth considering an investment where the return comes mainly in the form of capital growth rather than income. That's because the capital return is liable to capital gains tax, not income tax, and most people do not use their annual capital gains tax tax-free allowance.

■ *Making a pension contribution or charitable donation.* If you pay money into a pension, or donate to a charity under the Gift Aid scheme, you get tax relief on the payment at your top rate of tax. This is done by deducting the amount of the pension contribution or donation from your taxable income. So if it would make sense for you to contribute or donate anyway, parting with some cash may also mean that your overall taxable income stays below the relevant threshold.

> Trade secret

Keep track of capital losses

If you invest for growth, you run the risk of making a capital loss instead. If so, you can deduct the loss from your taxable capital gains made in the same or future tax years. However, you must tell your tax office about the loss within five years and ten months of the end of the tax year in which you make the loss. If you get a tax return, you will need to claim the loss on the special capital gains tax pages. Otherwise, contact your tax office – you may be asked to complete a return.

Beware of the age allowance trap

Your personal allowance (the first, tax-free, band of income) is increased if you are aged 65 or more during the tax year. In the 2005–06 tax year, the allowance is increased from £4,895 to £7,090 if you are aged at least 65, and £7,220 if you are aged at least 75. However, this extra allowance is reduced by £2 for each £1 of income above the age allowance limit (£19,500 in the 2005–06 tax year), until it reaches the minimum amount of £4,895. If your investment income takes you over this £19,500 limit, it could cost you up to about £500 in tax. See Example 4.5 and the Trade secret for ways of avoiding the trap.

This age allowance trap will also affect you if you or your husband or wife were born before 6 April 1935 and so are eligible for an age-related married couple's allowance. Once your personal allowance has been reduced to the minimum, your married couple's allowance will also be reduced. For most couples, the reduction in the married allowance depends on the husband's income, not the wife's – her income will determine how much of her own personal allowance she gets, but it will not affect the married couple's allowance. However, for couples who marry on or after 5 December 2005, either partner's income will be used, depending on who has the highest income.

Example 4.5: How extra income can cut your tax allowance

Angela is 70, and because her taxable income is £15,000 in 2005–06 – below the age allowance limit of £19,500 – she gets a full age-related allowance of £7,090 instead of the normal £4,895. She has an insurance bond that has built up a gain of £10,000. Angela will not have to pay tax on the gain when she cashes in the bond because she is not a higher-rate taxpayer (even after taking the gain into account). But the £10,000 gain will be added to her taxable income when working out her age allowance: £10,000 + £15,000 = £25,000. She will lose £1 of allowance for each £2 over the £19,500 limit (£25,000 – £19,500 = £5,500 divided by 2), although the allowance cannot be reduced below the minimum amount of £4,895. So Angela's allowance is reduced from £7,090 to £4,895 and her tax bill rises by £483 as a result (i.e. £7,090 – £4,895 = £2,195 × 22%).

Fortunately, there is a way round this. If Angela cashes in one-third of her bond this year, one-third next year and one-third the year after, she will stay below the age allowance limit in each year. However, she does risk a fall in the value of the bond during that time.

Trade secret

Ways to avoid the age allowance trap

The secret is to keep your income below the limit (£19,500 in 2005–06) above which the allowance is reduced. As well as choosing tax-free investments, such as National Savings Certificates, use the suggestions given on page 67. Other tips are:

- consider deferring your pension (see page 245)
- be careful when cashing in part of an insurance bond (see page 64)
- donations to charity through Gift Aid or pension contributions reduce your taxable income and so can increase your age-related allowances
- if you are married, and one person is above the £19,500 limit and the other is below, consider putting some income-producing assets in the name of the lower-income partner.

Work as a couple

Partners, married or unmarried, are taxed as two individuals for tax purposes. You each have your own tax-free allowances, tax bands and age allowance limit. This means that if one partner is in danger of slipping into a higher tax band, or one partner is a non-taxpayer, you can save tax as a couple by transferring investments into the name of the lower-income partner. There are a few things to note:

■ If you are married and own an investment jointly, you are normally each taxed on half of the income from it. Married couples who contributed unequal proportions to the investment can opt to have the income taxed in line with the proportion each invested, by asking their tax office for Form 17. However, you cannot use this for bank accounts or life insurance policies.

■ It is sensible to document a transfer to make your intentions clear – this is essential if you are unmarried. A dated letter to the other partner is all you need. (See page 118 for more on who owns joint investments.)

■ You do not have to pay capital gains tax or (usually) inheritance tax on gifts between a husband and wife, but you might have to on gifts between an unmarried couple. Unmarried couples should try to keep any transfers of investments within the annual tax-free allowances for both these taxes (£3,000 a year for inheritance tax, plus any unused balance of £3,000 from the previous year; £8,500 in 2005–06 for capital gains tax).

■ Any gift should be an outright gift, without strings. A gift in name only does not count for tax.

■ Rearranging your wealth between you may be particularly useful if you are likely to be liable for a large inheritance tax bill. But this is an increasingly complicated area, so if the sums involved are large you should get specialist tax advice.

■ Unlike tax, tax credits are worked out on your joint income, whether you are married or unmarried, or same-sex partners.

■ You cannot save tax by giving investments to your own child, even if he or she is a non-taxpayer, because if the investments produce income of more than £100 per parent per year it is all taxed as the parents' income anyway. You can give investments (or money to invest) to your grandchildren or relatives without this rule biting – but the gift may count as a gift for inheritance tax. (For more on investing for children, see Chapter 7.)

Example 4.6: **Working as a couple**

Adrienne and Bertie are a married couple both aged 65. Bertie has just retired; Adrienne works part-time. Adrienne is a starting-rate taxpayer, but Bertie's taxable income is £20,000, which means that in 2005–06 he is above the £19,500 age allowance limit (see Example 4.5). If Bertie gives Adrienne investments that produce £500 a year income, his age allowance will no longer be reduced. But they will have to make sure that the income does not push her into a higher tax bracket.

5

....

Planning: getting help

Faced with the complexity of modern-day savings and investments, you may feel that you need help. But don't forget that advice is a product like any other, even if you don't have to hand over any cash (because the adviser receives commission). Buy advice with care.

The full advice process takes you through all the steps that we recommend you should carry out yourself (see Table 5.1). However, advisers may offer different levels of service, or sell only a restricted range of products, or products from only a few companies. So it pays to think carefully about what sort of advice you need before you start to approach advisers.

This chapter explains how to decide whether you need advice, how the world of financial advice works, and how to choose and get the best out of an adviser. It also explains the two 'key facts' documents that can help you.

Jargon alert

Cooling-off
After buying an investment you may have a limited period within which you can cancel the agreement. The investment company should tell you what rights you have to a cooling-off period. Note, though, that if the investment is linked to the stockmarket, and stockmarket prices have fallen, you will not get back the full amount invested.

Do you need advice?

Using an adviser to tell you what you should buy means that someone else takes on the responsibility for the decision-making. A properly qualified financial adviser should also be up-to-date with all the tax rules, have a

Table 5.1: An ideal full advice process

What an adviser should do

Review	Go through a 'fact find' of your existing circumstances, covering your existing savings, pensions and insurance, your personal circumstances, possible changes in future, your attitude to risk and your savings goals. Ask to keep a copy of this for future reference.
Plan	Provide a report or letter with recommendations for how you should plan your money to meet your savings goals (e.g. how much money you should have in the different types of investments) and the reasons for these recommendations.
Choose	You may not need any new investment, and an adviser should not sell you anything if there is nothing suitable in their range of products. But if you need to buy, they should recommend and arrange a suitable savings account or investment scheme. For some types of investment, such as pensions, investment-type life insurance and unit trusts, you should get a document explaining the key features of the investment. The adviser should explain if you have a right to a cooling-off period.
Review	Conduct regular reviews to check whether your financial plan needs to change in line with economic and personal circumstances.

good knowledge of what is available on the market and the expertise to help you make your choice. They may also have access to special computer programs and databases.

Remember, though, that even if someone else is legally responsible for giving you suitable advice and pointing out the risks in investments they recommend, you will be the one living with the consequences. Advisers don't always get it right: many of the types of investment that have caused problems, such as with-profits bonds, were actively marketed by advisers.

So if you do decide to consult an adviser, it is in your own interest to find out as much as you can about a proposed investment plan, rather than relying entirely on someone else. In particular, it is worth doing as much as possible of the review stage yourself. This will help you keep on top of your finances, save you time and may save you money if your adviser charges a fee. Chapters 1 and 8 will help you.

If you decide to go it alone, there is a great deal of information freely available that explains savings and investments and helps you plan your money. A good place to start is the Financial Services Authority (FSA), which has a range of leaflets and a comprehensive website, but many other organisations have useful information (see the Fact file).

There are also many websites and magazines that list and compare financial products to help you choose – but take care. They may not be comprehensive, and you should check the basis on which the lists are compiled (for example, whether companies have to pay to be included) and how up-to-date the information is. An objective source of information is, again, the FSA website, which has comparative tables for a number of key investments, including savings accounts, endowment policies, investment bonds, stocks and shares ISAs, pensions and annuities. These tables compare what is on offer from most companies on a like-for-like basis and include information on rates and charges.

> ### Trade secret

You may be able to buy more cheaply through an adviser

If you buy an investment through an adviser you may save money by negotiating a commission rebate. An initial commission payment of up to 5% of your investment is usually built into the cost of the product, and advisers may agree to waive part or all of this. The adviser still gets any further commission payable later on in the policy's lifetime. The extra money usually increases the amount that is invested on your behalf. A firm that rebates commissions but does not provide advice is often called a discount broker.

Choosing an adviser

Don't assume that just because an adviser works for a well-known company, he or she is necessarily the right person for you. You need to take into account:

■ *An adviser's range.* An adviser may offer only limited advice, or sell the products of just one or two companies. An independent financial adviser (IFA) who can sell products from companies across the marketplace is usually the best option. (See Types of advice below, and Types of adviser on page 80.)

■ *Cost.* Even if you don't have to hand over any cash, your adviser still has to get paid somehow. (See How advice is paid for on page 83.)

■ *Expertise.* All advisers who give full investment advice must have a minimum qualification. (See Qualifications on page 85.)

■ *Availability.* Naturally, financial advisers are generally more interested in working for people with lots of money. But however little cash you have, do not assume that a high-street bank or building society is your only option. (See Finding an adviser on page 88.)

■ *Service.* An adviser may look great on paper but still not provide a good service. This is the most difficult quality to check (for some clues, see Questions to ask on page 89).

Types of advice

As explained in Chapter 2, anybody who sells or advises on investments in the UK must be authorised by the Financial Services Authority (FSA). This gives you some comeback if things go wrong. But how much protection you get depends on the type of advice – and advice doesn't necessarily mean what you think it does. You need to check what you are getting.

Financial advisers must usually give you a 'keyfacts about our services' document explaining:

■ how many companies' products they can offer
■ whether you are getting full advice from a qualified adviser, basic advice, or simply general information.

An extract from a typical keyfacts document is shown in Figure 5.1, and some of the key information on it is explained below.

How many products can an adviser choose from?
Financial advisers can sell products from just one company, a selected range of companies or the whole market. But advisers with a restricted range do not necessarily choose the companies on the basis of what is best for you – they also look at the commission and other services they might

Figure 5.1: 'Keyfacts' document 1 – the services on offer

keyfacts **about our services**

XYZ INDEPENDENT FINANCIAL SERVICES LTD	2 More Road, Any Town, W1 0TB

▼

1. The Financial Services Authority (FSA)

The FSA is the independent watchdog that regulates financial services. It requires us to give you this document. Use this information to decide if our services are right for you.

2. Whose products do we offer?

✔	We offer products from the whole market.
	We only offer products from a limited number of companies.
	We only offer products from a single group of companies.

3. Which service will we provide you with?

✔	We will advise and make a recommendation for you after we have assessed your needs.
	You will not receive advice or a recommendation from us. We may ask some questions to narrow down the selection of products that we will provide details on. You will then need to make your own choice about how to proceed.
	We will provide basic advice on a limited range of stakeholder products and in order to do this we will ask some questions about your income, savings and other circumstances but we will not: • conduct a full assessment of your needs; • offer advice on whether a non-stakeholder product may be more suitable.

4. What will you have to pay us for our services?

✔	Before we provide you with advice, we will give you our **keyfacts** guide **'about the cost of our services'**.
	We will tell you how we get paid, and the amount, before we carry out any business for you.

5. Who regulates us?

- **XYZ Independent Financial Services Ltd**, 2 More Road, Any Town, W1 0TB is authorised and regulated by the Financial Services Authority. Our FSA Register number is 123007.
- Our permitted business is **advising and arranging life insurance, pensions and unit trust business**.
- You can check this on the FSA's Register by visiting the FSA's website www.fsa.gov.uk/register or by contacting the FSA on 0845 606 1234.

6. Loans and ownership

- Bizee Life Office Ltd owns 25% of our share capital.
- We have 20% of the voting rights in Royal Edinburgh.

7. What to do if you have a complaint

- If you wish to register a complaint, please contact us:
  In writing: Complaints Department, XYZ Independent Financial Services Ltd.
  By phone: 0121 100 1234.
- If you cannot settle your complaint with us, you may be entitled to refer it to the Financial Ombudsman Service.

8. Are we covered by the Financial Services Compensation Scheme (FSCS)?

- We are covered by the FSCS. You may be entitled to compensation from the scheme if we cannot meet our obligations. This depends on the type of business and the circumstances of the claim.
- Most types of investment business are covered for 100% of the first £30,000 and 90% of the next £20,000 - so the maximum compensation is £48,000.
- Further information about compensation scheme arrangements is available from the FSCS.

get from the company. You can ask the adviser to provide you with a list of the companies and products offered.

For this reason, it makes sense to choose an adviser offering 'whole of market' advice (see Jargon alert). In addition, check the 'loans and ownership' section on the second page of the keyfacts document, which will tell you if the adviser has any significant links with other financial companies that could bias their advice (for example, they are partly owned by a financial company).

Note, though, that these rules apply to investment advice, not advice about savings accounts.

Jargon alert

Whole of market advice

If someone researches all the investment products of a particular type before selecting one for you, this is called whole of market advice. This does not mean that they have to carry out this research every time they make a recommendation, or know about every single product on the market, but they do need to have knowledge of a reasonably large proportion of the products available and keep their research up to date.

Advice and a recommendation

Only advisers who have gained a qualification can give advice about buying (or selling) a particular investment such as an investment fund, life insurance policy or personal pension (see page 85 for more on adviser qualifications). Before making a recommendation, the adviser must have taken full steps to understand your needs, and he or she must give suitable advice. If you later feel the advice was not suitable, you can complain to the Financial Ombudsman Service. Additional rules apply to some types of advice, for example on transferring a pension from one scheme to another.

No advice or recommendation

This does not mean that an adviser cannot give you any advice at all. As long as he or she doesn't advise you to buy or sell a particular investment, you can still be given factual information about a particular product, advice on a savings account, or general advice about different ways of investing (sometimes called generic advice). The problem is that you do not have any comeback against the firm if you think the advice was wrong, although you can usually still complain (to the ombudsman if necessary) if you bought a product on the basis of misleading information.

Basic advice

This may be offered if you buy some types of stakeholder product (stakeholder means that certain minimum standards are met; see page 95). An adviser will take you through a series of scripted questions, but the advice does not include a full assessment of your needs, the adviser does not have to be qualified, and although you can still complain to the Financial Ombudsman Service if you think you were poorly advised, the ombudsman will take into account the limited nature of the service on offer.

Jargon alert

Execution-only

If you ask a firm to arrange the purchase of an investment for you without taking any advice, this is known as execution-only business. For example, most internet services and many telephone services are execution-only. You are responsible for deciding whether the investment is the right thing to buy and have no comeback against the firm if you later regret your decision.

Investment management

You may want someone to manage a portfolio of investments on your behalf. If so, there are different types of management. A discretionary service means that you give your adviser the discretion to buy and sell on your behalf without consulting you, but within a specific brief. With an advisory service, however, they must ask you first. An alternative form of advisory service gives you simply the advice, and you organise the buying and selling of your investments.

How much money you need to have varies widely – it could be as little as £30,000 or as much as £200,000, depending on the organisation and the service.

Independent financial advisers, banks and stockbrokers may all offer management services. You should be given a 'terms of business' letter detailing the service on offer and how it is to be paid for. You will normally pay an annual fee based on the value of the investments under management, say 0.5%, and you will have to pay the costs of buying and selling investments on top of this. This can amount to quite a lot if your investments are changed frequently, so you should check the standard trading costs.

If you are looking for an investment manager, the Association of Private Client Investment Managers and Stockbrokers (APCIMS) and the Association of Solicitors and Investment Managers (ASIM) both have lists of members (see the Fact file).

> Trade secret

Alternatives to investment management

You will probably get a truly personal service, and a choice of a wide range of potential investments, only if you have a lot of money, say £100,000 upwards. For smaller amounts (£30,000–50,000, say), you may be offered a 'portfolio management' service, where your money is put into a range of unit trusts. An alternative worth considering is a multi-manager fund, a kind of off-the-shelf portfolio (see page 102). Your money is in a single fund, but the fund managers then spread all the money in the fund around a number of funds run by other managers, according to certain criteria. For example, you can choose a cautious fund or a more adventurous one.

Types of adviser

All the following types of organisation can offer financial advice. But beware: the boundaries between different types of adviser are breaking down, and there are fewer neat categories than there were in the past.

High-street banks and building societies

The bank manager who handled all a customer's business no longer exists. These days, branch staff are unlikely to be authorised to give full investment advice, although they should be able to help you choose between their employer's own savings accounts. If you want something more than this, most banks and building societies employ specialist financial advisers, but you will normally have to make an appointment to see one of these. Either you go to the branch, or they may offer to visit you at home. They are usually paid a basic salary, topped up by commission or bonuses.

Financial advisers working for banks and building societies usually sell products from a restricted range of companies: the firm that employs them and one or two others. Some of the companies whose products they sell may be owned by the bank. So while they can help you through the review and planning stages, banks and building societies are not the place to go for a truly independent viewpoint or a good choice of companies. A few may offer basic advice for stakeholder products (see page 79). Even fewer (usually building societies or ex-building societies) can offer independent advice from a subsidiary company or specialist division.

Note that if you have a lot of money, you might be offered a higher level of service, such as a personal wealth manager, private banking or investment management. You will usually pay for this extra service, so shop around before accepting.

Insurance companies

There are far fewer insurance company representatives about than in the past. Indeed, some major insurance companies do not offer full 'advice' at all, and refer you to an independent financial adviser. You may be able to buy some products direct from the company, but usually without advice.

Some companies do still employ advisers, but their services may be available only to people with large amounts to invest, or to businesses. Other insurance companies sell through appointed representatives, who run their own firms but are tied to just one or two companies.

In the past, insurance company representatives were able to sell only their own company's investments. These days, they are allowed to offer the products of other companies too, although most do not, and the choice they offer is likely to be limited.

Independent financial advisers (IFAs)

An adviser can use the term 'independent' only if he or she offers products from the whole of the market (not just a few companies) and allows you to pay by fee rather than by commission if you wish. However, within this definition, IFAs may offer a complete financial planning service or investment management, or just specialise in a particular area, such as investing to pay for healthcare or ethical investing.

There are still many small IFA firms, and many of these have banded together as networks. The network is responsible for ensuring that the adviser complies with FSA regulation and provides centralised services such as research. It may also have a 'panel' of recommended products that the adviser sells.

Some IFAs are qualified as financial planners, which means that they look at the whole of your finances, rather than just, say, investments. Unfortunately, anybody can call themselves a financial planner. Look for someone who is certified by the Institute of Financial Planning.

At the other end of the spectrum, discount brokers may not give you any advice at all. Instead, they provide a cheap service for buying and selling particular investments, by rebating part of the commission they receive.

Other financial advisers

Between the two extremes of company representatives and IFAs you will find many people calling themselves advisers. They are agents of a limited number of investment companies. Sometimes they are called multi-tied advisers. They may work through networks in the same way as IFAs.

► Jargon alert

Multi-tied advisers

These advisers can sell the products of a limited range of companies and they include many banks and building societies. A multi-tied adviser can give you more choice than an adviser that represents just one company, but do not assume that they are tied to the best companies on the market. Unlike IFAs, they have no obligation to look across the whole of the market (see page 78).

Solicitors, accountants and actuaries

These are types of professional adviser (actuaries are specialist number crunchers who advise pension funds and insurance companies). Most professionals are not regulated directly by the FSA. Instead, they are allowed to give limited investment advice to individuals under the supervision of their professional organisation.

Legal and accountancy firms may have staff who specialise in giving financial advice and who are FSA-regulated as IFAs. Specialist legal firms may be members of the Association of Solicitors and Investment Managers (ASIM). Smaller firms may also have links with IFAs to whom they can refer you. If you have a family solicitor, or use an accountant for work, it is worth asking them what services they have available, or who they recommend.

Actuaries work mainly for financial organisations, but a few firms of consulting actuaries offer services for individuals with more complex finances (such as people who are directors of their own companies). The Association of Consulting Actuaries has a list of members.

Stockbrokers

Not all stockbrokers accept private clients. However, those that do may offer investment management, a comprehensive financial planning service, or share-dealing services. The Association of Private Client Investment Managers and Stockbrokers (APCIMS, see the Fact file) has a directory of members that accept private clients and the services they offer.

How advice is paid for

Professional firms, such as accountants, stockbrokers and solicitors, have always charged fees for their financial advice. These days, you are increasingly offered the option of paying a fee for the services of other financial advisers, and IFAs must offer you this option. Even so, sales-related payments, such as commission from the investment company whose products you buy, remain the main method of payment.

Advice paid for through commission is not free. The commission is paid by charges that are deducted from your investment. There is usually an initial commission when you first buy, which can be between 3% and 7%

of your investment, depending on the type of product, and a smaller trail or renewal commission, which is paid every year that you have the investment. Figure 5.2 on page 86 shows average amounts.

Commission rates are falling for some types of investment, but research has shown that being paid by commission can still affect the quality of advice. It puts the emphasis on selling, rather than advising, and can give advisers an incentive to sell an unsuitable product.

A typical hourly fee might range from £100 to £200 an hour, depending on the experience and qualifications of the adviser, but it could be more. You may also be charged, say, £20–50 a month if you want continuing advice. You may hear it said that fees are liable to VAT, whereas commission is not. This is not the case. If you pay fees as an alternative to commission, you should not have to pay VAT. However, if you pay separately for other services such as, say, a pension valuation, you might have to pay VAT.

Fees sound high, but they might work out cheaper than commission because the adviser should ensure either that the commission is used to increase the amount invested on your behalf, or that a no-commission investment with lower charges is chosen. Do not be afraid to ask an adviser whether their fees are likely to come to more than the amount of commission they think they can save you. Some advisers may also be prepared to produce a financial plan for you on a fixed-fee basis.

If you are unwilling or unable to pay an up-front fee – which is likely to be several hundred or even several thousand pounds – a third option is commission offset. The adviser charges you a nominal fee, but any commission they receive reduces the fee. Sometimes, the adviser will agree not to charge you a fee unless you go ahead and arrange an investment through them, and promises that the fee, if you do buy, will not come to more than the commission. However, a 'no investment, no fee' deal doesn't get around the problem that the adviser gets paid only if you buy something, and so has a vested interest in getting you to do so.

Read the menu

Before you sign up with a particular adviser, he or she should give you a document called 'Keyfacts about the cost of our services'. This is a sort of menu of the payment options available from that adviser, including the amount of any fees or commission. It also tells you what the market average commission rate is, so that you can see how the amount that you are being asked to pay compares with average rates elsewhere. Figure 5.2 is an extract from a specimen keyfacts document showing average rates. For example, if you invest a lump sum of £10,000 in a unit trust, an average £370 of your money will immediately go in commission, but it is more likely to be £490 if you buy an insurance bond.

When looking at percentage commission rates, remember to take the likely value of your investment into account. An average annual commission rate of 0.25% on a monthly premium personal pension may not look like much, but if your pension fund reaches £50,000, the annual commission would amount to £125 a year, even if your adviser never gives you any advice after the initial sale.

Trade secret

Beware paying commission even if you get no advice

Commission is included in the charges you pay an investment company, and usually you pay the same charges even if you buy direct from the company. However, you can ask an adviser for a commission rebate, with the rebated amount paid into your investment on your behalf.

Qualifications

Anybody giving investment advice must have passed the Certificate in Financial Planning or its predecessor, the Financial Planning Certificate, or an equivalent exam, unless they are just giving basic advice. Advisers with this qualification will have the title 'Cert PFS' after their name.

Do bear in mind, though, that this qualification is at a basic level, and is regarded as roughly equivalent to an A level. Advisers are encouraged to work for higher-level qualifications, such as the Advanced Financial Planning Certificate (AFPC) or other optional exams run by the Chartered Insurance Institute, the Institute of Financial Planning, the Securities and Investment Institute, or the Chartered Institute of Bankers. Advisers may also have accountancy or legal qualifications.

Figure 5.2: Extract from 'Keyfacts' document 2 – the cost of advice

4. How much might our services cost?

If you choose the fee option

We will agree the rate we will charge before beginning work. We will tell you if you have to pay VAT.
Our typical charges are:

Director	**£150-200 per hour**
Financial adviser	**£100-150 per hour**

You may ask us for an estimate of how much in total we might charge. You may also ask us not to exceed a given amount without checking with you first.

If you choose the commission option

Tables 1 and 2 show examples of the amounts of commission we could receive (or the equivalent we earn through product charges) and compare those amounts with the market average (see notes 1 & 2 at the end of this section 4).

The amounts vary according to the type of product, the amount you invest, and (sometimes) how long you invest for, or your age when you start the product. We will confirm the actual amount to you before you buy a product.

Table 1 - Commission if you invest monthly

Products	Example term or age	Comparison of costs		Example based on £100 per month
		Our maximum	Market average	This shows the maximum costs of our sales and advice for a monthly investment or premium of £100, ignoring any changes in fund value
Savings and investments				
Collective investments (eg unit trusts)	Any	5% of all payments	5.2% of all payments	£60.00 each year
Endowments	10 year term	30% of each of the first 16 month's payments plus 2.5% of all payments from month 17	24.7% of each of the first 16 month's payments plus 2.5% of all payments from month 17	£480.00 spread evenly over the first 16 months plus £30.00 each year from month 17
Protection				
Whole of life assurance	Age 40	90% of each of the first 12 month's payments plus 2.5% of all payments from month 49	101.6% of the first 12 month's payments plus 2.5% of all payments from month 49	£1080.00 spread evenly over the first 12 months plus £30.00 each year from month 49
Saving for retirement				
Personal and Stakeholder pensions	25 year term	20% of each of the first 12 month's payments plus 0.25% of your fund value each year from year 1	20.3% of the first 12 month's payments plus 0.25% of your fund value each year from year 1	£240.00 spread evenly over the first 12 months plus £3.00 in year 1, £6.00 in year 2, and so on (The actual amount in later years will vary in line with your fund value)
	10 year term	15% of each of the first 12 month's payments plus 0.25% of your fund value each year from year 1	19% of the first 12 month's payments plus 0.25% of your fund value each year from year 1	£180.00 spread evenly over the first 12 months plus £3.00 in year 1, £6.00 in year 2, and so on (The actual amount in later years will vary in line with your fund value)

Table 2 - Commission if you invest a lump sum

Products	Example term or age	Comparison of costs		Example based on £10 000 lump sum
		Our maximum	Market average	This shows the maximum costs of our sales and advice for a lump sum investment of £10 000, ignoring any changes in fund value
Savings and investments				
Collective investments (eg unit trusts)	Any	3% of the amount you invest plus **0.25%** of your fund value each year from year **1**	3.7% of the amount you invest plus **0.25%** of your fund value each year from year **1**	**£300.00** initially plus **£25.00** each year from year 1 (The actual amount in later years will vary in line with your fund value)
Investment bonds	Any	7% of the amount you invest	4.9% of the amount you invest	**£700.00** initially
Saving for retirement				
Personal and Stakeholder pensions	Any	**0.5%** of your fund value each year from year **1**	**0.6%** of your fund value each year from year **1**	**£50.00** each year from year 1 (The actual amount in later years will vary in line with your fund value)
At retirement				
Annuities	Any	**1.5%** of the amount you invest	**1.4%** of the amount you invest	**£150.00** initially
Income drawdown	Any	3% of the amount you invest plus **0.5%** of your fund value each year from year **1**	1.8% of the amount you invest plus **0.5%** of your fund value each year from year **1**	**£300.00** initially plus **£50.00** each year from year 1 (The actual amount in later years will vary in line with your fund value)

Notes:
1. The market average figures are calculated by the FSA using actual data from a representative sample of regulated firms and are shown in a way that you may compare with our own maximum rates. The market average figures will be updated by the FSA from time to time based on new data.
2. Where a firm sells its own products, it must calculate its figures according to FSA guidelines.

5. Further information

If you need any more help or information
- ask your adviser; or
- visit www.fsa.gov.uk/consumer.

Last updated 1 April 2005

FSA rules require advisers to keep up to date. They should be happy to tell you about their qualifications, particularly if you are looking for advice on a specialist and highly technical area, such as pensions, investing for long-term care, or equity release schemes.

Jargon alert

Alphabet spaghetti

Don't be swayed by a string of letters after someone's name, sometimes known as alphabet spaghetti. The letters might just mean that the adviser belongs to a particular trade association.

Finding an adviser

For lists of advisers in your area, you can use the following websites and telephone helplines (contact details are in the Fact file):

- 'Find an Adviser' website run by the Personal Finance Society
- telephone helpline and website run by IFA Promotion
- website of the Institute of Financial Planning – this only includes advisers who have met demanding requirements to become a Certified Financial Planner
- online directories of investment managers and stockbrokers on the APCIMs website, and specialist solicitors on the ASIM website.

Not all advisers appear on these lists, and if you come across them through other routes you should check that they are authorised by the FSA. If they are not, and you have problems, you will not be able to use the Financial Ombudsman Service or Financial Services Compensation Scheme. The FSA's consumer helpline can tell you if an adviser is authorised, or you can check online using the Firm Check service. This service can also tell you if the FSA has taken any disciplinary action against the firm. However, since this information started to be included only recently, the lack of any recent action does not mean that the firm has always had a clean bill of health.

Recommendations from friends or family are a popular way of finding an adviser. Remember, though, that financial planning is a long-term process and someone's initial favourable impressions may fade over time if an adviser fails to live up to expectations. It is even more important to check the hard facts such as the adviser's range of services, to be sure that they suit your needs.

Help with sorting out problems

Many people have found that if they have problems with a particular investment – an endowment policy, say, or mis-sold personal pension – the adviser who sold it to them disappears like snow in summer, and it can be difficult to find someone else prepared to give advice on what to do. You are more likely to have to pay a fee for advice, but if you are really stuck you could also try a not-for-profit agency such as a Citizens' Advice Bureau or Money Advice agency. Some agencies have links with advisers or organisations, such as the Pensions Advisory Service. The Money Advice Trust is an umbrella organisation. Treat with caution commercial agencies that offer to help you pursue a complaint – their fees can be steep.

Trade secret

Advice arranged by your employer

Your employer may have links with a firm of financial advisers, and it is worth investigating whether your employer is prepared to pick up some or all of the cost of an advice session for staff. Pensions advice paid for by your employer is now a tax-free fringe benefit, as is debt counselling and other welfare counselling.

Questions to ask

Once you have some names of possible advisers, you should investigate their range of services, the number of companies they represent, their qualifications and how they charge for their services (fees or commission). Even if you find an adviser who appears to meet all your requirements on paper, how good will they be in practice? These are some questions to ask:

1 What experience do they have? However good their qualifications, they need practice at putting it into effect.

2 How do they keep up to date? What sources of information do they have, and are they working for higher-level qualifications?

3 Will they look at the whole of your finances, including your loans and protection needs, or do they advise only on the investment side?

4 What approach do they take to advising you? Can you see an example of their written advice? This will show you how clearly they can explain things.

5 Will the same person deal with you throughout?

6 What back-up is there if your adviser is off sick, run over by a bus, or leaves the firm? A larger firm is more likely to have back-up, but it may be more impersonal and your adviser may leave.

7 How many and what sort of clients does your adviser have? Do they have experience of handling your sort of situation? If your adviser has lots of richer clients, how can you be sure that you won't be at the end of their 'to do' list?

8 What tools does the adviser have to help you? For example, do they have access to online quotation systems and databases? If they refer you on to someone else for specialist help, what will it cost you and what will be in it for your adviser?

9 What about your existing policies and investments? What help can you expect with these?

10 What help will the adviser give you in future? How often can you expect to hear from them, and will it cost extra?

Beware of any adviser who is not happy to answer these questions.

> Trade secret

Watch where your money is going

If your adviser recommends that you buy an investment, they should ask you to pay the investment company direct. Be suspicious of advisers who ask you to make cheques out in their own name: some unauthorised advisers have conned people by pretending to invest in fictitious investments.

Jargon alert

Churning

If someone advises you to cash in an investment unnecessarily in order to buy another one for the purpose of generating more commission, this is called churning. Beware of an adviser who advises you to cash in an investment early, unless they give good reasons for doing so.

6

Choosing your tools

By now you should know what the gaps in your financial plan are, and Chapter 3 should have given you a broad idea of the type of saving or investment that you need to fill them, such as a savings account, British Government stock, or a stockmarket-linked investment. There is more information about each type of investment in Part 2. This chapter looks at:

- how to choose a savings account
- if you decide you want a stockmarket-linked investment, whether to invest via a life insurance or pension policy, unit trust or OEIC, or investment trust
- how to choose an investment fund.

Choosing a savings account

For information about different types of savings accounts, see page 266. You should also consider the accounts on offer from National Savings & Investments; see page 220.

Don't restrict yourself to accounts available from high-street branches of the big organisations as they are often the poorest value. Branch-based savings accounts generally pay less than accounts operated by phone, internet or post. But there are some branch-based accounts aimed at particular groups, such as pensioners, children or people who live locally, that pay good rates.

Smaller, newer organisations may also have to pay particularly good rates to establish themselves in the market. If you are worried that you haven't heard of the organisation before, you should check that it is regulated by the Financial Services Authority and is a member of the Financial Ombudsman Service (see Chapter 2 for how to check up on financial institutions).

Newspaper money supplements have regular round-ups of the best rates on offer, such as *Money Mail*'s Savings Watch, but there is also a wealth of information on the internet. The Financial Services Authority has useful tables on its website comparing savings rates. However, do be aware that not all internet sites cover all savings organisations, and each site may have slightly different criteria for what they choose as a best buy.

Whatever the organisation, you cannot count on good rates to continue (see Trade secret). Non-branch-based organisations with lower overheads may be able to sustain good rates for longer, but there is no substitute for shopping around and being prepared to move if necessary.

Trade secret

Beware the best-buy tactics

In the battle to appear in the best-buy lists, savings institutions may resort to tactics such as delaying a cut in interest rates until after the newspaper money supplements are published; boosting their headline rate by paying introductory bonuses, or having tiered interest rates with the highest rate available only if you deposit very large amounts; introducing restrictions such as limiting the number of withdrawals each year; or offering a very good rate and then dropping it to an uncompetitive level once it has drawn in the punters. To beat these tactics:

■ Always check the small print for nasty surprises, such as limited withdrawals or high rates only for large deposits. Beware of letting the balance in an account drop below the minimum. If it does, no interest or a negligible amount may be paid.

■ After the Bank of England changes its base rates, wait for the dust to settle before choosing an account.

■ Be sceptical about bonuses and introductory rates. The interest rate may not be competitive once the bonus or introductory period is over, and you won't necessarily be reminded when the period runs out.

■ Look for guarantees – such as a guarantee to stay within 0.5% of the bank base rate – or a tracker account, which is guaranteed to change in line with base rates.

■ Stay on top of interest rates, and be prepared to move your money to a more competitive account. Under the terms of the Banking Code, which most account providers have signed up to, you should be sent a list of current interest rates at least once a year if your account has more than £500 in it.

Life insurance, pensions, unit trusts or investment trusts?

If you want to invest in things like shares, corporate bonds and property, it makes sense to buy them through a packaged investment unless you have enough money and expertise to invest in these things directly.

Packaged investments are life insurance policies, personal pensions, unit trusts, OEICs (see Jargon alert on page 46) and investment trusts. They all offer similar types of investment fund, but their legal structures and tax treatment are very different, so it is important to choose the right type of package for you. This is what you should take into account:

- what you get out (a lump sum or income?)
- what you must pay in
- types of fund available
- tax treatment.

There is more detail about each type of product package in Part 2, but Table 6.1 on page 99 summarises the principal differences. Once you have decided what sort of package suits you best, you will need to choose a fund to put your money in (this is covered on page 98).

Jargon alert

Key features

If you are thinking of buying a savings-type life insurance policy, unit trusts/OEICs, a personal pension, a stocks and shares ISA or an investment trust savings plan, the company must give you a document setting out the key features of the investment. This should cover most of the information below, as well as the risks associated with the investment. In some cases it may include a personal illustration (see Trade secret on page 102). Note, though, that key features documents are not required for cash-based products, or (under current rules) investment trusts bought outside a savings plan. The FSA is also considering changes to key features documents.

Jargon alert

Stakeholder products

Stakeholder products meet certain minimum standards laid down by the government. You can choose the following types of stakeholder products for short-term, medium-term and longer-term savings:

- *Short-term*: a cash savings account (see page 268 for an explanation of the minimum standards).
- *Medium-term*: an investment fund with a maximum of 60% in shares and property. The fund may be set up as a unit trust/OEIC or as a life insurance policy. The annual management charge is capped at 1.5% for ten years and 1% after that.
- *Long-term*: a stakeholder pension (see page 253).

Because of the maximum charges (or minimum interest rate, for the savings account) it is worth including stakeholder products on your shopping list. But you may only get basic advice when buying (see Chapter 5 for more on this). The short-term and medium-term products can be bought within an ISA.

What you get

Packaged investments are all medium to long-term, and you should be happy to leave your money invested for a minimum of 5–10 years.

With unit trusts/OEICs and investment trusts, you can usually cash in part or all of your units or shares at any point (provided you are willing to realise a loss if prices have fallen), although some unit trusts/OEICs now charge exit fees. You may also get regular dividends (called distributions for unit trusts), but these will vary in amount. If you don't want the income, you can automatically reinvest it. Some funds are also designed to provide higher-than-normal income.

Pensions are designed to provide an income in retirement (although you don't have to stop work to draw your benefits). So you usually cannot get your money out before age 50 (increasing to 55 by 2010), and although you can take part of your pension as a lump sum, most of it must be paid out as income over the rest of your life.

Regular-premium life insurance policies are designed to pay out a lump sum and usually run for a minimum of ten years.

Single-premium insurance bonds do not usually have a formal maturity date. You can leave your money to grow, or cash in part as needed or on a regular basis. But there are often charges on cashing in within the first five years, and with-profits bonds may charge 'market value reductions' at any time (see page 201). You should not rely on any stockmarket-linked fund for a fixed income (see page 30).

With some types of life insurance or pension policy, part of your premium is deducted to pay for life insurance on your death or illness, rather than being invested. Generally, though, it is more efficient to buy a separate insurance policy to cover you in the event of illness or death (see Chapter 1).

What you pay in

Only regular-premium life insurance policies, such as endowments, require you to make regular payments. With them, you are making a significant commitment.

With the other packages, it's usually up to you whether you save regularly or invest a lump sum. Life insurance bonds are set up for one-off payments, but will accept further investments later on. Unit trusts/OEICs and investment trusts are also designed for lump sums, but many management companies have savings plans which you can set up to accept regular payments.

With personal pensions, you can choose a regular premium or single premium pension plan, but if you choose a regular premium plan check whether there are any penalties for stopping contributions.

The minimum investment varies according to the management company and the fund. If you want to save regularly, some companies will accept monthly payments of £20 or £25, but a £50 minimum will widen your choice. For lump sums, £500 is a typical minimum, but some companies require a larger amount, sometimes up to several thousand.

If you are investing the minimum amount, the cost of any investment becomes even more important. Beware of flat-rate charges that will take a greater proportion of a small investment than a large one.

Jargon alert

Pound cost averaging

You will often hear it said that regular investing into a share-based or unit-linked investment (such as unit trusts, unit-linked life insurance or investment trusts) has the edge over investing a lump sum, because when prices are low, your regular investment buys more units or shares – so-called pound cost averaging. But it all depends on how the price fluctuates. Regular investing can reduce the impact of stockmarket falls, but also stockmarket gains.

Types of fund available

All packaged investments put your money into investment funds that are usually linked to the stockmarket (although some cash funds are available). This exposes your money to the risk of capital loss (see Chapter 2). Whether you invest via a unit trust, OEIC or insurance bond, the risks you face depend largely on the type of fund you choose, and some types of fund are considerably more risky than others. However, the different types of packaged investment have slightly different rules about how the fund can be structured which may affect your choice:

■ *Life insurance and pension funds* are allowed to hold a broad range of investments within one fund, although not all funds use this freedom. Insurance companies also offer with-profits funds. As described on page 198, these work in a unique way, although many are no longer attractive.

■ *Investment trust funds* are significantly different from other funds, so you should approach them with caution. First, the trust fund is a company in which you buy shares, and the share price depends on how popular the trust is, not just the value of its investments. Second, the fund can borrow to buy investments. This gearing, as it is known, magnifies the effect of any change in price (see page 34). Third, investment trusts are not regulated to the same extent as other packaged products (see page 189). They can have some advantages, such as low costs, but you need to choose your trust with care.

■ *Unit trusts and OEICs* are probably the simplest type of fund. The price of each unit reflects the value of the underlying investments, and they are easy to buy and sell directly from the fund manager.

Tax treatment

Tax is covered in detail in Chapter 4, and see the summary in Table 6.1. But these are the factors to take into account when choosing between different types of packaged investment:

- *Personal pensions*, if you want to invest for your retirement, have big tax advantages. The pension company claims basic-rate tax relief to add to your investment, even if you aren't a taxpayer. You can draw part of your fund on retirement as a tax-free lump, although the rest has to be drawn as an income. There is no capital gains tax to pay.
- *Life insurance policies* also have a special tax regime. But this does not mean that the policy is tax-free. Life insurance really only saves tax for higher-rate taxpayers or people who would otherwise be liable to pay capital gains tax.
- *Unit trusts/OEICs and investment trusts* are usually taxed in the same way as company shares. Dividends and distributions are liable to income tax, and any gain is liable to capital gains tax.

You can avoid almost all the tax by buying unit trusts/OEICs, investment trusts and some types of life insurance policy through an Individual Savings Account (ISA). However, you cannot invest much in ISAs each year (see page 183).

Choosing an investment fund

Each insurance company or unit trust company, say, has its own range of funds, run by its in-house fund managers, but increasingly companies also offer funds run by other managers. You can switch your money between the funds.

The types of fund available are categorised slightly differently according to whether you buy the fund through an insurance policy, pension policy, unit trust, OEIC or investment trust, but the most common types of fund are shown in Table 6.2.

Table 6.1: Product packages compared

	What you get	Restrictions	Tax
Life insurance (see page 196)	Regular savings policies: lump sum on maturity. No income. Lump-sum bond: can cash in part or all of your investment.	Regular savings policies last at least ten years. Most lump-sum bonds expect you to invest for at least five years. May be steep penalties on early withdrawal.	Fund pays equivalent of basic-rate tax; no further tax for basic-rate taxpayers, but payouts may affect your tax if you're a higher-rate taxpayer or aged 65 or over. Payout not liable to capital gains tax. Can buy some types of policy through an ISA.
Personal pension plan (see page 250)	A lifetime pension for you and, if you wish, a partner. Part of pension may be taken as a lump sum.	Can't usually get your money out before age 50 (increasing to 55 by 2010). Money must largely be taken as an income; you can take only up to a quarter of the fund as cash.	Tax relief at your top rate of tax on contributions; favourable tax treatment of pension fund. Can withdraw part of fund as tax-free lump sum, but income is taxable. Not liable to capital gains tax.
Unit trust/ OEIC (see page 287)	Lump sum on cashing in units. Can normally cash in part or all of investment. Variable income, depending on type of fund chosen.	Can normally cash in on demand, except with some types of fund or if the fund is suspended.	Fund pays some tax on income. Income is paid with some tax deducted; higher-rate taxpayers may have to pay more. May have to pay capital gains tax (unless held in an ISA).

Table 6.2: Investment funds – a spotter's guide

Income funds	Fixed interest funds, also known as bond funds, gilt funds, high-income funds	Invest mainly in British Government stocks (a gilts fund) or in a mixture of gilts, other government bonds, and corporate bonds, either in the UK or internationally (see also page 154).
	Distribution funds	Invest in a mixture of assets, such as shares, bonds and property, but they aim to produce and pay out (or 'distribute') a relatively high income.
	UK equity income, also known as growth and income funds	Invest mainly in UK shares, but aim to produce an income from them that is higher than the normal income from equity funds.
Growth funds	With-profits funds	Special life insurance funds (see page 198).
	Managed or balanced funds	Can invest in a range of stocks and shares; managed insurance funds can also hold property and cash deposits. Defensive and cautious managed funds aim to reduce risk by putting comparatively little money into shares; balanced managed funds can invest nearly all the fund in shares to increase the potential return; stockmarket, growth and active managed funds can invest the whole fund in shares.
	UK equity funds, also known as UK growth funds	Invest up to 80% of their money in shares in UK companies, either any UK company (all companies funds), or smaller companies.
	Index tracking funds	Aim to track a particular share index, usually a UK share index but sometimes a global or regional index (see page 103).
	Geographical funds, e.g. North American	Invest in shares of companies in a particular region (e.g. Europe) or in a single country (e.g. Japan).
	Global growth	Invest mainly in shares, but with not more than a certain percentage from any one region.

Capital protected funds	Money market funds	Invest in special accounts used by financial organisations as short-term homes for surplus cash. Because the fund is investing large sums, it can get good interest rates.
	Guaranteed or protected funds	Guarantee to return a set amount, or more limited protection (see page 172).
Specialist funds	Ethical funds	Aim to invest in line with a particular ethical stance, e.g. in environmentally friendly enterprises (see page 166).
	Industry sectors	Specialise in shares of a particular industry, e.g. technology, healthcare.
	Property funds	Invest in commercial property, or in the shares of property companies (see page 261). Currently mainly insurance funds.

> Trade secret

Income funds are not just for income investors

As Table 6.2 shows, some funds are classified as income funds because they aim to pay out a higher-than-normal income. The fund managers do this by investing in companies or stocks that they expect to pay out good dividends. If you invest in such a fund, you don't have to draw the income, you can reinvest it. This is worth considering. The income can roll up to provide a good return even if the stockmarket is in the doldrums.

Don't be dazzled by past performance

Don't choose a fund purely on the basis of how it has performed in the past. A lot of research shows that just because a fund has performed well in the past, it will not necessarily do so in future, although research does suggest that funds that have performed poorly will continue to do so.

Some individual fund managers have produced consistently good results, and putting your money with a successful manager is a popular strategy. The problem is that good managers are often poached by the opposition, and moving your money from one fund to another to follow the manager is likely to be expensive because you may incur initial charges each time. One way round this might be a 'manager of manager' fund (see Jargon alert).

Jargon alert

Manager of managers and funds of funds

There are two ways of sidestepping the difficulty of choosing a fund:

- *Manager of managers funds* subcontract the management of different portions of the fund to managers from other fund management companies. The managers work to a brief, for example you might get a cautious fund, or a riskier growth fund.
- *Funds of funds* invest directly in other funds. Some have to stick to the funds run by the same management company, but others can invest in any funds.

Funds of funds usually have a more aggressive approach, while manager of managers funds are more risk-averse. Both types of fund have a big disadvantage: you are paying two sets of managers and this puts the charges up. Manager of managers funds are usually better value, but they are relatively new so it is difficult to predict their future performance.

Trade secret

Limitations of illustrations and projections

Your adviser – or the investment company – may give you an illustration of what your investment might be worth in the future. Treat this with caution. Illustrations are based on standard assumptions of how much, on average, your investment might grow. It may grow by more or less. But these illustrations are a useful way of demonstrating the effect of charges, because they include the amount that might be deducted – again, assuming your investment grows by a certain amount each year. Don't forget, though, that the company may change its charges later on, and there is a possibility that the rules for projections may also change (the FSA is reviewing their use).

Choose the right type of fund for you

Funds are invested in different sectors – for example, UK shares or global shares – and some sectors are more risky than others. As explained in Chapter 2, there are lots of different types of risk, but a useful indicator of how far the fund value might swing up and down is its volatility (see below).

Novice investors might want to start with a fund with low volatility, such as a managed fund which spreads your money across several different types of investment. You could also consider a lifestyle fund, which automatically moves your money into less volatile fund sectors over time (see page 54), or a medium-term stakeholder fund (see page 95).

Look at the volatility

Volatility is a way of measuring the extent to which an investment is affected by changes in the stockmarket. For example, a defensive balanced or cautious managed fund is designed not to fall too far in value if stockmarket prices fall, but you may not get such a good return when prices rise. Such a fund is said to have low volatility. Figure 6.1 below shows the relative volatility of some types of investment funds, with 1 being very low volatility and 5 or more being very high. But volatility is just part of the picture, and you should treat volatility ratings with caution. They are worked out on the basis of what has happened in the recent past, and there is no guarantee that this will continue.

Decide whether you want an active or passive fund

An index-tracking fund that simply copies a stockmarket index is said to be a passive fund; one where the manager makes a positive decision to buy or sell investments is an active fund. Supporters of passive funds point out that the majority of active managers do not beat the index, partly because their charges are much higher than those for most passive funds. Fans of the active approach, however, argue that their greater freedom is particularly helpful when the stockmarket falls.

Given the difficulty of choosing an active fund, a tracker fund is a good first step. Note, though, that:

Figure 6.1 Volatility of various types of investment fund

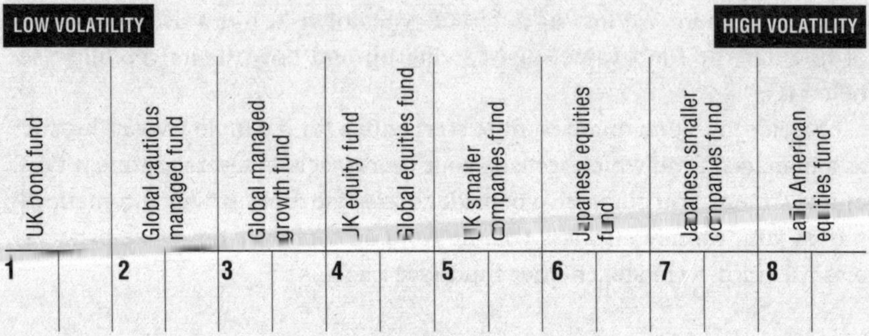

Source: *Money Management*, May 2005

- index-tracking funds will not completely reflect the performance of the index, because of small differences in their tracking techniques
- most funds track the FTSE 100 (or Footsie) index, which is made up of only the top 100 shares, but some track other indices, such as the FTSE All Share, which spread your investment more widely
- most tracker funds have low charges and deduct no initial charge. Avoid the exceptions – a few have initial charges up to 4%.

An alternative to a conventional tracker is an Exchange Traded Fund (see page 289).

Look behind the labels

Once you know what sort of fund you want, you can consult the newspapers for lists of funds in that category. For unit trusts and OEICs, the Investment Management Association has a fund directory, available free either in paper form or on their website (see the Fact file). For investment trusts, the Association of Investment Trust Companies can provide similar information. There is also a wealth of information on the internet, but you should be careful to check that it comes from a reputable source.

Do not assume that all the funds in one category offer a similar level of risk or volatility: it depends on the specific investments in the fund, how much of it is invested abroad and vulnerable to exchange rate changes, and so on. Be particularly careful when investing in bond funds. These have often been cited as low risk, but this depends on what types of bonds the fund is investing in. Some can be quite high risk, particularly if they are aiming to pay a high income.

Many companies rate their own funds in terms of relative riskiness, and there are also many organisations such as Standard & Poor's that rate funds. Just remember that the fund manager is far more likely to tell you about their fund's rating and past performance if it is good than if it is bad.

Go for a low-charge fund

Fund charges can make a significant difference to your investment. Good performance may make up for high charges, but as it is impossible to predict future performance with any certainty, you are advised to check the following:

■ *The initial charge.* When you first invest, a slice of your money is taken to cover the costs of selling and administering your investment, including any commission to the salesperson. This is typically 3–6% of your money (so only £9,400–9,700 of a £10,000 investment is actually invested for you). However, initial charges vary a lot: some types of fund have lower charges, and some products have lower initial charges plus exit charges when you cash in your investment. You can often get a discount on the charge (see Trade secret on page 74). Note that with life insurance policies, part of your premium may also go to pay for any benefits payable on your death.

■ *The annual charge.* Each year, around 1–2% of the value of your investment is taken to cover fund management charges and any further commission payable to the salesperson. Some funds adjust their fees depending on their performance (see page 291).

■ *Surrender penalties or exit charges.* When you cash in an insurance policy you may have to pay a surrender penalty. A few unit trusts also make an exit charge that gradually reduces for each year you keep your investment, but if so there will be no initial charge or a low one. Other unit trusts and investment trusts have no charges on cashing in.

However, charges are not the only costs of investment. Other costs are deducted from the value of the fund as a whole, such as fees for the fund trustees, auditors or registrars, and the costs of buying and selling investments.

In general, insurance policies have had higher charges than other funds, and some investment trusts have had low charges. But insurance policies have been under pressure to trim their costs, while charges for some unit trusts have been gradually drifting upwards. The type of fund also makes a big difference: an index-tracking fund is likely to cost less to manage than a fund specialising in Latin American investments, say. In all types of package there are good-value and bad-value investments, and you may also be able to negotiate lower initial charges.

The key features document you get before you buy most packaged investment policies will show the effect of charges on your investment, and you can use this to compare different companies. You can also find the effect of charges for each company on the Financial Services Authority's comparative tables, available on its website.

Jargon alert

Reduction in yield and total expense ratio

There are two ways of showing the cost of charges:

- The reduction in yield (RIY) tells you the extent to which charges will reduce the potential return from your investment. So, for example, an RIY of 1.5% will reduce the return on an investment from, say, 5% to 3.5%. The larger the RIY, the greater are the charges. RIYs for some types of packaged product have to be shown in key features documents.
- A total expense ratio (TER) may also be shown for unit trusts and OEICs. But this reflects only the year-on-year charges of a fund; it doesn't include initial charges when you first invest, or exit charges when you leave. TERs for individual funds can be found on the website of the Investment Management Association and the Association of Investment Trust Companies.

> ## Trade secret

Cost is critical
Your investment needs to grow by more than the cost of investing before you make any money at all. So if you pay an initial charge of 5%, your investment needs to grow by at least 5% or you will lose money.

Annual charges may look insignificant, but they can have a big impact. A £5,000 investment growing by 7% a year should grow to be worth £19,348 after 20 years (with no annual expenses). But if the annual expenses are just 1% these will drag down the return to £16,036.

Be careful how you buy and sell
Each time you buy into an investment fund, you incur an initial charge. Remember that if you buy through an adviser, you can negotiate the charges you pay. Advisers may waive part or all of their commission so that you pay a smaller initial charge. If you have access to the internet, a fund supermarket is another cheap way of buying (see Chapter 8). However, with the lowest-cost ways of buying, you will not generally get advice.

7

....

Choosing different tools for different jobs

This chapter considers the needs of people in different situations, such as parents, couples, pensioners and people who depend on their savings to top up their income, and suggests ways of making their money work harder for them.

Saving for your child's future

The diagnosis

Children may need financial help from their parents for much longer than in previous generations. Once school is out of the way, you may have to support your son or daughter through college and then, possibly, contribute towards their first home.

If you have young children and only small sums to save, it can be difficult to build up a significant lump sum. For example, a standard high-street savings account may give a return of only 1% a year, after taking tax and inflation into account. At 1%, if you start to save £25 a month when a child is born, by the time he or she reaches 18 you will have about £5,500, for an outlay of £5,100. In these circumstances, the lessons of sensible investing – keeping the tax bill low, looking for the best return, and saving long-term – apply more than ever. For example, if you can push the return up to 3%, you will get about £6,600.

The prescription

- *Regular saving, starting when your child is young.* Consider having your child benefit paid directly into a separate savings account as a way of building up a lump sum, even if you have to dip into it to pay one-off expenses. Some banks and building societies offer good rates on regular savings accounts, and there are now one or two special high-interest accounts for people saving their child benefit.

- *Low-risk savings if you are a taxpayer.* There are several tax-free
  schemes with no risk of capital loss. Banks, building societies and
  National Savings offer tax-free cash ISAs, which usually allow you
  instant access to your money (but children must be at least 16 to open
  an ISA in their own names). If you are prepared to tie up your money
  for five years, the government-backed National Savings & Investments
  offers children's bonus bonds (which can be opened in the child's
  own name from birth), savings certificates and index-linked savings
  certificates.

- *Topping up a Child Trust Fund.* A child born after 31 August 2002
  should receive a Child Trust Fund voucher from the government,
  which can be used to open a special tax-free account. Family and
  friends can pay up to £1,200 a year into the account for the child,
  although the money cannot be withdrawn until the child is 18 (see
  page 150).

- *Don't assume that special 'children's plans' will always offer the best deal.*
  You need to check what exactly you are buying – it may be a savings
  account, unit trust or OEIC or life insurance policy. A stakeholder
  child trust fund account has caps on charges which make them good
  value, but the money is invested in the stockmarket and could fall in
  value. And special life insurance policies may have high charges.

- *Don't rule out stockmarket-linked investments if you are investing long
  term.* There is the risk of a capital loss but also the chance of capital
  gain. Consider one of the more cautious types of investment fund,
  such as an index-tracking unit trust fund (see Chapter 6). If you invest
  through a stocks and shares ISA, there will be no further tax to pay. A
  few funds are marketed specifically for children, but it is important to
  check the charges.

- *If you want to help an older child buy a home.* Several lenders now
  offer loans for this purpose, but think about the tax consequences
  first. If you buy a house in your own name, it may become liable to
  capital gains tax when you pass it on to your child (whereas your
  main home is usually tax-free). And if your child pays you rent, it is
  taxable (although you can deduct the mortgage interest and any other
  expenses). You may instead be able to guarantee a loan for your child
  to buy in his or her own name, so that it is classed as their main home.

■ *If you can afford to put money away for decades.* You can pay up to £2,808 a year into a stakeholder pension for a child, of any age, and the government will add a further 28% in tax relief, but your child cannot get at the money until they reach 55. If you can afford to do this, you should also consider a self-invested personal pension (SIPP, covered on page 276).

Trade secret

Using the child's own tax allowance

Children have their own tax allowance, like anybody else, and most children are non-taxpayers. If your child has his or her own savings, you can ask to have the interest paid tax-free (see page 274). But parents cannot save tax by giving children money to invest in their own names. This is because income arising from a gift to your child is taxable as yours and must be declared on your tax return, unless it comes to less than £100 a year (per parent per child). However, this doesn't apply to gifts from other people, such as grandparents. Parents can also avoid tax in these circumstances by choosing tax-free accounts such as children's bonus bonds from National Savings & Investments, or by topping up a Child Trust Fund account.

Trade secret

Saving inheritance tax

If you want to give money to a child who is too young to have an account in his or her own name, you can designate investments in the name of a particular child if you want to, but the money still counts as belonging to you. Alternatively, most savings accounts, and some investments, allow you to set up the account as a 'bare trust' for a child. This belongs to the child, and is often said to fall outside your estate for inheritance tax purposes. However inheritance tax is now so complicated that it is worth getting a trust properly drawn up, and taking professional advice if much money is at stake. There are also other tax implications to how you pass on your money (see above).

A child's own savings

If you want your child to have day-to-day control of a savings account in his or her own name, the minimum age is usually seven, sometimes older. However, you can open an account in trust for younger children. This means that the account belongs to the child, but you operate it on their behalf until they are old enough to control it themselves.

A bank or building society is the automatic first choice, and good deals are available (see page 264). Unless your child has at least £100, forget the Post Office: the old-fashioned Post Office account, the National Savings & Investments (NS&I) ordinary account, is no longer available, and the alternative NS&I easy access account requires a minimum balance of £100.

Children cannot buy a unit trust or investment trust in their own name until they reach 18, but you can designate one for them, or (depending on the company) hold it in trust for them (see above). However, a child born after 31 August 2002 can save in the stockmarket through a Child Trust Fund account, although they cannot get the money out until they are 18. (See page 150.)

Saving for retirement

The diagnosis

The state pension will provide a man earning £21,500 with less than one-third of his pre-retirement earnings, and that assumes that he pays National Insurance Contributions for the whole of his working life (44 years). If you want to top your retirement income up to, say, two-thirds of what it was, you will need to save around 9% of your earnings if you start to save at age 25, 14% if you start to save at age 35 and 19% if you wait until you are 40. This assumes that you get a rate of return of 3.3% and you retire at 65 – you'll need more if you're hoping to retire earlier.

As this shows, starting to put money aside for retirement in your 20s should be less painful than waiting until later on. Unfortunately, 9% of your salary at age 25 may be a bigger sacrifice than 19% at 40, and 9% may seem an unattainable figure at any age, particularly since you cannot generally draw cash from your pension until you retire. Many people also question whether pensions are as good a home for their money as property, as economic changes have led to lower incomes from private pensions and employers' schemes are seen as less secure than in the past.

On the plus side, pensions' inflexibility also means that you aren't tempted to dip into your retirement fund. As explained on page 259, relying on property alone can be a high-risk strategy. And the affordability of saving when you are older will depend on your personal risk factors: your job prospects, and whether you have children to support and a large mortgage to pay off.

However, you don't have to confine yourself to pensions, and it is possible to save in the long term while still finding the cash for shorter-term spending. (For further information on pensions, see page 240 for state pensions, page 230 for employers' pensions, and page 250 for personal pensions.)

The prescription

- *Start by estimating how much income you will need in retirement.* Half or two-thirds of your current income is a common starting-point, but if you are married look at your needs as a couple. Now work out how close to your target you already are, taking into account your state pension entitlement (see page 240) and any existing employer's or personal pension. If you are divorced or separated, you may have a claim on your ex-partner's pension. Once you know how far short of your target you are, consult the online calculator at www. pensioncalculator.org.uk to find out how much extra you need to save. For example, a man saving £100 a month might get a pension of around £80 a week at age 65 (with no inflation-proofing, lump sum or pension for a dependant) if he starts saving at 40, and around £130 if he starts at 30.

- *Does your savings shortfall look hopeless?* Don't despair. Look more closely at your target. Is it realistic? Will you really need that much? If you still think you have a shortfall, your options are to rely on the state, top up your pension or look for alternative long-term savings.

- *Relying on the state may be the best option for low earners.* It may not be worth saving if it reduces your eligibility for the means-tested state Pension Credit (see page 243). This is most likely if you are fairly close to retirement, with small savings to date, and your ability to save more is limited.

- *Consider topping up your pension.* Your money works harder for you in a pension. You get tax relief at your top rate of tax on private pensions, and although pension funds can no longer reclaim dividend tax credits, they are still favourably taxed.
- *Look at your employer's pension scheme.* If you do not join a scheme to which your employer contributes, you are effectively turning down extra pay, and possibly eligibility for other benefits such as life insurance and sick pay insurance. A salary-related employer's scheme is particularly valuable, but with any scheme you should keep an eye on the health of the pension fund.
- *If you are worried about tying up your money in a pension.* A more accessible form of saving may give you a shorter-term safety net as well as getting you some way towards your longer-term goals. The most important thing is to build up a regular pattern of saving. Consider opening an account which doesn't allow you immediate access to your money, to avoid the temptation of spending it, or consider five-year investments, some of which have tax advantages, such as tax-free National Savings Certificates. You can move your money into a pension later on (you can buy a personal pension with a single lump sum – monthly premiums are not necessary), and forthcoming changes to the pension rules mean that most people will be able to pay in as much as they earn.
- *Alternative longer-term investments.* If you won't need the money for 5–10 years or so, you should also consider investing in British Government stocks and stockmarket-linked investments. Regular saving in a stocks and shares ISA will give you some tax advantages (though they are only guaranteed to be available until 2010) while still allowing you access to your money if necessary. But you should consider moving your money into safer investments as you get closer to retirement, so-called lifestyling (see Jargon alert on page 54).
- *Substantial pension fund? Family business?* New rules make self-invested personal pensions (SIPPs) more flexible (see page 276). Just remember that this is a fast-developing market, to be approached with care.
- *Remember the effect of inflation.* If you are saving for ten years or more, you should not rely just on savings accounts. The return from these

may struggle to beat inflation. See page 31 for inflation-beating investments.

■ *Review your plans regularly* to ensure that they keep up with any changes in the pension or tax rules, and with any changes in your circumstances. You should get regular statements for your private pensions, but you have to request a forecast of your state pension (available from the government Pension Service, see the Fact file).

Investing for income

The diagnosis

The point of investing, for many people, is to supplement income when necessary: in a financial crisis, or when you retire, or to tide you over a period of heavy spending, such as when your children are at college. So at some point you will probably have to find ways of producing an income from your investments.

You will have to steer a careful course around three particular pitfalls:

■ *Inflation*, which reduces the purchasing power of your money (see page 30). You should plan to draw an increasing amount of income each year.

■ *Eating into your capital*, particularly if you are not sure how long you will need to draw income. For example, as Table 7.1 shows, if you draw £50 a month from a lump sum of £10,000, and invest the rest at a rate of 3% (after tax), your money will run out during year 18 if the income you draw increases by 2.5% a year.

■ *Taking on more risk in the search for income*. Falling interest rates at the end of the 20th century led to the development of new income-producing schemes that were riskier than they seemed, in particular stockmarket-linked precipice bonds (see page 181). Don't rule out having some money in the stockmarket, as long as you go into it with your eyes open.

Table 7.1 shows how many years your money will last, if you have a lump sum of £10,000 growing at an after-tax rate of 3% and draw various levels of income.

Table 7.1: When will £10,000 run out?[a]

Monthly starting income (£)	If income increases by	
	2.5% a year	5% a year
	Your money will be exhausted during year	
25	38	27
50	18	15
75	12	11
100	9	8
125	7	7

a Assuming growth of 3% (after tax) each year.

The prescription

- *Avoid putting all your eggs in one basket.* No investments are risk-free, inflation-protected and produce a high income. Unless you have only small sums at your disposal, think about your money in terms of pots: one pot to provide capital security and easy access to cash; one to protect you against inflation; and one to provide the income.
- *Do you need a fixed regular income?* Annuities, fixed interest savings accounts with a monthly income option, National Savings & Investment income bonds and British Government stocks provide this, but they may not give the best return and are vulnerable to inflation. Some stockmarket-linked investments provide regular income, but may eat into your capital if the stockmarket falls (see page 179).
- *Don't restrict yourself to traditional income-producing investments* (listed in Table 7.2). You could just invest for growth and cash in investments as needed. Alternatively, you can arrange your investments so that they mature, or pay out income, at times when you are likely to need an income top-up. For example, if you will need income in about five years' time, you could make regular investments in five-year Savings Certificates from National Savings & Investments, so that they mature in sequence.
- *Take specialist advice if you need income to pay for long-term care.* Your investments may affect your state benefits. Members of the organisation IFACare (see the Fact file) specialise in this area.

Table 7.2: Investments for income

Investment	Income	More information
Annuities	A regular lifetime income (fixed or increasing) in return for a lump sum	page 129
Cash-based	*An essential bedrock for your savings; low risk of loss, but may not provide a high enough income on their own*	
Savings accounts	Monthly income and fixed income options are available	page 264
National Savings & Investments	Income bonds and pensioners' income bonds are available	page 219
Guaranteed income bonds	Special insurance policies that pay out a fixed rate of interest	page 208
Fixed-interest stocks	*Usually pay fixed interest twice-yearly and a fixed sum on maturity, but can be sold on the stockmarket before maturity for a price that may rise or fall, depending on demand*	
British Government stocks	A loan to the UK government	page 136
Corporate bonds	Loans to companies; varying degrees of riskiness	page 154

Stockmarket-linked	*Income either variable or you risk eating into your capital, but stockmarket investments offer the chance of higher growth than a savings account, in return for higher risk*	
Pension income withdrawal	Regular withdrawals from a pension fund instead of buying an annuity; amount depends on stockmarket performance	page 254
High-income bonds	Many different types. Income may be fixed (in which case it may eat into your capital) or variable but with a minimum return of capital	page 179
Income funds	Unit trust or investment trust funds that specialise in providing a higher-than-normal level of income	page 287 for unit trusts, page 189 for investment trusts
Insurance bonds	Lump-sum investments in an insurance fund. Can make regular withdrawals but income is variable unless you are prepared to eat into capital if stockmarkets fall	page 206
Property	Rents can provide income. Equity release allows you to draw income from your home	page 259

Investing as a couple

The diagnosis

You can usually invest jointly with someone else (you don't have to be married), except for some investments with special tax rules such as pensions or ISAs. However, joint investment has its pros and cons, and the rules differ depending on whether you are talking about income tax, inheritance tax, state benefits and your rights on death or divorce. See below for some things to take into account. Useful information is also available from the charity One Plus One (see the Fact file). Note that the legal rules may be slightly different in Scotland and Northern Ireland.

The prescription

■ *Think about whether you need speedy access to the money.* With some investments, both of you may have to sign the paperwork to withdraw money. However, this does not apply to most bank or building society accounts, which are set up to pay out on just one signature (see page 271).

■ *Make sure that you each have something to live on if one of you dies.* There are legal formalities before most jointly owned investments, such as unit trusts, can be put into the survivor's name. However, money in a joint bank or savings account automatically goes to the other partner (whether or not you are married) without having to wait for the full legal formalities to be completed. And if you have nominated someone to receive a payout from your pension, or as the beneficiary of an insurance policy 'written in trust' (see page 15), this also goes directly to them. However, a joint life insurance policy may be either 'first death' or 'last death'; if it is the latter, it carries on until both of you die.

■ *Make a will to say who you want to inherit your money.* This is particularly important if you are not married. If you don't make a will, the laws that apply mean your partner will get nothing if you are unmarried. And even if you are married, your husband or wife will get only a limited amount.

■ *Arrange your investments to save tax.* You can save tax by putting some investments in the name of the lower-income partner, but if you are not married this might mean both a capital gains tax and an inheritance tax bill if you give away more than the tax-free limits. See Chapter 4 and page 70 for more on how joint investments are taxed. (Note that same-sex couples who have registered as civil partners are treated in the same way as married couples for tax purposes.)

■ *Be clear about ownership.* The question of who actually owns a joint investment is not straightforward. If you are married and you split up, your legal advisers (or the courts, if it comes to that) will look at your finances in the round, including your pension. They can rearrange your investments – for example, assigning a joint endowment policy to one partner, or earmarking part of your pension for your ex-spouse on your retirement. If you are not married, and you contributed equally to an investment, you each own half; if you contributed unequal amounts, you own the investment in the same proportions. However, these general rules may be overridden by something you have done or said – for example, if you promised or implied that you had given something to your partner, the courts could hold you to this. And some types of investment may be set up so just one person's signature is needed to withdraw the money. It is important to spell out at the outset what you agree, and the charity One Plus One has useful advice on cohabitation agreements.

Trade secret

If a demutualisation is on the cards

If you have a joint investment with a mutual building society or insurance company, check the terms and conditions to see which of you is entitled to any payouts. It is often the investor whose name happens to be first on the documents.

Trade secret

Simple ways of saving inheritance tax

Your share of any jointly owned investment counts as part of your estate for inheritance tax purposes, even a joint bank account which goes automatically to the survivor. However, if you have nominated someone to receive a pension payout on your death (see page 235), or put a life insurance policy in trust, the amount paid out does not form part of your estate, so these steps are worth considering as ways of reducing inheritance tax.

Investments that you leave to your husband or wife are also tax-free, but you may save more tax by leaving them to someone else or to a trust. The first part of your estate is exempt from inheritance tax (£275,000 for deaths in the year to 6 April 2006), but this exemption is wasted if you leave everything to your spouse. Note that if large amounts of tax are at stake you should get professional advice.

8

Keeping track

Sorting out your finances is not a one-off task. You should review your plans regularly – at least once a year, but more often if, say, you depend on your savings to provide you with an income. This chapter looks at how you can monitor the progress of your money.

Make a list

It sounds obvious, but making a list of every account, pension and investment you own could save you money. An estimated £15.3 billion lies forgotten and unclaimed in pensions, bank accounts, investments and lottery winnings (see Trade secret for how to trace them). Table 8.1 gives an example of headings you might want to use, but you will need to adapt this to your own needs. Tell your family where you keep your list.

Remember to tell all the companies on your list if you move. These days, companies change their names, get taken over or merge with alarming frequency.

Trade secret

Tracing missing financial assets

The Unclaimed Assets Register has a database of unclaimed life policies, pensions, unit trusts and shares. However, not all companies are members and a search costs £18. The following organisations (addresses in the Fact file) also have free tracing services:

■ for personal or occupational pension schemes, the Pension Tracing Service
■ for savings and current accounts, the British Bankers' Association or Building Societies Association
■ for National Savings schemes or Premium Bonds, National Savings & Investments.

Table 8.1: Possible headings for your list of financial assets

	Organisation	Account number	Documents kept in
Cash savings			
Current account			
Instant access accounts			
Credit union			
Cash ISAs			
Cash-based Child Trust Fund			
National Savings & Investments			
Other savings accounts/bonds			
Fixed-interest stocks			
British Government stock			
Corporate bonds			
Life insurance policies			
Mortgage endowment			
Other endowments			
Insurance bonds			
Other policies			
Pensions			
Employer's pensions			
Personal or stakeholder pension			
State pension			
Other pensions			
Annuities			
Stockmarket-linked investments			
Shares			
Unit trusts/OEICs			
Investment trusts			
Stocks and shares ISAs			
Stocks and shares Child Trust Fund			
Enterprise Investment scheme			
Venture Capital Trusts			

Monitor progress

It is a good idea to draw up a simple progress sheet for your investments, as shown in Example 8.1. Remember, if you are comparing interest rates, to do so on a like-for-like basis, whether this is before or after tax.

Whatever the investment, you should get regular statements, but you can ask the company involved for a valuation at any time. Alternatively, there are now a number of one-stop tools for tracking your investment (see page 125).

For stockmarket-linked investments, prices are published regularly in newspapers, or are usually available on the management company's website. However, just knowing the value won't tell you how the investment has done. You can work out the percentage by which your money has grown by taking the value at the end of the period, dividing it by the value at the start of the period, deducting 1 and multiplying by 100. For example, if you invest £1,600 in a unit trust, which grows to £1,720, your percentage return is worked out as follows:

$$£1,720 \div £1,600 = 1.075$$
$$1.075 - 1 = 0.075$$
$$0.075 \times 100 = 7.5\%$$

Remember to take into account any income you have drawn from the investment (any income reinvested should already be included in the value); see Example 8.1.

However, you can't take the percentage return at face value:

- *What period is it over?* You will need to adjust it if you want to compare it with annual interest rates on other investments. For example, a return of 7.5% over six months is equivalent to an annual return of 15.5%, but a return of 7.5% over 18 months is equivalent to an annual return of just 4.9%.
- *How does it compare with other investments of the same type, in the same sector?* For example, other Ruritanian equity funds. A return of 7.5% may not look good if the average fund of the same type has produced 10%. Average performance figures are available from trade associations such as the Investment Management Association, and are

Example 8.1: An investment progress sheet

Savings	Value at (date) (£)	Value at (date) (£)	Current interest rate (%)	Income drawn (£)
Internet savings account	3,500	4,675	5	–
Cash ISA	6,100	9,300	4.4	–

Investments	Value at (date) (£)	Value at (date) (£)	Growth over period (%)	Income drawn (£)
Ruritanian equities unit trust	1,000	825	–17.5	–
UK index-tracking fund	1,600	1,720	7.5	–
Life insurance bond, managed fund	28,746	29,824	3.75	1,000

often printed in the press. An online fund tracking service (see Trade secret on page 125) can be helpful if you are happy to use the internet.

■ *What has the rate of inflation been over the same period?* If inflation has been 2.5%, your 7.5% return is reduced to a real return of 5%.

■ *What would it cost to cash in your investment?* Your return is a paper return only until you do, and with some types of investment, such as a life insurance policy, there may be penalties for cashing in early (it may not be possible at all with a pension fund).

Dump the dogs

Armed with your progress sheet, you can start to review your investments.

For savings accounts, the information given regularly in *Money Mail* will help you check whether the interest rate is still competitive. If it isn't, you should consider moving to a new account, if it is possible to do so without incurring penalties.

It can be harder to decide whether to dump any under-performing investments, such as the Ruritanian equities unit trust in Example 8.1 above. The temptation is always to hang on in the hope that things will improve; and you certainly need to take into account the fact that selling and reinvesting will cost you money, in the form of charges. But sooner or later you will have to bite the bullet, and it helps to look at the performance of other funds in the sector to see whether the fund is under-performing the sector as a whole. If it is, you should definitely consider moving. Remember that it might be cheaper to switch to another fund offered by the same organisation rather than selling and reinvesting.

It can help to look at your investments as a whole. Do you still want some money in Ruritania? Did you invest in the fund as a gamble and are you prepared to lose the money? If you are looking for an overseas investment, a fund that is invested in a number of different countries, not just one, would reduce the risks. Or would you be happier switching into a different type of fund altogether, or even just moving your money into a savings account?

Records you should keep

Keep as much documentation relating to your investments as you can. This can help if you have a problem to sort out. If you do have to part with any documents – simply to reduce the amount of paper – the things to dispose of first are non-personal circulars such as annual reports or investment newsletters. Hang on to anything personal, and certainly anything that forms part of your contract with the investment company, such as insurance policy documents or account terms and conditions. It is also worth keeping any marketing literature provided when you first bought the investment, to show the basis on which you invested.

For tax purposes, even if you do not have to fill in a tax return, you are required by law to keep records of your income for at least one year and ten months after the end of the tax year, or five years and ten months if you have a business.

You should keep the following:

- *Shares and unit trusts*: tax vouchers sent with any dividend or distribution (you should get one even if the dividend is paid direct to your bank account).

> Trade secret

A fund supermarket or wrapper can simplify things

Many financial organisations now provide services to help you keep track of your investments – usually, but not always, internet-based. When you register with the service, you enter details of your savings and investments into something called 'My account' or 'My portfolio'. The service then automatically updates the values of your investments so that you can track their performance.

■ *Fund supermarkets* allow you to buy and sell investment funds online. They are usually free to use and you are likely to get reduced charges if you buy. Note, though, that they may not offer every fund on the market and some are limited to investments in stocks and shares ISAs. Nor do they usually cover other investments or savings accounts. Some are accessible only through financial advisers.

■ *Wrap accounts* are offered by some financial advisers. They put all your investments under one roof and you get a single statement of what you own. They are likely to cover a wider range of investments than fund supermarkets, but they are in their infancy and the adviser will receive commission or charge you a fee.

■ *Aggregation services* download the information from all your online accounts for you to view on one website, usually free. It sounds great, but this is legal grey area, and you need to check whether your online accounts allow you to use the service without breaching your agreement with them, and what comeback you have if things go wrong.

With any online system, you should check what use the service provider can make of your personal information, and what security is in place to protect it.

■ *British Government stock*: you will get an annual statement of interest if the interest is paid direct to a bank, otherwise a tax voucher is attached to the cheque. Keep any contract notes when you buy or sell.

■ *Enterprise Investment Scheme or Venture Capital Trusts*: certificates provided by the company.

■ *Interest and annuities*: you may get a certificate of tax deducted at the

end of each year, otherwise the after-tax amount of interest paid will
be shown on your statements or passbook.

■ *Life insurance*: policy documents; notes of date and amount of any
withdrawal; any 'chargeable event' certificates from the insurer.

If you have stockmarket investments, you may also become liable to
capital gains tax if you make a profit on parting with them. You should keep
a record of:

■ the number of shares or units you bought, the date of purchase, the
purchase price and the total amount you paid (including charges)
■ the number of shares or units sold, the date of sale, the sale price and
the total proceeds after deducting selling costs
■ details of any extra shares you received, either as part of a rights issue,
or as the result of reinvesting dividends
■ details of any losses, which can be set against any possible future
gains.

Part 2
The tools

! This symbol means that an investment carries some risk of capital loss

Annuities

In return for a lump sum, annuities provide a regular income, usually for life. ❗ (although you can pay extra to protect your capital)

Good for
- A regular income.
- Providing certainty (except for investment-linked annuities).
- Protecting you against inflation (index-linked annuities).

Bad for
- Flexibility – once you have bought an annuity, you cannot usually change it or get your lump sum back.
- Passing on money – if you die earlier than expected, your family will lose out unless you buy a guaranteed annuity.

Risk factors
- In terms of providing a secure income, a normal annuity is low risk. However, you are taking a gamble on how long you will live.
- An investment-linked annuity is much riskier. Your income could go up and down, so buy one only if you have substantial amounts to invest, and don't put all your money into one.
- If the insurance company cannot meet any claims against it, you are covered by the Financial Services Compensation Scheme (within limits – see page 34).

Timescale
An annuity is usually a lifetime purchase.

How they work

Annuities are usually used to provide an income in retirement. You can buy them from an insurance company, using either your pension fund (a pension annuity or compulsory purchase annuity) or a lump sum built up in some other way (a non-pension annuity, sometimes called a purchased life annuity). The annuity then pays you a regular income, usually monthly.

Annuities generally pay out for life, but from April 2006 short-term annuities, lasting for just five years, will be introduced as an alternative for pensions (see page 254).

The income you get depends on your life expectancy at the time you buy (the older you are, the more you get, and men get more than women). With the simplest type of annuity, once you have bought you are stuck with the same income for the rest of your life. But you can also buy:

- *a joint life annuity*, which pays out until both you and your partner have died
- *a guaranteed annuity*, which pays out for a minimum period of, say, five or ten years
- *an escalating or index-linked annuity*, where the income increases by a certain percentage each year, or in line with inflation (important if you live to a good age)
- *a care fees annuity*, designed to cover the costs of long-term care
- *investment-linked annuities*, where the income depends on the performance of a linked investment fund, so it could rise or fall. Variants are available, such as schemes where you buy a five-year annuity with some of your money, and in the meantime the rest of your money is invested.

Note that forthcoming tax changes will allow insurance companies to design more flexible annuities in future.

Trade secret

Always mention any health problems
If you have an impaired life expectancy – because of diabetes or heart disease, say, or if you are a smoker – you can get better annuity rates from an enhanced annuity, available from some companies. For example, a diabetic could get 30% higher income.

Rates and charges

Annuity rates (the income you get for each pound invested) depend on life expectancies, inflation and interest rates. Rates have fallen over recent years, because of changes in the economy and increasing life expectancies. This means you need a larger lump sum to get a worthwhile income, but doesn't necessarily mean that annuities are bad value. If you delay buying an annuity, you could lose out if annuity rates fall further or if the value of your investments reduces in the meantime.

How to buy

Annuity rates change frequently and shopping around is essential. The best company may pay 25% more than the worst, and once you have bought you are stuck with that company for life (although this may change in future). If your lump sum comes from a personal pension plan, you do not have to buy the annuity offered by the pension company; you have the right to buy it from another company.

Rates for pension annuities are given in the Financial Services Authority's comparative tables (see page 74). However, not all annuity companies will deal with you directly. Contact an independent financial adviser or one of the annuity supermarkets that operate by post, phone or internet.

Tax treatment

- The income from a pension annuity is taxed as a pension, so all the income you receive is taxable in the same way as earnings from a job, normally under PAYE.
- With a non-pension annuity, part of the income is treated as a return of your lump sum and is tax-free. The tax-free amount depends on your age at purchase. The rest of the income is taxed as interest, with 20% tax deducted before you get it (but non-taxpayers can ask to have it paid out before tax).
- The income from a care fees annuity is tax-free provided it is paid directly to the care provider.

Alternatives to consider

- If the money comes from a pension scheme, instead of buying an annuity you may be able to draw an income directly from your pension fund. However, this could be an expensive and risky option, and should be considered only by people with large pension funds or alternative sources of income (see page 254). From April 2006, people with very small pension funds – under £15,000 in total – can draw the whole amount in cash.

■ For lump sums that don't come from a pension, see Chapter 7 for other ways of using your investments to provide an income.

Bonds

Almost any type of investment may be called a bond, ranging from the highly risky to the ultra-safe, but the term usually refers to investments with a maturity date and your money may not be repayable on demand. Use the table below as a guide to the main types.

Types of bonds

	Timescale	Type of investment	The return you get	More information
British Government stock (gilts); Corporate bonds	Maturity dates range from a year or two away, to 15 years or even longer	Bonds issued by the British government, a local authority, or a company (corporate bonds) as a way of raising money. Also called fixed-interest securities. You can also buy bonds issued by foreign governments and companies.	Regular fixed interest. You can either keep till maturity for a set payout, or sell before at a price that varies with demand. ❗ (except for British Government stock kept to maturity).	page 136 for British Government stock; page 154 for corporate bonds
National Savings & Investments bonds	1–5 years	Government-backed savings accounts; guaranteed equity bond also available	Usually fixed-term, the bonds return your original deposit in full and pay either fixed or variable interest. Return from guaranteed equity bond depends on share prices.	page 219

	Timescale	Type of investment	The return you get	More information
Savings bonds	6 months–5 years	Savings account with a bank, building society or other account-provider	Usually fixed-term, the bonds return your original deposit in full and pay interest, usually fixed-rate.	page 264
Index-linked bonds, high-income bonds, guaranteed stockmarket bonds	Usually 5 years	Your money is invested in either a special savings account or a special investment fund or insurance policy.	Fixed-term investment linked to an index of share or other prices. May offer some protection against falling prices, e.g. a guarantee. Some types ❗	pages 172 and 179
Guaranteed income bonds	Usually 1–5 years	Single-premium life insurance policies	Guaranteed fixed income for fixed term, plus return of original investment.	page 208
Guaranteed growth bonds	Usually 1–5 years	Single-premium life insurance policies	Guaranteed return at the end of fixed period; no income in the meantime.	page 208
With-profits bonds	No set maturity date, but 5 years is usual minimum in practice	Single-premium life insurance policies	Depends on the performance of the with-profits insurance fund in which your money is invested. No income, but you may be able to make withdrawals. ❗	page 207

	Timescale	Type of investment	The return you get	More information
Investment bonds	No set maturity date, but 5 years is usual minimum in practice	Single-premium life insurance policies	Depends on the performance of the unit-linked insurance fund in which your money is invested. No income, but you can make withdrawals. ❗	page 206
Baby bonds	May refer to either a Child Trust Fund account (see page 150) or a friendly society insurance policy (see page 169). ❗ (some types)			

Note: ❗ means that an investment carries some risk of capital loss.

British Government stocks (gilts)

A government bond that pays fixed interest and a fixed sum on maturity, but that can be sold on the stockmarket before maturity for a price that depends on demand. ❗ (unless kept to maturity)

Good for
- Providing a secure fixed income. Remember, though, that a gilt may cost more to buy than its repayment value on maturity, so you are effectively sacrificing part of your capital for the higher income.
- Certainty – if you hold a gilt until maturity, you know exactly what you will get.
- Protection against inflation for both your capital and your income, if you buy index-linked gilts.
- Providing a counterbalance to share-based investments. Investors seek the security of gilts when stockmarkets are doing badly.

Bad for
- Providing high overall returns, taking into account both the income and the cost of the gilt. Although there are periods when gilts outperform shares, over the long term shares have performed better.
- The fixed income provided by gilts looks low when inflation is high, but the cost of buying the gilt will usually fall to compensate. You can buy index-linked gilts if you are worried about inflation.

Risk factors
- Because gilts are issued by the British government, the risk that they will not pay out the promised amount is infinitesimal.
- This does not mean that you personally cannot make a loss on them. If you sell a gilt on the stockmarket before maturity, you may get less than you paid for it.
- If you buy an index-linked gilt, its value will fall below its face value if there is a prolonged period of deflation (see Jargon alert on page 32).

Timescale
Most gilts have a maturity date: gilts maturing between 2005 and 2055

were available in mid-2005. Gilts with less than seven years to run are called 'shorts', those with 7–15 years 'mediums' and those with more than 15 years 'longs'.

However, you can sell gilts on the stockmarket before maturity, and a few gilts have a range of possible maturity dates (e.g. 2012–15) or are undated, with no maturity date (these are sometimes called perpetuals).

Jargon alert

Gilts

British Government stocks were originally nicknamed gilts because the loan certificates used to be edged with gold leaf. However, such is the creditworthiness of the British government that gilt-edged is sometimes used generally to mean any really safe investment.

Trade secret

What's in a name?

The name of a gilt will tell you a couple of important things about it. A typical gilt is '5% Treasury Stock 2014'. This would be quoted in the newspaper as:

Tr 5pc '14

| Stands for Treasury stock – the **name** of this stock. Gilts may also be called Exchequer (Ex), Conversion (Cn), Consolidated (Cons) or War Loan, but the name has no significance for investors. | The **coupon**, or annual rate of interest payable on the **nominal** value of your stock (the nominal value is the amount the government will pay you when the gilt matures). In this example, for each £100 of nominal value you would receive interest of £5 a year. | The **maturity year** (2014). Some stocks are undated and have no set maturity date; others are double-dated (e.g. '13–17'), which means that the government can redeem them within a period (e.g. 2013–17). |

How they work

Gilts are issued at intervals by the British government as a way of raising money to finance government spending. This is why the government agency charged with issuing them is called the Debt Management Office (DMO). These debts are repaid (or redeemed) at a set value (the nominal value), usually on a set maturity date, and in the meantime they pay out a fixed rate of interest twice a year. This makes them sound rather like a building society fixed-rate, fixed-term bond, but they are different in two important ways:

- Gilts are tradeable. This means that you don't have to buy them when they are first issued and then wait until they are redeemed; instead you can buy and sell them on the stockmarket at any time before maturity. The stockmarket price depends on demand – you may pay more or less than the nominal face value of the gilt. If you pay more and keep the gilt until it matures, you make a capital loss; if you pay less and keep it until maturity, you make a profit.
- You can also buy index-linked gilts. Unlike the returns on conventional gilts, with the index-linked variety both the interest payment and the value at redemption are adjusted in line with inflation. There is more about index-linking below.

Because gilts' returns are fixed, their appeal to investors depends on interest rates available on other investments. If you can get an income of 5% on a building society account, for example, a gilt paying 8% for each £100 of nominal value looks very attractive. But what if the gilt would cost you £120 to buy each £100 of nominal value? The yield is a tool for helping you work it out (see Jargon alert).

Note that gilts do not always have fixed rates. Floating-rate gilts are occasionally issued, with interest rates that reflect short-term interest rates.

You can ask for the income from a gilt to be paid directly into a bank or building society account, otherwise a special cheque called a dividend warrant will be sent to you.

> ## Jargon alert

The yield
The yield is a way of measuring the true return from a gilt or bond, but there are various different types.

Say you want to compare a building society account which pays out 5% a year (£5 for each £100 deposited) with 8% Treasury Stock 2013 (paying £8 for each £100 of nominal stock), but current market conditions are such that each £100 of nominal stock costs £120 to buy. So for an investment of £120, you receive £8 each year, which is equivalent to an interest rate of 8/120 × 100 = 6.6%. This is called the 'Running Yield' or 'Interest Yield'.

However, the interest yield doesn't take into account any profit or loss you make by buying the gilt at more or less than the nominal value. For that you need the 'Redemption Yield', which assumes that you hold the gilt until maturity and reinvest the income by buying more stock at the same yield. The calculation is not as easy for the redemption yield, but you will see it quoted alongside the gilt price in the newspapers as the 'Red Yield' or 'Red Yld'. In this case it works out as 5.1% – about the same as the building society account.

Note that both yields ignore tax so actual returns will be less for taxpayers.

Index-linked gilts
Index-linking means that the value of the interest payments and the final payout on redemption are both increased in line with the retail prices index (RPI) since the gilt was first issued.

Assume you have an index-linked gilt with a 4% coupon, and retail prices are 25% higher than when the stock was first issued:

- The next six-monthly payment will be half of the annual coupon (i.e. 2%) increased by 25%, i.e. 2.5% in total.
- If prices are 25% higher when a gilt matures, the payout that you receive for each £100 of nominal value that you hold will be £125.

The RPI is used to measure how far prices have risen, but to allow time for the calculations to be made, the increases are linked to the level of the index eight months before the payment is due.

Because of the protection against inflation offered by an index-linked gilt, the coupon (or interest rate for each £100 nominal value of stock held) is on the low side. Effectively the coupon is the guaranteed amount above inflation, so when comparing a gilt with another type of interest-paying investment you need to add the expected rate of inflation. If you expect inflation to average 3%, say, you would expect a gilt with a 2% coupon to pay out 2 + 3 = 5% income each year, before tax.

One thing to be aware of is that it is possible for the income from an index-linked gilt to fall if the RPI falls between one payout and the next. And, if prices are lower when the gilt matures than when it was first issued (i.e. the index is at a lower level), you will get back less than £100 for each £100 nominal value that you hold. Note, though, that this does not apply if the rate of inflation falls – this just means prices are rising more slowly. It applies only if prices overall fall, over the whole term of the gilt.

Rates and charges

Although the nominal interest rate on a gilt and the eventual payout are fixed, the amount you might have to spend to get them could fall or rise. So when the competition is strong – that is, when variable interest rates on other investments rise, or are expected to rise – gilt prices fall. But because it now costs you less to buy a gilt providing a certain level of income, yields generally rise. When interest rates fall, gilt prices rise but yields fall. So, very broadly, yields generally move in line with interest rates. The financial section of the main newspapers will show prices and price changes.

The price paid also reflects the length of time until the next income payment is due (see Jargon alert).

The costs of investing in gilts are:

- if you buy or sell on the stockmarket, the difference in price between the selling price and the buying price; sellers get a bit less than buyers pay (this is called the spread). The price quoted in newspapers is usually half-way between the buying and selling price
- commission payable to whoever organises the sale for you (see below). No commission is payable if you buy a stock in an auction when it is first issued.

Jargon alert

Clean or dirty? Accrued interest

The whole of an income payment usually goes to the person who is registered as the holder of the gilt a week or so before the payment date, even if that person has just sold the stock. The cut-off date is called the ex-dividend date. The price the buyer pays is adjusted in line with the number of days' interest he or she is actually entitled to (the adjustment is called accrued interest). The accrued interest will be shown on the contract note that records the sale.

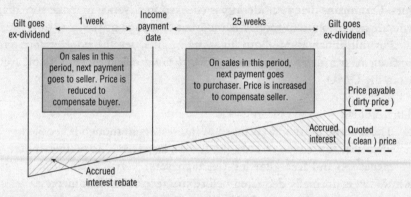

The price the purchaser pays is known as the dirty price. The prices quoted in the paper are clean prices, ignoring the accrued interest, but if a stock has passed its ex-dividend date you will see 'xd' beside its price to show that purchasers will not get the next payment.

How to buy and sell

You can buy gilts when they are first issued, in one of the gilt auctions organised by the DMO, or after they have been issued, on the stockmarket.

In a gilt auction, investors bid for stocks, but private investors can bid on a non-competitive basis. They pay the average price paid by successful competitive bidders, which may be more or less than the nominal value of the stock. Note that the minimum application at auctions is for £1,000 nominal of gilts.

If you want to buy or sell a stock that has already been issued, you can either contact a stockbroker or other organisation offering broking services (such as a bank), or use the Gilt Purchase and Sale Service run by Computershare on behalf of the DMO. In both cases you will have to pay commission. The commission charged by the Gilt Purchase and Sale Service is likely to be cheaper for small transactions and there is no minimum investment, but note that it is a postal service. This means that you cannot be sure exactly what the price will be.

If you want to buy gilts in an auction, or use the Gilt Purchase and Sale Service, you will have to join what is known as an 'approved' group of investors. This means that your identity is checked in advance to make sure that you are not involved in money-laundering (see page 273).

For full information about investing in gilts, see the booklet *Investing in Gilts: the private investor's guide to British Government Stock* available free from the DMO.

Tax treatment

- The income from a gilt is taxed as interest, even though it is called a dividend. Tax is paid at 20% (basic-rate taxpayers), 40% (higher-rate taxpayers) and 10% (starting-rate taxpayers).
- No tax is normally deducted before you receive the income; it is collected either through PAYE or through your tax return. However, you can opt to have 20% tax deducted by asking the Gilts Registrar, Computershare.
- Any accrued interest you receive when you buy a gilt is also taxable if it falls within the accrued income scheme (see Jargon alert).
- You will receive an annual statement of interest after the end of the tax year which will give you the information you need to fill in your tax return. Also keep your contract notes on sales and purchases – these show the amount of accrued interest.
- There is no capital gains tax on gilts.
- Gilts are free of income tax if held in a stocks and shares ISA.

Jargon alert

Accrued income scheme

This is a tax scheme that stops investors using gilts and bonds to turn (taxable) interest into (tax-free) capital gains. However, you fall within the scheme only if, at any point within a particular period, you own gilts, corporate bonds and other similar bonds with a total nominal value of more than £5,000. The relevant period is the tax year in which the next payment of interest after the purchase falls, and the previous tax year. You can deduct from your interest any rebates of accrued interest that you received if you sold a gilt. The government is reviewing this method of taxing accrued income, but in the meantime see HM Revenue & Customs leaflet IR68 *Accrued income scheme*.

Alternatives to consider

- If you are going for absolute security, bonds from banks and building societies, or National Savings & Investments, are probably the most suitable and easily available alternatives. Local authorities also issue fixed-interest bonds that work like gilts, but there are few of them around these days. Guaranteed stockmarket-linked bonds protect your capital but may have other disadvantages (see page 172).
- Alternatively, you can spread your money over a range of gilts by investing in a unit trust gilts fund. This is one of the least risky types of unit trust fund, but you won't have the certainty of knowing exactly how much you will get back, because the fund managers may buy and sell gilts on the stock exchange. The fund managers' charges will also reduce your return.
- If you are happy to accept a greater level of risk of losing your capital, you could consider corporate bonds (see page 154).
- If your main aim is to provide income, see Chapter 7.

Buy to let

Investing in residential property by becoming a landlord. ❶

Good for
- The possibility of good long-term capital growth if house prices rise.
- People who already have a good range of safer investments as an alternative to stockmarket-based investments (see Chapter 1).

Bad for
- Providing a reliable income, particularly if you need a mortgage to buy the property. The income from letting may be less than the outgoings.
- People who have only small amounts to invest, or who might need to cash in their investment in the next ten years or so.

Risk factors
- Putting all (or too many of) your eggs in the property basket.
- The possibility of falling house prices. The effect is magnified by gearing if you borrowed to buy (see the example on page 147). At the worst, you could end up in negative equity – that is, with a mortgage that is more than the value of the property.
- The possibility that the property will be unlet for long periods, which, if you are having to pay a mortgage, is no joke.
- Rising interest rates, if you need a mortgage.
- Investment and mortgage advice is regulated by the Financial Services Authority. However, this does not include advice on buy-to-let investments or mortgages.
- Letting agents who manage lettings on a landlord's behalf do not have to be regulated and vary in quality. Only use an agent who belongs to a professional body that requires minimum codes of practice and has rules to protect your money, such as the Association of Residential Letting Agents (ARLA), National Association of Estate Agents or Royal Institution of Chartered Surveyors. Agents who meet certain standards may also be accredited by the National Approved Letting Scheme.

Timescale

Buying to let is a long-term investment. Research has found that landlords expect to be in property investment for an average of 16 years.

How it works

Buying a house or flat with the aim of letting it out has become hugely popular in recent years because of the spectacular growth in house prices (about 15% a year between January 2000 and January 2005). However, house prices have stopped rising at this rate, and are now falling in some areas.

As well as property values, you need to take the level of rents into account. As the example on page 146 shows, you cannot assume that the rents will exceed the outgoings, particularly if you have to take out a mortgage to buy the property. According to the ARLA, most rentals are short-term (six months to three years, say) and you should assume an average of 30 days' rent lost a year while your property is standing empty (or void). Not receiving any income may not bother you too much if you are hoping to make a profit when you sell your properties, but the rest of your finances must be secure enough for you to afford the difference between what you are paying out on the property and what you are earning from it. You are running a business, and as with any business, you must have some working capital.

Once you have found your tenants, you will need to collect their rents, deal with any problems and keep an inventory of furnishings in case of damage. You can hire a professional lettings agent to take on some or all of these tasks for you.

Complying with the law

Currently anybody can be a buy-to-let landlord. However, this could change, and there are proposals to require all private landlords in Scotland to be licensed. There are also some important regulations that you need to know about, including:

■ the fire safety regulations for any soft furnishings you supply (such as mattresses and sofa cushions)

- safety requirements for gas and electrical installations and appliances
- special rules about suitability and overcrowding for homes in multiple occupation (e.g. if a property you own is rented out to people who do not form a single household). Your local authority may require you to register such a property with them, and the government plans to tighten the rules in future
- your rights and your tenants' rights, for example how to evict a troublesome tenant without falling foul of the law
- landlords will soon be required to join a scheme to safeguard tenants' deposits.

Example: Do not count on the income from a property

Albert bought a £150,000 property at a time when market conditions led him to expect a rent of just under £8,000 a year, with an annual average of 30 days' unoccupancy. He uses a letting agent who charges 15% of rents for a full management service. Albert wanted a 75% mortgage, but this and the management fees would have left him £665 out of pocket (ignoring the other costs of letting). So Albert scraped together a larger deposit and took a 65% mortgage. When he bought, the interest rate was 6%, which would have left him with a small excess of income over expenditure (£235). But then interest rates rose to 6.5%, producing a £253 loss over the year. Even if he finds a letting agent charging only 10%, the net income would only increase to £106 a year.

	75% mortgage, interest rate 6% (£)	65% mortgage, interest rate 6% (£)	65% mortgage, interest rate 6.5% (£)
Gross annual rent	7,800	7,800	7,800
Minus			
Rent lost through unoccupancy	641	641	641
Mortgage interest	6,750	5,850	6,338
Management fees	1,074	1,074	1,074
Net income	−665	235	−253

Example: **How gearing can magnify gains and losses**

Borrowing to buy a property is an example of gearing (also known as leverage). Gearing means that because the mortgage is a fixed amount, you get the whole of any increase or fall in the value of the property above the value of the mortgage. The effect of gearing is to magnify your potential gains, but also your potential losses.

Take the example of Albert, opposite, who borrowed £97,500 to buy a £150,000 property, and see what would happen if house prices rose by 5% a year for the first four years, and then fell by 4% a year. The graph below compares the annual rate of growth with a mortgage (the dark line), with the rate of growth he would have experienced had he not had a mortgage (the light line).

The graph shows that without a mortgage, Albert's return after the first four years (5%) would be the same as the change in house prices. With a mortgage, he receives a much higher return of 13% on his £52,500 deposit; but when house prices fall, the value of his investment drops far more steeply than house prices. Of course, this ignores any income Albert might receive from the property, and if house prices had continued to rise, Albert would have been very happy to have a mortgage.

The effect of gearing[a]

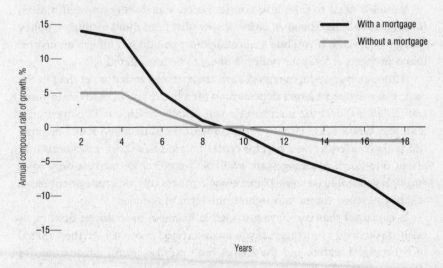

a Assuming house prices rise at 5% p.a. for 4 years, and then fall at 4% a year.

Rates and charges

In early 2005, the average annual rent available on buy-to-let properties was about 5% of the property value, after taking unlet periods into account. From this you would need to deduct:

- all the normal costs of buying and owning a property
- the cost of the mortgage – say 1.75% more than normal mortgage rates, although cheaper deals may be available
- the costs of letting, e.g. rent collection, legal and accountancy fees. If you use a letting agent, the agent's fees could cost you 10–17% of the gross rental income from the property.

How to buy

You need to find a property that will appeal to prospective tenants, not to your personal taste. When you are thinking about the market you are aiming at, remember that a significant percentage of tenants (around 15%) are either students or on benefits, and check current rental values in the area in which you are thinking of investing. The ARLA publishes useful data.

You also need to take into consideration stamp duty and renovation, furnishing and maintenance costs. A specialist household insurance policy may be necessary. If you buy a normal policy and do not inform an insurer that a property is let, your policy is likely to be invalidated.

Although buy-to-let mortgages are cheaper and easier to get than in the past, you will need a larger deposit than for a home you plan to live in yourself (25%, say) and the interest rate will usually be higher. The maximum loan may be based on either your income or the anticipated rental income, but usually a lender will require rental income to exceed the interest by about one-third. Mortgages are available on either an interest-only basis (though you will need some plan for paying them off), or a repayment basis, where you repay capital throughout the term of the loan.

It is crucial that you have a workable business proposition first, especially if you need a mortgage. If you are interested in buy-to-let, the Council of Mortgage Lenders and the ARLA both publish useful information for prospective landlords.

Tax treatment

■ You are liable to income tax on rental income at 22% (basic-rate taxpayers) or 40% (higher-rate taxpayers), but you can deduct mortgage interest, letting agents' fees and other costs. If you make a loss, you can set it against other profits from letting UK property, or carry it forward and set it against any future profits.

■ You will probably have to pay capital gains tax at 20% (basic-rate taxpayers) or 40% (higher-rate taxpayers) on any profit you make when you sell the property. However, the first slice of total gains in each tax year is tax-free (see Chapter 4) and the taxable gain is reduced the longer you keep the property. If you have lived in it at some point you may also be able to claim various reliefs.

■ From April 2006, it will be possible to hold residential property in your own Self-Invested Personal Pension (see page 276). This may save you tax, but it reduces your flexibility. Get advice from a financial adviser with specialist qualifications.

■ Get advice from a qualified accountant or tax adviser on the best way to set up your property business, for example whether to own it jointly with your spouse or partner, and what costs you can deduct from the rents.

■ The usual property taxes apply, namely stamp duty on the purchase price and council tax (although the tenant normally pays the council tax).

Alternatives to consider

■ Rather than investing directly in property, you could consider a property fund (see page 261).

■ If you are looking for capital growth and are willing to take a risk, stockmarket-linked investments are the main alternative.

■ If producing an income is your aim, see Chapter 7.

Child Trust Fund

A special savings and investments account for children born after 31 August 2002. ❗ (some types)

Good for
- Any eligible child – they will get a minimum of £250 from the government.
- Parents who want to give money to their children free of tax. Normally, if interest on money given by a parent comes to more than £100 a year per child, the whole amount is taxed as the parent's. This does not apply to the Child Trust Fund.

Bad for
- Disadvantages depend on the type of account you choose (you can choose between cash-based savings and stockmarket-linked investments).
- Money that might be needed before the child turns 18 – the account cannot be cashed in until then.
- People who want to control how their children spend the money – they can spend it as they wish at age 18.

Risk factors
- If you make no other choice, your child's money will go into a stockmarket-linked account. These accounts can fall in value and their performance is not guaranteed by the government.
- When choosing an account for your child, you will need to weigh up the security of a cash-based account against the possibility that a stockmarket-linked account might produce a higher return over 18 years. You can transfer between types of account, but if you get it wrong your child could lose out.
- Child Trust Fund accounts are covered by the Financial Ombudsman Service and Financial Services Compensation Scheme.

Timescale
Money cannot be taken out of a Child Trust Fund until the child reaches age 18.

How it works

This scheme started in April 2005 with the aim of helping children to build up a pot of savings by the time they are 18. To kick-start their savings, the government gives children born after 31 August 2002 a voucher that must be used to open a special account called a Child Trust Fund. Until the child reaches 16, a parent or other responsible adult must operate the account, but the money always belongs to the child and can be spent as he or she wishes at age 18.

The voucher is worth £250, plus a bit extra if the child was born between 1 September 2002 and April 2005, and so had to wait for the voucher. A further £250 is payable if the family receives Child Tax Credit and has a household income below the Child Tax Credit threshold (£13,910 in the 2005–06 tax year), but this will be paid only after the end of the tax year, when your tax credit is finalised. The government also plans to give further vouchers when children reach age seven and at secondary school age.

To be eligible, a child must be registered for Child Benefit and living in the UK. The scheme is administered by HM Revenue & Customs, so contact their special helpline if you think your child is eligible but you haven't yet received a voucher (see the Fact file).

There are three types of account:

- *Savings account* – this works like any normal savings account.
- *Stakeholder account* – this must invest mainly in stockmarket-linked investments such as unit trusts, investment trusts and insurance policies, but to reduce the risks the investment company is required to ensure that there is a spread of investments, and to gradually move the money into less risky investments in the five years before the child reaches 18 (see Jargon alert: Lifestyling on page 54). There is also a 1.5% cap on the amount the company can charge each year for managing the money.
- *Non-stakeholder account* – any stockmarket-linked account that does not meet the conditions to be a stakeholder account.

A child can have only one account, and you can choose whichever one you think is most suitable for your child. If the voucher is not invested in an account within a year of being issued, the Revenue will automatically put it in a stakeholder account. However, money can be transferred between accounts (including accounts of a different type) and between financial organisations, without a penalty (apart from the normal costs of buying and selling investments, if necessary). You will get an annual statement to help you track the progress of the account.

Trade secret

How to avoid risk

If you make no other choice, your child's money will automatically go into a stakeholder account, which is stockmarket-linked and could rise or fall in value. The justification for this is that over the long term, stocks and shares might be expected to produce a better return than cash-based savings. If you want to avoid risk altogether, it's important to nominate a cash-based saving account.

Extra contributions

Anyone, whether they are relatives or not, can make additional payments into a child's account (with a £10 minimum), but all additional payments must not exceed £1,200 a year per child (using the child's birthday year). Remember, though, that the money cannot be taken out until the child is 18, unless the child dies or becomes terminally ill. If the full additional payment is not made in one year, the unused amount cannot be carried forward to the next year.

Rates and charges

These vary depending on the account provider and the type of account:

- Stakeholder accounts have a maximum 1.5% annual management charge.
- There are no restrictions on the charges for a non-stakeholder account so these are likely to be the same as for other accounts of the same type.

■ Not many companies offer cash savings accounts. Those that do may require you to make extra contributions in order to get the best rates.

How to buy

A Child Trust Fund account can be opened through some banks, building societies, credit unions, friendly societies, life insurance companies and investment companies. Lists of companies offering accounts are listed on HM Revenue & Customs' website. Note that these organisations may not provide advice about which type of account is best for your child (if you want help, see Chapter 5).

Tax treatment

The interest or capital growth from a Child Trust Fund account, including any extra contributions, is free of income tax and capital gains tax. The money in a child's account will not affect the family's right to claim any state benefits, such as tax credits.

However, you cannot invest as a way of avoiding inheritance tax. Any extra contributions you make count as a gift, although for most people there will be no tax to pay as the money will fall within one of the categories of tax-free lifetime gifts.

Alternatives to consider

■ Before you make extra contributions to a child's account, you should consider the other alternatives covered in Chapter 7. The main benefit of the account is that the money is tax-free, but most children don't have to pay tax in any case.

Corporate bonds

Bonds issued by a company as a way of raising money. They are repaid at a fixed value at a fixed date in the future, and usually pay out fixed interest in the meantime. They can be sold on the stockmarket before maturity for a price that depends on demand. ❗

Good for
- Providing a higher income than savings accounts at a time of low interest rates.
- Providing a counterbalance to share-based investments, because investors seek the relative security of bonds when stockmarkets are doing badly.

Bad for
- Performance – although there are periods when bonds outperform shares, over the long term shares have generally performed better.
- You may get less for your bond than you paid for it. You may be content with this if it pays a high income in the meantime, but if so, remember that you are effectively sacrificing part of your capital for the income.

Risk factors
- A bond is only as secure as its issuing company. If the company becomes less creditworthy, or defaults on its promise to repay its bondholders, your investment could be worth little or nothing. There is no compensation scheme if this happens, although if you were wrongly advised to buy the bonds by an authorised adviser, you may have a case against them for compensation.
- Bonds are more secure than shares because bondholders will be paid out before shareholders in the event of bankruptcy (although bondholders will be competing with other creditors for their money). Bond prices on the stockmarket also usually fluctuate less than share prices, because of the fixed income payable. However, this makes them vulnerable to changing interest rates – the price of fixed income bonds generally falls when interest rates elsewhere rise.

- You reduce the risks of choosing the wrong company if you invest through a fund such as a unit trust, but then you lose the benefits of fixed interest and a fixed sum on maturity, and you are still vulnerable to price drops caused by rising interest rates. Also some funds take a riskier approach than others (e.g. by putting more money in high-yield or 'junk' bonds, see below, or also investing in shares).
- The bond market is international and bond issues may be priced in pounds sterling, dollars, yen, euros or other currencies. Buying a bond that is not denominated in sterling exposes you to currency risk (see page 40).

Timescale

Corporate bonds have a maturity date (sometimes referred to as the redemption date) of anything from a few years to 30 years. You can sell them on the stockmarket before maturity, but if some disaster has befallen the company it might be difficult to find a buyer. You should be prepared to leave your money invested for at least 5–10 years.

From time to time a company might buy back existing bonds or exchange them for new issues, before the maturity date, if it wants to restructure its finances.

Jargon alert

Investment grade or junk?

A bond issued by Solid-As-A-Rock plc will be a much better bet than one from DodgyCo. Companies' credit ratings are assessed by various specialist agencies, of which the best known are Standard & Poor's (S&P) and Moody's – you will see their ratings (AAA is the safest) quoted in some of the newspapers' listings. Bonds issued by companies with the best safety ratings are known as investment grade; those issued by companies with the worst ratings are called junk bonds or – more politely – high-yield bonds (because they have to offer better terms to attract investors). However, ratings do change and some large, well-known companies have bonds that are classed as junk.

How they work

Corporate bonds are issued by companies as a way of raising money to finance their businesses. For this reason, another common name for some types of bond is loan stock. These debts are repaid (or redeemed) at a set value (the nominal value), on a set maturity date, and in the meantime most bonds pay out a fixed rate of interest (the coupon), usually twice a year.

All the key facts about the bond – the issuing company, the maturity date and the coupon – are included in the name of the bond. For example, BondCo 8.5% 25/05/2009 will be redeemed on 25th May 2009 but in the meantime will pay out £8.50 a year for each £100 of nominal value held.

You can buy and sell bonds before maturity on the stockmarket. The stockmarket price depends on demand – you may pay more or less than the nominal face value of the bond. For example, a bond paying 8% for each £100 of nominal value might look attractive when interest rates elsewhere are about 5%, but on the stockmarket it could cost you £120 to buy each £100 of nominal value. If you pay £120 and keep the bond until it matures, you make a capital loss; if you pay less than £100 and keep it until maturity, you make a profit. However, if the price subsequently rises to £130, you can sell the bond before maturity for a profit.

In all these respects, corporate bonds work in a very similar way to British Government stocks (gilts – see page 136). As with gilts, the yield is used as a tool for helping you compare returns (see Jargon alert on page 139).

However, there are some important differences between bonds and gilts:

- *Quantity* – there are many more bonds and much more variety.
- *A company's creditworthiness* affects the terms on which it issues the bond and its stockmarket value (see Jargon alert on page 155).
- *Bonds may be secured or unsecured.* With a secured bond (sometimes called a debenture), assets of the company can be seized to repay the debt if the company fails to do so. This makes them less risky than unsecured bonds.
- *The income may be variable instead of fixed*, offering interest rates that reflect short-term interest rates at the time of issue. These are called floating-rate notes.

■ *Some bonds pay no or very little interest*, and instead pay out a larger sum at maturity (these are called zero coupon or deep discounted bonds).

■ *The bond market is international*, and bond issues may be priced in pounds sterling, dollars, yen, euros or many other currencies.

Trade secret

How to tell if the income is eating into your capital

Investors often buy bonds in the hope that they will provide a higher income than a savings account. But if the price of the bond falls, you are effectively eating into your capital. If you buy a bond direct, rather than a bond fund, always look at the redemption yield (see page 139). If it is lower than the interest yield, it will show that you are eating into capital.

Jargon alert

Permanent interest bearing shares (PIBs)

Building societies can issue bonds called PIBs, which work in a similar way to corporate bonds but have no fixed maturity date. You can also buy PIBs issued by banks which were previously building societies. There aren't many PIBs about, but if you are interested you can buy them through stockbrokers and independent financial advisers. They are exposed to more risk than other building society accounts (or other corporate bonds), because in the event of a bankruptcy PIB-holders rank behind savers in the queue for repayment.

Rates and charges

As with gilts, companies that issue bonds are competing with other investments for your money, so the interest rate on offer will have to be on a par with rates available elsewhere at the time of issue. However, they are not as safe as gilts, which have the backing of the British government, so bonds have to offer better returns in order to compete. But the stockmarket value will reflect all the latest news about the company, so if, say, it runs into trouble, you might find that the value of its bonds (as well as its shares) plummets.

The financial sections of the main newspapers show only a selection of bond prices. The London Stock Exchange website and other websites also give bond prices, but for private investors information is not as easy to come by as it is for shares.

The costs of investing in corporate bonds are:

■ if you buy or sell on the stockmarket, the difference in price between the selling (or bid) price and the buying price; sellers get a bit less than buyers pay (this is called the spread). The spread is likely to be wider than that for gilts

■ commission payable to whoever organises the sale for you (see below).

How to buy and sell

The corporate bond market is extremely varied, and unless you have the time and expertise to research it carefully, it is not one to enter without assistance. You can buy through a stockbroker or a financial adviser. Unless you are experienced in buying bonds, it is sensible to get advice rather than buying on an execution-only basis (see page 79).

To reduce the risk of buying corporate bonds in a company that fails, you should invest in several companies' bonds, but the costs of buying may eat up a high proportion of your money. A corporate bond fund (available from a unit trust manager, for example) is the most practical solution. However, the income and eventual payout from such a fund will not usually be fixed, and the fund manager's charges will reduce the value of your investment.

Tax treatment

■ The income from corporate bonds is taxed as interest, but the income is paid out before tax. Tax is paid at 20% (basic-rate taxpayers), 40% (higher-rate taxpayers) or 10% (starting-rate taxpayers).

■ If you receive accrued interest when you buy a bond (see Jargon alert on page 141), it is taxable if, at any point within a particular period, you own gilts, corporate bonds and other similar bonds with a total nominal value of more than £5,000.

- There is no capital gains tax if you make a profit when you sell most corporate bonds (or when they are redeemed).
- Corporate bonds and corporate bond funds are tax-free if held in a stocks and shares ISA.

Alternatives to consider

- If you are looking for a secure fixed income, consider gilts or fixed-interest savings accounts from a bank or building society, or from National Savings & Investments. Also see Chapter 7 for more on how to produce an income from your investments.
- If you are happy to take a risk and are looking for capital returns, consider investment funds, particularly those which take a more cautious approach (see Chapter 6). Guaranteed stockmarket bonds protect your capital but may have other downsides.

Credit unions

Savings and loans 'co-ops' owned and controlled by their members.

Good for
- Building up savings if money is tight – they will accept very small amounts.
- Providing cheap loans to members.

Bad for
- You may not be eligible to join a credit union, although you can band together with other people to set one up.

Risk factors
- If the credit union is poorly run or fails to attract enough members, the dividend payable to savers may be poor or non-existent.
- The value of your savings may fail to keep up with inflation.
- Credit unions can go bust and a few have done so. However, they are regulated by the Financial Services Authority (except in Northern Ireland), and if they go bust you will be covered by the Financial Services Compensation Scheme (see Chapter 2).
- Credit unions in Northern Ireland are regulated by the Registrar of Credit Unions, but the registrar's powers are limited. Some credit unions belong to a voluntary compensation scheme.

Timescale
Credit unions are designed to help people build up regular savings, but you can usually get at your money without having to give a minimum period of notice.

How they work

Credit unions are set up to provide access to good-value savings and loans for people with a 'common bond' – for example, people who work for the same employer or in the same trade, who live or work in one area, or who belong to a particular organisation, such as a church or trade union.

They can be small and run by volunteer members, or have a membership of several thousand people and be run professionally. The larger credit unions offer access to other financial products, such as discounted insurance, Child Trust Fund accounts and even mortgages.

To join a credit union, you must share its common bond. You open a share account with the union and are usually expected to make regular savings into it (though the minimum amount is often as low as £1 a week). Credit unions will also accept extra deposits. The accounts pay a dividend, usually annually.

You can withdraw your money on request (but you should allow a bit of time for cheques to clear and so on). And once you have built up a record of savings with the union (usually a minimum of three months), you can apply for a loan – the maximum amount usually depends on your savings. However, an increasing number of credit unions are breaking the link between loans and savings. People can then apply for a loan without having had to save for a specific amount of time.

Membership usually also gives you a small amount of free life insurance. If you die, this will pay out up to twice the amount saved and also pay off any loan outstanding.

Rates and charges

The dividend payable to savers varies depending on the financial performance of the credit union. By law, the maximum dividend payable is 8%, but in practice it is likely to be roughly in line with bank and building society accounts.

Interest on loans is low. By law, credit unions can charge a maximum of 1% interest per month on the money they lend to their members. This is equivalent to an annual percentage rate (APR) of 12.7%. However, this limit is under review. The maximum amount you can save is also under review – it is currently £5,000.

How to join

Credit unions are stronger in some parts of the country than in others, so you may not have access to one. But if you do not, and you can find a large enough group of like-minded people, you can set one up with help from the Association of British Credit Unions Ltd (ABCUL). The ABCUL can also tell you if there is one you might be able to join.

Tax treatment

The dividend payable to savers is taxed as interest at 20% (basic-rate taxpayers), 40% (higher-rate taxpayers) and 10% (starting-rate taxpayers). No tax is deducted before you receive the income; instead it is collected either through PAYE or your tax return.

Alternatives to consider

- Savings accounts or cash ISAs with a bank, building society or National Savings & Investments.

Enterprise Investment Scheme (EIS), Venture Capital Trusts (VCTs)

Schemes that give you tax relief for investing in smaller, high-risk companies. ⓘ

Good for

- Rich people who are willing to take on a high-risk investment in return for tax advantages.
- People who are selling something that is liable to capital gains tax – they can put off paying the tax if they reinvest in the Enterprise Investment Scheme.

Bad for

- Anybody who cannot afford to lose the money invested and has not already got substantial amounts in safer investments.
- Cost – some schemes may have high costs.

Risk factors

The smaller high-risk companies that you invest in can easily go bust. There is no compensation for this, unless (possibly) you invested on the advice of a UK-authorised adviser and weren't made aware of the risks.

Timescale

These are long-term investments. With both schemes, you must keep your investment for at least three years to get the tax advantages, but you may find it difficult to get your money out at any point.

How they work

These schemes give you tax advantages for investing in qualifying companies, which include most types of unquoted trading company and some companies listed on the Alternative Investment Market (AIM).

Under the Enterprise Investment Scheme (EIS), you buy shares in a qualifying company itself, either directly or through an EIS fund or portfolio, which buys shares in several companies. With Venture Capital Trusts

(VCTs) you do not buy shares in the company itself. Instead you buy shares in the VCT, an investment company set up to invest in qualifying companies (but it can hold some other investments as well). VCTs work like investment trusts (see page 189) and are listed on the London Stock Exchange.

The main tax advantage is that if you buy shares in an EIS company or VCT when they are first issued, you get a rebate on your tax bill. But there is no tax relief for investors who buy shares after they have been issued, and as a result it can be difficult to find buyers when you want to sell. The VCT or EIS company itself may agree to buy back the shares, but at a discount.

Rates and charges

The cost of investing in a VCT or EIS fund can be high. The initial charge for VCTs is usually over 5%, and a typical annual management charge is 2%. There may also be performance fees if the investment performs well.

How to buy

The minimum investment for many VCTs starts at £3,000, but it is likely to be around £25,000 for an EIS fund. It is best to buy through independent financial advisers who may rebate some of their commission. Check an adviser's expertise in this area, though, and invest with care. If a new VCT or EIS fund fails to attract enough investors, it may be burdened with high costs. Also ask about the fund manager's track record and the policy on buying back shares.

Tax treatment

- The normal tax rebate on investment is worth 20% of the amount you paid, but VCTs qualify for a special rate of 40% until 5 April 2006. With both schemes, the tax rebate will be clawed back by HM Revenue & Customs if you dispose of your shares within three years, or if the company ceases to qualify under the scheme.
- Dividends from VCT shares are tax-free. Dividends from EIS shares are taxable.
- If you make a capital gain when you eventually sell your EIS or VCT shares it is free of capital gains tax. However, you must keep

EIS shares (but not VCTs) for at least three years for this exemption to apply. You can claim capital gains tax relief if you dispose of EIS shares (but not VCT shares) at a loss. Special rules apply if you defer a capital gain by reinvesting in an EIS.
- EIS shares (but not VCT shares) may qualify for exemption from inheritance tax as business property, if held for at least two years.
- For more information see leaflets IR137 *The Enterprise Investment Scheme* and IR169 *Venture Capital Trusts*.

Alternatives to consider

- If you are looking for an adventurous investment, consider a unit trust, OEIC or investment trust that specialises in small companies or a specialist industrial sector.
- If the tax relief is what attracts you, the only other investment with comparable tax advantages is a private pension. Self-invested personal pensions (SIPPs) offer considerable investment freedom (see page 276).

Ethical savings and investments

A savings account or an investment fund that promises to use your money in line with environmental, social or ethical principles. ❗ (usually)

Good for
- People who want to invest in companies whose ethics they approve of.

Bad for
- Cost – charges are likely to be a bit higher than for similar funds without an ethical commitment.

Risk factors
- The same as for any other investment of the same type (for savings accounts see page 264, for life insurance or pension funds see page 196, for unit trusts see page 287).
- In theory, ethical investments shouldn't perform any worse than other investments of the same type; in fact, investments in companies with good practices should do better. Some funds have done very well. But fund managers have a limited choice of companies to invest in, and the extra costs of investing ethically mean that a company has to perform better than its counterparts to produce the same return.
- It could be difficult to find a fund with investment criteria that match your own principles completely. In addition, some funds are more successful than others in meeting their ethical aims.

Timescale
Broadly similar to other investments of the same type.

Jargon alert

Socially responsible investment (SRI)
This is an umbrella term for almost any investment approach that takes social, ethical and environmental issues into account.

How they work

Most ethical homes for your money are unit trust funds and unit-linked life insurance or pension funds, although there are a few ethical bank and building society accounts. There are two basic approaches:

- The fund or account managers may avoid investing in companies involved in particular industries, such as tobacco, the arms trade, the nuclear industry, or in companies that have a poor environmental record or are associated with oppressive regimes. This is called negative screening.
- The managers may seek to invest in companies that make a positive contribution to the environment or to society, or have good employment practices.

However, it is not so clear-cut in practice. Most funds combine these two approaches. Some companies have a very clear policy. Others may say only that they seek to avoid certain practices, or that they will take other factors into account, or that they will use their investment muscle to encourage companies to improve their practices. It's up to you to read their literature carefully and decide what is important to you.

Until recently, most UK financial institutions have not catered for people who wish to avoid certain investments on religious grounds. Nowadays, products that comply with Shari'a law are increasingly available, both from specialist Islamic financial organisations and high-street organisations.

Trade secret

Influencing your employer's pension fund

The trustees of an employer's pension fund must have a statement of investment principles, which includes information on how far the fund takes social, environmental and ethical concerns into account when deciding how to invest. This gives concerned employees an opportunity to ask trustees to change their policy.

Rates and charges

You pay the same sorts of charges as for other investments of the same type. But charges on ethical investment funds are usually a bit higher than normal because of the extra research that is needed to pick their investments.

How to buy

A good first step is to look at the websites of the Ethical Investment Research Service and the UK Social Investment Forum (see the Fact file). The EIRIS publishes a guide to ethical funds and also has a directory of independent financial advisers who have experience of dealing with ethical investments (see the Fact file). There is also an Ethical Investment Association whose members are advisers with an interest in this field.

The Institute of Islamic Banking and Insurance has a list of its members operating in the UK (see the Fact file).

Tax treatment

This is the same as for any other product of the same type. However, you can get a special tax relief if you invest in an accredited Community Investment scheme, such as social banks. Investors can claim a community investment tax credit of 5% of the amount invested for up to five years – 25% in total.

Alternatives to consider

- You can do it yourself by investing directly in companies whose aims you support, or in social projects such as regeneration schemes.
- Alternatively, you can use your voice as a shareholder to encourage companies to act as you believe they should.
- However, these alternatives are only likely to be suitable if you have plenty of time, money and experience, and are prepared to take the extra risks of direct investment.

Friendly society tax-free savings plans

Life insurance policies with tax advantages, designed to run for at least ten years. !

Good for
- People who really need a tax-free investment – for example, people who have used up all their other tax-free chances to invest, higher-rate taxpayers.
- Parents who want to give substantial amounts to a child. Normally, if interest on money given by a parent comes to more than £100 a year per child, the whole amount is taxed as the parent's. This does not apply to tax-free savings plans.

Bad for
- Inflexibility – only buy one if you are sure you can keep the policy going until maturity.
- High charges that may cancel out the tax benefits.

Risk factors
- The same as for life insurance endowment policies (see page 214).

Timescale
These are ten-year savings plans. If you cash in a plan early, you may get a very poor return.

How they work

Friendly societies developed as a form of self-help during the 19th century. Most of them are small, but the biggest are virtually indistinguishable from life insurance companies and offer the same types of products, particularly with-profits life insurance policies, bonds, pensions, and healthcare and income protection policies. These work in exactly the same way as policies issued by standard insurance companies (see page 196). Some societies specialise in providing savings schemes for children, including Child Trust Fund accounts (see page 150).

There is one type of friendly society plan that you cannot get anywhere else: the tax-free savings plan. This works in the same way as a life insurance endowment plan (see page 214), but the maximum you can put in is £25 a month, or £270 a year if you are paying annual premiums.

Jargon alert

Mutuality

Mutual organisations are owned by and run for the benefit of their members. They include building societies, credit unions and friendly societies, and a few life insurance companies. Because mutual organisations are not companies, and do not have to pay part of their profits to shareholders, they should be able to produce better returns. Some mutuals have offered consistently good deals. Unfortunately, others have proved to be pretty inefficient organisations and some have had to demutualise in order to inject new funds (see Jargon alert: Carpetbagging on page 272).

Rates and charges

How much the policy pays out on maturity depends mainly on the company's investment performance. But policy charges will reduce your return and can be high, partly because the low premiums make plans expensive to run.

How to buy

You can buy plans directly from a friendly society, or through financial advisers. You can find out which societies offer plans, and their charges, from the FSA's comparative tables.

Tax treatment

You don't get tax relief on the premiums, but they grow in a fund that is largely tax-free, and all the proceeds are tax-free.

Alternatives to consider

■ If you want the discipline of regular saving, you can set up a regular standing order into a savings account, or a cash ISA if you are a taxpayer.

■ If you want some exposure to the stockmarket, consider a stocks and shares ISA (see page 183).

■ Parents saving for children should see Chapter 7, and people who want to save tax should see Chapter 4.

Guaranteed and protected stockmarket bonds

Bonds linked to the performance of the stockmarket, with some protection if the stockmarket falls. ❗ (some bonds)

Good for
- Safety – the best bonds, such as National Savings & Investments equity bonds, can be a safe way into the stockmarket for people who would otherwise be tempted to leave their money in a savings account.

Bad for
- The cost of the guarantee or protection means that you will lose some (and possibly a lot) of the potential growth if the market rises. The potential return may not be much more than investing in a savings account.
- You are unlikely to get dividend income, which can make up a large part of the return from a stockmarket investment.
- If the stockmarket falls and all you get back is your original deposit, you will be worse off than if you had invested in the worst savings account.
- People who are prepared to accept less than 100% protection – they should consider whether the cost of the bonds is really worthwhile.

Risk factors
- The firm offering the guarantee or protection may be unable to meet its liabilities. This is not a risk with the National Savings & Investments guaranteed equity bond, backed by the UK government, but with other bonds you should read the small print carefully to see who is providing the protection (it may not be the organisation whose name is on the bond). At least one company issuing bonds has been unable to pay out on the due date.
- Not all bonds guarantee that you will get all your money back.
- You are taking a gamble on whether the stockmarket will go up or down.
- Complexity. Even some advisers admit that they find the most complicated bonds difficult to understand. Do not buy unless you

have read all the small print.

■ Withdrawals are often not allowed at all during the term of the bond, and if they are, there may be a penalty.

■ Whether or not you are covered by the UK Financial Services Compensation Scheme and Financial Ombudsman Service depends on how the bond is set up. You should be covered if it is set up as a UK deposit account, insurance policy or fund, but you may not be if it is set up as an offshore bond (see page 40). But beware – bonds may be set up through a web of different companies, some UK and some overseas. The small print should say if you are covered.

Timescale

These are typically five-year investments, but they may last from two to 15 years. Some bonds have no fixed maturity date, but you should still check for penalties on withdrawal.

How they work

Guaranteed or protected bonds are issued by banks, building societies, insurance companies and fund managers, National Savings & Investments and even supermarkets and the Post Office. They work in many different ways, but what they all have in common is that their return is linked to some form of stockmarket index and they include some form of protection in case the index falls. But there the similarities between them end.

They can be set up as single-premium insurance policies, deposit accounts or investment funds and this can make a big difference as to how they are taxed (see page 176). (But don't confuse these bonds with the type of guaranteed growth bonds offered by a few insurance companies and covered on page 208 – they are completely different.)

Many bonds are designed to provide capital growth and offer no income during the term of the investment. A few give the option of taking some income, perhaps from a linked savings account. A few concentrate on providing income, but these may have limited protection (they are covered under High-income bonds on page 179). This section concentrates on bonds designed for growth.

Jargon alert

Structured products

Guaranteed and protected stockmarket bonds are known in the trade as structured products, because they are structured to provide a return linked to a particular investment index, without needing to invest directly in the investments that make up that index. For example, a bond might keep most of your money in a safe investment, but use some to buy derivatives, such as options and futures, to bet on the stockmarket. Options and futures allow you to buy investments at a future date at a price fixed now; so if the market price is more than the fixed price, the bet pays off.

Trade secret

You can buy bonds linked to property indices

From time to time bonds are issued that link all or part of the return to property prices, including UK house prices. But bear in mind that these products started to be issued at a time when house prices were forecast to stabilise or even fall.

What happens if the index falls

Some bonds guarantee to return the amount you deposited; others guarantee to return a set amount, which may be more (or less) than the amount deposited. The guarantee may be conditional on the index reaching a certain level. Other bonds offer only limited protection, for example you might get back a minimum of 80% of the amount you invested.

Avoid bonds that offer protection only if the market falls by less than a certain amount. You are protected if the market falls by a little, but have no protection if things get really nasty.

What happens if the index rises

Most bonds pay out no interest during the period of your investment. Instead, the return comes in any number of forms. This makes it difficult to compare the value of bonds. For example, a bond might:

- increase in value in line with the chosen index up to a certain limit (a cap)
- give you (say) 60% of the rise in value of the index over the period
- also offer some fixed interest
- offer extra growth in return for less capital protection
- offer the best or worst of two possible options.

Don't be dazzled by potential large percentage increases – this is the total increase over the period of the investment. For example, a five-year bond might offer you up to 150% of your original investment over five years. This is equivalent to an annual interest rate of 8.5%. Great, you might say, but this is the maximum – if the index rises to 125% of its initial value it is equivalent to a return of 4.5%, similar to what you could receive in savings accounts. Had you invested directly in a share-based investment you might also have received dividends.

Trade secret

Watch out for which index is used and how the growth is calculated

Bonds may be linked to an index of UK shares (such as the FTSE 100), European shares (such as the Dow Jones Euro Stoxx 50), or a 'basket' of, say, four worldwide indices. The more difficult it is to forecast the performance of an index, the better the terms you should get, to compensate for the extra uncertainty. Don't buy a bond linked to an index you've never heard of and know nothing about.

Bond issuers can also make their bonds look more attractive by offering a high percentage of an index which is not expected to grow very much – for example, a basket of indices that averages out the overall return. Averaging can be a good thing, as it reduces the chance of being affected by a one-off blip (the start point or end point of the index might be averaged over a few days or months to avoid this, for example), but do make sure you are comparing like with like when choosing a bond.

Rates and charges

The percentage of any growth offered depends on future expectations of how the related index will perform, and the cost of providing the protection (which can be quite high). How the charges are collected depends on how the bond is set up. Often they are not separately stated, but built into the return.

How to buy

The bonds are normally sold in issues, available for a limited period (typically, a couple of months), and the terms of each bond differ depending on market conditions. The minimum investment can be anything from £500 to £30,000.

If you are interested in a stockmarket bond, check first what is on offer from National Savings & Investments, which has the backing of the UK government and offers deposit-based bonds from time to time. Other bonds are often sold by direct mail, but it's worth buying through a financial adviser who subscribes to a specialist database.

Tax treatment

This depends on how the bond is set up. Currently, most bonds are issued either as deposit accounts, single-premium insurance policies or ISAs (see the table opposite for a summary). However, there are also many offshore products, which may be set up as virtually anything – deposit accounts, special insurance or investment companies, or funds.

You need to take the following into account when choosing a bond:

■ With a deposit-based bond, the whole of your return, minus your original investment, will be taxed as interest in the year the bond matures. For basic-rate taxpayers, this means a tax bill of 20% of the return, but receiving a large amount of interest in one year could push you into a higher tax band or affect your age-related allowance if you are aged 65 or over (see page 68).

■ The payout from a life insurance bond will not incur a further tax bill if you are a non-taxpayer, starting-rate taxpayer or basic-rate taxpayer, but it may reduce your age-related allowance if you are aged 65 or over. A higher-rate taxpayer may have further tax to pay on any gain over the original investment (see page 63).

■ An ISA bond is tax-free, but remember that you have only a limited

ISA allowance each tax year and you should check whether any other ISA investment is more suitable.

- An offshore product is not tax-free. An offshore deposit account or insurance bond provides taxable income that must be declared to your tax office, and an investment fund is likely to provide a return in the form of a capital gain, potentially liable to capital gains tax (see page 64).
- If a bond only pays out interest, this is unlikely to be liable to capital gains tax; otherwise you might have to pay capital gains tax, but only if your gains exceed your annual tax-free allowance (£8,500 in the 2005–06 tax year).
- Read the small print and do not assume that a bond offered by, say, an insurance company will necessarily be set up as an insurance policy. If in doubt, ask the bond issuer.

How the various types of bond are taxed

Type of bond	Type of income	Liable to income tax?	Liable to capital gains tax?
Deposit-based	Interest	Yes	No
ISA	Usually tax-free	No	No
Life insurance bond	Life insurance gains	Possibly	No
Unit trust/ OEIC	Capital gain only	No	Possibly
Offshore bond	May be interest, insurance gains, or capital gain only	Possibly	Possibly

Alternatives to consider

- If you are a really cautious investor, and haven't got much money to invest, stick to savings accounts offered by banks and building societies (see page 264) and National Savings & Investments (see page 219). Some unit trust and OEIC funds are also guaranteed or protected.

- If you are prepared to accept a bit of risk, and already have a reasonable amount in savings accounts, you should consider investing directly in stockmarket-linked investments, such as an index-tracking or lifestyle investment fund (see page 54), bought through an ISA if you are a taxpayer.

High-income bonds

Different types of investment may be marketed as high income. With many of these products you may not get back all your original investment. ❶ (some bonds)

Good for
- People who have thoroughly researched what is on offer, are prepared to risk their capital, and already have substantial amounts in other, safer investments.

Bad for
- People who need to depend on their investments to provide a substantial proportion of their income, or who have a restricted amount of savings.
- People who cannot afford to lose part of their original investment – look for a bond which guarantees to return at least the amount you invested.

Risk factors
- These products are linked to the value of corporate bonds or the stockmarket. They may not return your original investment if these fall in value.
- The amount of income may not be fixed. If it is fixed, you cannot usually withdraw your money, so you risk losing out if interest rates rise elsewhere.
- High-income bond funds may invest in corporate bonds from firms with a higher risk of default. You are unlikely to be covered by the Financial Services Compensation Scheme in the event of default, although if you were wrongly advised to buy the bonds by an authorised adviser you may have a case against them.
- Stockmarket-linked high-income bonds may promise a complete return of your capital, but companies can, and occasionally do, break their promises.
- Some high-income bonds are complex. Do not buy unless you have read all the small print.

- With a high-income bond, withdrawals are often not allowed at all during the term of the bond, or if they are, there may be a penalty.
- A high-income bond set up in the UK should be covered by the UK Financial Services Compensation Scheme and Financial Ombudsman Service, but these may not protect you if the bond is set up offshore, as many bonds are (see page 40). The small print should say if you are covered.

Timescale

High-income bond funds have no set maturity date, but you should expect to keep your money tied up for at least five years, preferably more. Other high-income bonds are usually set up to last for a fixed period, typically five years.

How they work

The two main investments marketed as high income are high-income bond funds and stockmarket-linked bonds.

High-income bond funds

These are unit trusts, OEICs or investment trusts that invest in corporate bonds. Their value fluctuates and they do not offer a fixed rate of interest. (See page 154 for more on corporate bonds and bond funds.)

Stockmarket-linked bonds

These are structured in the same way as guaranteed or protected stockmarket bonds (see page 172), with the following important differences:

- Some bonds do not promise to return all your original investment if the stockmarket falls. Instead, they offer you a fixed income that is higher than you can get on a savings account. There may be limited protection if the stockmarket falls by a little.
- Some bonds do promise to return all your original investment. In this case, though, the amount of income may not be guaranteed and may fall, or stop altogether, if the investments to which the bond is linked perform badly.

Jargon alert

Precipice bonds

These are a type of stockmarket-linked bond where you get the full amount of your initial investment back only if the index to which the bond is linked does not fall below a certain level. If the index falls over this 'precipice', you could lose a substantial part, or even all, of your initial investment – the value of your capital could even drop at a faster rate than the fall in the index.

Many people lost money in these bonds when the stockmarket fell at the beginning of this century. The bonds affected were mostly intended to provide income, but growth bonds may also be designed this way. Bond issuers are now more cautious about the bonds on offer, but there are still bonds available where your capital falls by 1% for each 1% fall in the value of the index below, say, 30% of the index's original value. And new types of bond are coming onto the market all the time.

Rates and charges

Rates on stockmarket-linked income bonds change frequently, in the same way as other stockmarket bonds (see page 176).

The same types of charges are payable on bond funds as on other invest-ment funds of the same type (such as unit trusts, see page 287). Often charges are not separately stated but built into the return. And in order to give a higher return, charges may be deducted from the fund's capital, rather than the income received by the fund. If so, the charges may erode the value of fund, so check the fund's policy on this. Also be careful when comparing funds – to achieve a high income, the fund may be investing in riskier high-yield bonds (see page 155).

How to buy

Because high-income bonds and bond funds vary so much, it is probably worth buying through an independent financial adviser. Bonds may be sold by direct mail, but be cautious about buying this way.

Tax treatment

■ For high-income corporate bond funds, see page 292.

- For stockmarket-linked high-income bonds, the income may be paid before tax, or with tax taken off, depending on how the bond is set up (see page 176, and make sure you are comparing like with like when you buy).

Alternatives to consider

- See page 114 for more on investing for income.

Individual Saving Accounts (ISAs)

A tax-free wrapper within which you can hold a cash savings account or various types of stockmarket-linked investments. ❗ (if stockmarket-linked)

Good for
- Taxpayers – there is no income tax or capital gains tax to pay on the income or gains from an ISA, except for the dividend tax credit payable on share-based investments, which cannot be reclaimed.
- People (including non-taxpayers) whose investment income might push them into paying a higher rate of tax (see page 58).
- Charges – if you invest in an investment fund through an ISA, the normal initial charge may be reduced (with some companies).

Bad for
- Money you need to take in and out of your account frequently. The tax rules only allow you to put in a certain amount each year.

Risk factors
- The government has committed itself to keeping the income and gains from an ISA tax-free only until April 2010. It is not clear what will happen then.
- Other risk factors depend on the type of investment you hold within your ISA.

Timescale
You can withdraw all or part of your money at any time, although the ISA manager may impose a minimum investment period. Stocks and shares ISAs are best kept for the long term, ideally a minimum of 5–10 years.

How they work

ISAs are run by an ISA manager, such as a bank or building society, National Savings & Investments, and many unit trust companies and other investment firms. There are two types of ISA:

- *Cash ISAs.* These are savings accounts that work in the same way as a normal bank or building society account. Many instant-access ISAs are available, but there are also fixed-term accounts, or ones where you have to give, say, 90 days' notice of withdrawal.
- *Stocks and shares ISAs.* These can include shares and corporate bonds, British Government stocks, unit trusts, OEICs and investment trusts, as well as many European investment funds and stocks and corporate bonds of companies listed anywhere in the world. Stocks and shares ISAs can also include some types of insurance-based investment, but few companies offer this option. At one end of the spectrum, you can choose just one investment fund to go in your ISA; at the other end, you can have a self-select ISA within which you can buy and sell company shares, or a wide range of investment funds from both the ISA manager and other investment companies. In the middle, many managers offer you a range of their own investment funds. There may also be a cash fund or deposit account, within which you can keep cash while you are waiting to invest it.

How much can you invest?

You can invest up to £7,000 in ISAs in each tax year (running from 6 April in one year to 5 April in the next). You can put up to £3,000 in a cash ISA, but how much you can put in a stocks and shares ISA depends on whether you choose a mini- or maxi-ISA. Each year, you can choose either one maxi-ISA or one mini-cash ISA plus one mini stocks and shares ISA, but you cannot take out both a maxi and a mini in the same year (see the chart on page 187 for a summary of your choices).

Your choices start afresh the next tax year, and you don't have to stick with the same ISA manager, so you could end up with a collection of mini- and maxi-ISAs from different companies.

You can also transfer your ISA to a different ISA manager, or switch your money from one investment to another offered by the same ISA manager, provided that you keep your money in the same category (either cash or stocks and shares). However, these are only the tax rules. In practice, your ISA manager may impose other restrictions.

Jargon alert

Mini-ISAs and maxi-ISAs

A mini-ISA is an ISA that is invested either in cash, or in stocks and shares, but not both. A maxi-ISA allows you to invest in cash, stocks and shares or life insurance, all within the one ISA. In practice, most maxi-ISAs are effectively stocks and shares ISAs, but people choose them because the most you can invest in a mini stocks and shares ISA is £4,000 a year, whereas you can put the whole of your £7,000 annual ISA allowance into stocks and shares through a maxi-ISA. The advantage of choosing two mini-ISAs is that you can put your money with two different ISA managers. But the most you can put into cash savings through an ISA is £3,000 a year, whether you go down the mini route or the maxi route.

Trade secret

Investing in the stockmarket through ISAs

If you have investments in an ISA that pays dividends, your ISA manager used to be able to reclaim the 10% dividend tax credit on your behalf. This is no longer possible. However, investing in shares through ISAs still saves you tax if you are a higher-rate taxpayer or at risk of losing your age allowance (see page 68), or if you are likely to pay capital gains tax. Investing in corporate bonds or cash-based unit trusts through ISAs still has tax advantages, though, as these pay interest which remains tax-free.

Trade secret

Keep an eye on your ISA

Particularly with cash ISAs, it is important to ensure that your ISA is still offering a good deal. If it isn't, transfer it to a better account. But your new ISA manager must organise the transfer for you. If you just close your old account and then open a new one with the cash, the money you pay in will count as a new investment and use up your ISA allowance for the year.

Rates and charges

Interest rates for mini cash ISAs are comparable to the before-tax rates available on savings accounts with similar conditions, and sometimes beat them. But read the terms and conditions carefully for one-off charges and restrictions – for example, a charge may be made if you want to transfer to another ISA manager.

With a stocks and shares ISA, you usually just pay the normal charges for the underlying investment (though sometimes the initial charge may be less than normal). However, if you want a self-select ISA, you may have to pay a separate administration fee.

You can buy special stakeholder ISAs that meet minimum standards (see page 95).

How to buy

Cash ISAs are available from any UK bank or building society or from National Savings & Investments.

You have a wide range of options if you want a stocks and shares ISA. These are offered by most big banks and building societies, and by investment companies (such as unit trust and investment trust management companies). You can also buy from fund supermarkets (see page 125). Some types of ISA are covered in the comparative tables on the Financial Services Authority website.

You can invest a lump sum, but many ISA managers have regular savings schemes. However, you have to invest cash. You cannot transfer existing investments into an ISA without selling them first, except for shares from some employers' share incentive schemes.

Tax treatment

The tax rules are summarised below – full details are in HM Revenue & Customs leaflet IR2008 *ISAs and PEPs*. Note that if you buy more than one maxi-ISA in a tax year, or more than one mini-ISA of the same type, or both a mini-ISA and a maxi-ISA, you have broken the rules and you will be liable for tax on the most recent ISA investment.

Your ISA choices

You can invest up to £7,000 overall in each tax year.
You can choose to invest through either of the two routes below:

Either	*Or*
THE MAXI ROUTE Put all your money in one maxi-ISA, from one ISA manager, with: ■ Up to £3,000 in cash ■ The rest in stocks, shares and life insurance, i.e. up to £7,000	**THE MINI ROUTE** Split your money between two mini-ISAs, one for each component, from separate ISA managers, and with: ■ Up to £3,000 in cash ■ Up to £4,000 in stocks, shares and life insurance*

*Before 6 April 2005 you could put up to £3,000 in a stocks and shares mini-ISA, and £1,000 in a separate life insurance mini-ISA.

> ## Trade secret

Withdrawing money from an ISA

Think twice before withdrawing money from an ISA in the same tax year in which you invest it. If, say, you put the maximum £3,000 in a cash ISA in May 2005, and then withdraw £1,000 in July 2005, you will not be able to put in another £1,000 in the 2005–06 tax year.

Alternatives to consider

■ For other tax-free investments, see the list on page 57.
■ Self-invested personal pensions (SIPPs) are another type of tax wrapper that might suit some people who are saving for retirement.

Jargon alert

PEPs, TESSAs and TESSA-only ISAs

PEPs and TESSAs are tax-free schemes that were replaced by ISAs in 1999. Personal Equity Plans (PEPs) were stockmarket linked: if you still have one, it will continue to be free of income tax and capital gains tax (but, as with ISAs, the dividend tax credit is not reclaimable). You can transfer an existing PEP to a new provider, and so you may still see investments mentioned as homes for PEP transfers.

Tax Exempt Special Savings Accounts (TESSAs) were cash-based savings accounts. TESSAs have all matured by now, but you could transfer the money you put into them into a special ISA, provided you did so within six months of maturity. If you have one of these TESSA-only ISAs (or 'TOISAs') you should avoid cashing it in unless you have to, because you cannot open another. However, you can transfer a TESSA-only ISA to another ISA manager, in the same way as for other ISAs.

Investment trusts

Special companies that are set up to invest in the stockmarket. ❗

Good for
- Chance of a capital gain – you pool your money with other investors to invest in a wide range of stockmarket investments.
- Charges – some trusts have lower charges than other types of investment fund.

Bad for
- Novice investors – only venture into investment trusts when you have the rest of your finances sorted out and a sound basis of less risky investments.
- Flexibility – only invest money you can afford to tie up for 5–10 years.

Risk factors
- Like all stockmarket investments, the performance of investment trusts cannot be predicted. You may get back less than you put in.
- There are important differences between investment trusts and other investment funds that may give the potential for higher returns, but also higher risks.
- There is a huge range of trusts, from quite conservative to very risky. You need to do enough research to find one that suits your needs, or buy through an independent financial adviser.
- Many trusts have investments overseas whose values are affected by changes in exchange rates.
- Investment trusts are regulated differently from other investments, and you can only be sure of being covered by the Financial Ombudsman Service and the Financial Services Compensation Scheme if you invest through an authorised financial adviser, or through a wrapper such as an ISA or investment trust savings plan.

Timescale
You should be prepared to keep your investment for a minimum of 5–10 years. In theory, you can sell shares in an investment trust at any time, but

if you are forced to sell at a bad time you may make a loss. The ability to sell an investment trust's shares may be suspended at certain points, for example during trust reconstructions.

How they work

Investment trusts are special companies, quoted on the London Stock Exchange, that buy the stocks and shares of other companies. You invest by buying shares in the investment trust company; the value of your investment is the value of your shares, and you may get regular dividends. Effectively, you are buying into an investment fund, as described in Chapter 6.

However, because investment trusts are companies they differ from other investment funds in some important ways:

- *The share price depends on demand from investors.* The number of shares is fixed, so the price adjusts to reflect not just the value of the trust's investments, but also investor demand. They usually trade at a discount to the actual value of the shares the trust has invested in (see Jargon alert on page 193). Another name for this sort of fund is a closed-end fund (see Jargon alert on page 289).
- *The trust can borrow to buy investments.* A trust that borrows (not all do) is said to be 'geared', and this increases not only the potential for a high return but also the risk of greater falls in value. (See the example on page 147.)
- *Some trusts issue different classes of share.* These are called split capital trusts (see Jargon alert on page 192).
- *You have voting rights.* Investment trusts are governed by a board of directors. Boards can either employ their own fund managers or subcontract the management to other fund management companies (although, confusingly, trusts are often set up by fund management companies). Unless your shares are held in a nominee account (see Jargon alert on page 282) you have voting rights, and you may occasionally receive weighty legal documents asking you to vote on matters such as, for example, company restructuring plans. You also have the opportunity to question decisions by attending the Annual General Meeting.

■ *Investment trusts are regulated as companies.* They must comply with company law and the rules of the UK Listing Authority, which is part of the Financial Services Authority (FSA). But the FSA rules that apply to most investments do not apply to investment trusts. This is under review, but at present you cannot take a complaint against the investment trust company itself to the Financial Ombudsman Service, nor are you covered by the Financial Services Compensation Scheme if the trust goes bust. But you are likely to be covered by these schemes if you buy through an adviser who is authorised by the FSA, or if you buy through a wrapper such as an ISA or an investment trust savings scheme.

As these differences suggest, it is essential to know what you are getting into when you buy investment trust shares. For example, there are some big, long-running generalist trusts that invest in a wide spread of different companies, but also some much smaller specialist trusts that are likely to be far more volatile.

You can hold investment trusts in an ISA, SIPP or Child Trust Fund. A few companies also offer investment trust personal pensions.

Savings schemes

Investment trust savings schemes aren't just for regular savers – you can use them to invest lump sums. They operate as a centralised buying and selling service for a particular trust. The manager amalgamates all the orders received during a particular period and bulk buys (or sells) the shares. This is cheap and convenient. The disadvantage is that your transaction won't go through immediately – it may be only weekly or monthly – so you can't be sure of the price that will apply. And you may have to put your shares in a nominee account with the fund manager (see Jargon alert on page 282).

However, savings schemes have other advantages. You may be able to use them to invest in a wide range of investment funds run by other investment managers (not just investment trusts). You may also be able to transfer investments you already own into them, so that they can act as a portfolio tracking service and fund supermarket (see Jargon alert on page 125).

Jargon alert

Split capital investment trusts (splits)

These issue different types of share, each designed to produce a different type of return. The trust is usually designed to last for a limited period.

- *Zero dividend preference shares (zeros)* pay no dividends. You hope to get your return in the form of capital growth when the trust is wound up, or if you sell your shares earlier.
- *Income shares*, by contrast, are designed to provide income. The amount of capital you get depends on the trust structure, but in some cases you may get little or no capital growth.
- *Capital shares* get whatever is left over from the other shareholders when the trust is wound up.

The amount of income and capital growth is not guaranteed. Unfortunately, when the stockmarket fell at the turn of the century, split capital trusts were a major casualty and several went bust. The problems arose because some splits were very highly geared (had very large borrowings), and they had tended to invest in each other (so-called crossholdings), so when one got into trouble others followed. The situation became even worse because zeros in these trusts had been widely touted as low-risk investments, and so many investors who were far from wealthy lost large amounts of money.

However, not all splits were affected, and, ironically, the furore caused by the scandal is likely to have improved the regulation of investment trusts. The whole sorry episode shows just how important it is to understand what you are getting into.

Jargon alert

Real Estate Investment Trusts (REITs)

The government is proposing to allow a new type of investment scheme that will invest in commercial and/or residential property. This will make it easier for individuals to invest in property.

Jargon alert

Discounts, premiums and NAVs

The NAV, or net asset value, is the value of the underlying investments owned by the investment trust. Usually, however, the shares of the trust cost less to buy than the value of the underlying investments (the NAV). The gap between the two values is called the discount. For example, if the discount is 15%, you get £100-worth of investments for £85. Occasionally, if the trust is really in demand, the shares cost more than the NAV, and then the difference is called the premium.

Over time, the gap between the share price and the NAV may widen or narrow. If the discount narrows after you buy, it generally boosts the value of your shares; if it widens, your shares generally shrink in value. However, what matters most is the price of the shares over the period of your ownership, so discount variations should not make too much difference to long-term investors. A trust can manage its discount to some extent by buying back shares to reduce the supply.

Rates and charges

There are two types of charges: charges deducted from the fund to cover the costs of running it, and the costs you pay.

Charges paid within the fund include the fund manager's fees, payments to the trust's directors, accountants' fees, and so on. Funds quote a total expense ratio or TER (see page 106), which will help you compare funds. A big generalist trust may have a TER as low as 0.3%, while that for a specialist trust might be ten times as much (3%, say). Remember, though, that the TER doesn't include the dealing charges the fund has to pay when it buys and sells shares.

Then there are the charges you have to pay:

■ stockbrokers' commission or other dealing costs, which can be up to about 1.75% for telephone deals through a stockbroker (see page 283). If you buy or sell shares in a trust through the trust's own savings scheme, there are special cheap rates, or a flat fee of, say, between £2.50 and £15
■ the spread between the price buyers pay and the price sellers get (see Jargon alert on page 283)

- for purchasers only, stamp duty of 0.5% of the value of the shares
- the cost of any wrapper, for example administration charges. In practice, ISAs and savings schemes may not have any regular charges, just one-off charges such as a transfer fee if you transfer existing investments into a savings scheme
- advisers' charges, for example an annual fee if an adviser is managing a portfolio for you (see Chapter 5).

How to buy (and sell)

Investment trust shares can be bought through a stockbroker in the same way as other shares (see page 284). But to get the protection of the Financial Ombudsman Service and the Financial Services Compensation Scheme, it is best to buy either through an independent financial adviser, or through a wrapper such as an ISA or investment trust savings scheme.

If you buy through a wrapper, you can invest a monthly amount or a lump sum, or a combination of both. The minimum investment may be £25 a month for regular savings (but £50 is more typical) or a few hundred pounds for a lump sum. However, if you are not investing through a wrapper with cheap dealing fees, the minimum costs of dealing mean that larger investments (around £1,000, say) are more cost-effective.

There are about 350 investment trusts to choose from. The Association of Investment Trust Companies publishes useful information about member trusts, available both online and in monthly publications. But not all trusts are members, and information on specific trusts is also available from several internet databases and some fund supermarkets.

Tax treatment

- Investment trusts are taxed in the same way as shares – see page 286. A 10% tax credit is deducted from dividends before they are paid, and you have no further tax to pay unless you are a higher-rate taxpayer. But any profit you make when you sell your shares may be liable to capital gains tax.
- However, you can avoid capital gains tax, and any higher-rate income tax on dividends, if you buy through an ISA.

Alternatives to consider
- If you want investments with a chance of capital gain or loss, consider unit trusts or OEICs (held in a stocks and shares ISA if you are a taxpayer).
- Keen investors may want to consider investing directly in shares.

Life insurance-linked saving

A way of pooling your money with other people to invest in stocks, shares and other investments. ❶

Good for
- Special tax treatment, which may suit some taxpayers.
- A managed insurance fund or smoothed fund allows you to put your money in a broad spread of types of investments with a possibility of capital growth, even if you have only modest amounts to invest.

Bad for
- Cost – insurance company charges may be higher than those on similar pooled investments (see page 44).
- Complexity – make sure you know exactly what you are buying and where your money is invested.
- Restrictions – for example, you may be charged a penalty if you want to get your money out early.

Risk factors
- Although some insurance funds are invested in low-risk investments, most have at least some money in stocks and shares, so your investment will be affected by stockmarket ups and downs. You may get back less than you paid in.
- Many traditional with-profits funds have closed to new policyholders: both these and some open funds are likely to give low returns. A few funds are still strong, but it is not easy to tell which these are, so a traditional with-profits fund is probably best avoided unless you have expert advice.
- The return from unit-linked funds depends purely on the value of the fund's investments. Unit prices go up and down, so if the value is low when you cash in the policy you will get a low payout.
- A new-style with-profits fund can even out some of the stockmarket ups and downs, but you are not totally insulated: the value of your policy can fall and exit penalties may still apply. If you really cannot afford to take a risk, put your money in a savings account.

■ If you are a policyholder in an insolvent UK life insurance company, you get limited protection from the Financial Services Compensation Scheme (see Chapter 2). However, it can take years for an insolvency to be resolved and it is more likely that a fund will close to new policyholders first.

Timescale

Two main types of insurance policy are used as a way of investing:

■ policies designed for regular saving over a period of ten years or more, generally known as endowments, savings plans, maximum investment plans (MIPs) or regular-premium policies.
■ policies for one-off payments, called bonds or single-premium policies.

How they work

Endowment policies are covered in detail on page 214, and single-premium bonds on page 206. This section concentrates on the three main differences between life insurance and other investments:

■ Some of your premiums are used to pay for any life insurance that the policy has promised to pay on your death. With a protection-type policy (see page 7), all of your premiums are used to provide cover. An investment-type policy might pay out a set amount on your death (if it is an endowment policy) or simply the value of your investment (for most bonds).
■ The rest of your premiums go into a life insurance fund, which pools your money with that of other investors. There are two main types of fund – with-profits and unit-linked (see overleaf) – which differ in how the return to investors is shared out. However, a new type of with-profits fund is now available (see page 201).
■ Special tax treatment. You do not usually have personal tax to pay on the proceeds from most regular-premium life insurance policies, and there is tax to pay on a single-premium insurance bond only if you are a higher-rate taxpayer. However, this does not mean that the returns from a policy are tax-free – the life insurance fund has already

had some tax deducted. The tax rules also give rise to various other restrictions and disadvantages.

Jargon alert

Pension funds

A pension policy is a special type of insurance policy. A pension fund run by a life insurance company may be either unit-linked or with-profits and works in the same way as a life insurance fund of the same type (see below). The difference is that a pension fund is favourably taxed, so should grow faster.

Unit-linked funds

Your money buys 'units' in an investment fund. The fund may invest in a range of different types of investment, including shares, property and fixed-interest stocks, depending on the objectives of the fund (see Chapter 6 for some common types of fund).

The value of your units is directly linked to the value of the investments owned by the fund, so if those investments rise in value, so does the value of your units. However, if the value of the fund falls, your units will be worth less. In this respect, a unit-linked fund works in a similar way to unit trusts. You can choose to invest in a range of funds and switch between them, while still keeping your money within the one policy.

With-profits funds

The fund managers can choose to invest in stocks and shares, bonds, British Government stocks or property, or keep some in cash. The value of the investments owned by the fund can go up or down. But with a traditional with-profits fund, the return you get is not directly tied to the value of these investments. Instead, each year, the company reviews the health of the fund and declares an annual bonus to policyholders (sometimes called a reversionary bonus).

Each year's bonus is added to the value of your policy and paid out when the plan matures (or on death). You may have been told that these bonuses are guaranteed, because once added they cannot be taken away. This is misleading, because if you cash your policy in early, there may be a surrender penalty or market value reduction (see Jargon alert on page 201) that could be larger than your bonuses to date.

If you keep your policy up until it matures, you may also get an extra terminal or final bonus. Until recent years, final bonuses could be substantial. However, following poor stockmarket returns, recently some companies have not paid any final bonus.

The amount of each bonus depends on how the investments in the fund are doing (if the fund is doing badly, there may be no bonus at all). However, not all the returns from investing are declared as bonuses:

- The fund has to keep back enough to be able to pay what it has already promised its policyholders in the form of life insurance and existing bonuses.
- The company keeps back some of the profits of good years so it can pay a bit extra in poor years. This is called smoothing (see Jargon alert overleaf).
- Some funds also share in the profits or losses made by the insurance company as a whole. So if the company makes losses, the fund may not be able to pay out so much in bonuses.
- If the insurance company has shareholders, some of the profits (typically, 10%) have to be shared with them.

In the past, insurance companies have had a great deal of discretion over how they run their with-profits funds. For example, some companies made their maturity payouts look good by paying out low surrender values to people who cashed in early.

In recent years, investment returns have dwindled and bonuses generally have fallen. Although there are still a few strong funds, following the stockmarket falls of 2000 onwards other funds had to introduce steep surrender penalties to stop people taking their money out and weakening the funds still further. Many traditional funds have closed altogether (for more information on closed funds see page 202).

Jargon alert

Smoothing

Smoothing means that the fund managers keep back some of the fund's profits in good years in order to keep returns up in lean periods. This is the concept behind all with-profits funds whether they are traditional or new-style (many new funds do not call themselves 'with-profits' at all). But how the fund is smoothed varies widely:

- With a traditional fund, it is up to the company to decide, and you will not usually be told how the underlying investments in the fund perform.
- With a new-style fund, the actual performance of the fund is disclosed, and how much of any profit or loss is passed on to you will be set out in the product literature.

So before you buy any form of insurance policy or insurance bond, make sure you know what type of policy you've got. Each company running a with-profits fund now has to publish a guide to how it manages the fund, called its 'Principles and Practices of Financial Management'. From the beginning of 2006 a consumer-friendly version should also be made available.

Note, too, that smoothing cannot protect you from a prolonged stockmarket downturn – policy values will have to fall eventually.

Jargon alert

Unitised with-profits policies

Some traditional with-profits policies work out bonuses as a percentage of the minimum amount that the policy will pay out (the sum assured). However, most funds are now unitised. With a unitised policy, the company still declares bonuses, but when you invest you are allocated a certain number of units in the fund. The bonus is shared out in line with the number of units you have, in the form of bonus units. A unitised fund may allow policyholders to switch their money to any unit-linked funds run by the insurance company; this is not possible with a conventional with-profits policy.

> ### Jargon alert
>
> **Market value reductions**
>
> If a with-profits fund falls in value it could be worth less than the amount the company has promised to pay each policyholder in the form of bonuses. So to stop people being able to take out more than their share of the fund, the terms of the policy may entitle the company to apply a penalty when funds are withdrawn.
>
> These penalties may be called market value reductions (MVRs), market value adjustments (MVAs), market level adjustments (MLAs), policy value adjustments (PVAs) or unit price adjustments. Following the stockmarket falls from 2000 onwards, many companies applied MVRs that could be as much as 30% of the value of a policy. Things have improved a bit recently, but before you cash in a policy, check:
>
> - the current MVR for your policy – it may apply to only some types of policy, or only to withdrawals above a certain amount
> - whether there are any dates stated in the policy when an MVR does not apply. Some policies allow you to get out penalty-free after, say, five or ten years.
>
> Check the penalty regularly – it may be increased or decreased in line with stockmarket conditions. And note that some unitised policies do not charge an MVR but may instead be entitled to reduce the value of your units, which comes to the same thing.

New-style with-profits funds

With-profits funds have fallen out of favour in recent years, partly because of problems with closed funds, but also because policyholders cannot see how the fund is performing or what the charges are. In an attempt to deal with this, a new type of with-profits fund, sometimes called a smoothed investment fund, has been introduced.

With these new funds, your money will buy units in the fund, but the return does not come in the form of bonuses. How the return is calculated depends on the company, but, for example, the company may estimate an expected growth rate (or EGR) for the fund, which it adjusts from time to time. How the fund performs relative to the EGR is taken into account the next time the EGR is adjusted. You will be informed of the actual performance of the fund, and how much of any fall or rise in its value will be passed on to you. But do not use the level of the EGR to choose a policy. It is effectively just a yardstick to work out the smoothing, and the fund will still be able, in some circumstances, to make some sort of market value reduction charge or adjust the value of your units to reflect the actual value of the fund.

Some smoothed funds qualify as stakeholder funds (see page 95). This means that smoothing will be carried out on a daily basis, the fund must not share in the profits or losses of the company, and if anything is deducted from the fund for shareholders, it must be as a specific charge rather than at the company's discretion.

Closed funds

If an insurance fund is closed, it means that the fund will not accept new policyholders, but if you already have a policy invested in the fund, it can continue until maturity. A fund may close because the company is taken over, because it is not profitable to issue new policies in the fund or because the fund is weak.

The investment strategy of a unit-linked fund will not necessarily change if it closes, although its performance may suffer if a company has no incentive to manage it well, or if the fund becomes too small to run efficiently. However, if the company is still running, you may be able to switch to another fund without too much cost.

However, once a with-profits fund closes, it may have to buy safer investments that produce a lower return. These days, about half of with-profits funds are closed, and some are not paying bonuses at all. Moreover, to stop policyholders taking their money elsewhere, they may apply steep surrender penalties or MVRs (see Jargon alert on page 201). Not all funds are in this position. But if you are in a closed with-profits fund that pays no bonuses, you are losing money after taking inflation into account. Before you decide to pay the penalty and go, check the following:

- Does the policy give you any valuable guarantees, for example a guaranteed minimum pension if it is a pension policy?
- How strong is the fund? It will take some time for funds to make up for the stockmarket losses of the past few years, so bonuses are

unlikely to improve in the short term, but the penalties might be reduced. An independent financial adviser may be able to give you some information (see Chapter 5).

■ Can you transfer to another fund with the same company, and if so what penalty would apply?

If you feel you were misled into buying the policy, complain to the company that sold it to you. Another company might offer to pay the penalties for you if you reinvest with them, but do not be swayed by this unless you are sure that the new deal is right for you.

Recently, some closed funds have been bought by specialist companies that think they can do a better job of administering the funds. It is too early to say whether they will succeed, but policyholders have no say in what happens. The terms of their policies are unchanged by the move to the new owners.

Jargon alert

Traded Endowment Policies (TEPs)
It is sometimes possible to sell an endowment policy if you do not want to keep it yourself. And, if you are looking for a life insurance investment, you can buy one second-hand rather than taking out a policy on your own life. A specialist firm called a market-maker acts as a go-between to help sellers find buyers. However, falling returns from life insurance policies make this a less attractive investment these days, and some big market-makers have left the business. If you are interested, contact the Association of Policy Market Makers (see the Fact file).

Rates and charges

When you buy an insurance policy as an investment, part of your money is deducted to pay the company's expenses – for example, fund management costs, the cost of any life insurance, and commission payable to the person who sold the policy to you.

If you have a traditional with-profits policy, the overall expenses are deducted from the fund and you won't usually be told what they are (although see Chapter 5 for more on commission payments). With other types of policy, charges are disclosed but can be very complicated:

- A company may charge you slightly more to buy each unit (the offer price) than you get when you cash it in (the bid price). This is called the spread. A 5% or 6% spread is typical, so you might pay £1 and get 95p or 94p back. But different companies allocate units in different ways in order to recover some of their up-front costs. Some companies may give you extra units (a '102% allocation', say). This sounds good, but, because of the spread, the cash-in value of your units will still come to less than the amount you paid in. You may not be allocated any units at all to start with because your first few premiums go to pay charges. Other funds deduct a set charge for the first five years, say.
- Instead of having different prices for buying and selling units, some funds have a single price for units and a separate initial charge (see Jargon alert on page 290).
- Some policies may issue capital and accumulation units. Capital units are issued at the start of a policy and carry high management charges, making these policies very expensive. Not many new policies have these now, but you may still be paying into a policy that does have them.
- Once your money is invested, a set amount of, say, 1–1.5% of the value of your plan is deducted each year or month as an annual management charge.
- If you switch between funds, the first switch each year may be free, but further switches may cost, say, £25.
- There may be a penalty if you cash in a plan early.

To work out the overall cost of any policy, you need to look at the illustration provided by the company. This should show you the effect of charges on your investment – look for the figures headed 'effect of deductions'. The amount of charges is also shown in the comparative tables on the FSA website (see the Fact file). Note, though, that these figures are not guaranteed – they are worked out assuming that your policy grows at a set rate, and companies may change their charges.

Insurance company charges can be high. However, if you buy a stake-holder insurance product, the annual charge will be capped at 1.5%, falling to 1% after ten years (although an extra smoothing charge may be made if necessary).

How to buy
See page 214 for more information on endowment policies and page 206 for single-premium insurance bonds. You can find out which companies offer them, and details of the policies, from the FSA's comparative tables. Few companies now offer endowment policies.

Tax treatment
- The life insurance fund in which your money is invested is taxed. When the money is paid out to you, you are treated as if you have already paid notional tax of 20% of the amount received. This tax cannot be reclaimed even if you are not a taxpayer. If you are a lower-rate or basic-rate taxpayer, you have no further tax to pay. But you may have more tax to pay if you are a higher-rate taxpayer (i.e. your taxable income, including the taxable gain, is above the basic-rate tax band; see page 59) and you cash in a single-premium policy (or bond), or surrender a regular-premium policy early.
- For more information on the taxation of bonds see page 211. There is usually no tax to pay on the proceeds of an endowment policy or a protection-type policy unless you cash it in early (see page 217).

Alternatives to consider
- For regular saving, see page 218.
- For lump sums, see page 213.

Life insurance bonds

A special insurance policy designed for investing lump sums, usually for a minimum of five years. ❶

Good for

- Getting exposure to a wide choice of stockmarket and other investments which offer the chance of capital growth for modest amounts. Easy to switch between different investment funds within the one policy.
- Can be used to provide regular income, or cashed in as necessary (though there may be a penalty).
- Special tax treatment, which may suit people who expect their tax rate to fall in future and people who have used up their capital gains tax allowance.
- A special type of guaranteed bond, which might suit people who want a fixed rate of interest over a set period.

Bad for

- Insurance company charges, which may be higher than charges on comparable investments.
- If you cash in a policy early (usually within the first five years), there may be penalties. Market value reductions may apply at any time if you cash in a with-profits bond.
- Non-taxpayers and people aged 65 or over who qualify for the higher age-related tax allowance. They could find that cashing in a bond means an increased tax bill, even if there is no tax on the gain itself (see page 211).

Risk factors

- Unless you buy a guaranteed bond, the value of the policy cannot be predicted and depends on how the insurance fund in which your money is invested performs (see page 196 for more on insurance funds in general).
- Although you can cash in a policy at any time, penalties may be charged. On with-profits bonds a market value reduction may apply

(see page 201), effectively trapping you in the policy for an unknown period.

- Drawing an income from your bond can eat into your capital if investments are falling in value.
- If you are a policyholder in an insolvent life insurance company or were mis-sold a bond by a company that is no longer in business, the Financial Services Compensation Scheme may pay limited compensation (see Chapter 2).
- You can usually complain to the Financial Ombudsman Service if you were advised to buy a bond that was unsuitable for you.

Timescale

Guaranteed bonds have a set maturity date that can be anything between six months and five years. Although most other bonds have no set maturity date, they are best kept for at least five or even ten years. Unless the bond is guaranteed, it can go up and down in value, and a long-term investment allows time for losses to be recovered. In addition, some bonds make a charge if you want to leave in the first five years; and many with-profits bonds only guarantee that you will be able to leave without penalty on, say, the fifth or tenth anniversary of your investment.

Jargon alert

With-profits bond

A with-profits bond is simply a single-premium insurance policy invested in an insurance company's with-profits fund (explained on page 198). These bonds were sold heavily when interest rates fell in the late 1990s, as they seemed to offer an answer to the problem of providing higher income with reduced risk. But there is no easy answer, as events proved when stockmarkets fell and with-profits funds began to run into difficulties, and high market value reductions (an adjustment the company can make to the value of your policy; see page 201) left many people trapped in poor funds. At the end of 2004, the cash-in value of the average with-profits bond taken out in each of the previous seven years was less than you would have got from a building society.

How they work

Any type of insurance policy for which you pay a single one-off premium may be called a bond, including unit-linked bonds, with-profits bonds, guaranteed bonds and so on. They are marketed under all sorts of weird and wonderful names; the insurance bond family tree opposite will help reduce the confusion.

The minimum investment is usually £5,000, although some companies accept smaller amounts. You can sometimes add extra lump sums later on, or else you can buy a separate bond. Most bonds have no set maturity date, but they are designed to run for at least five years and there will be penalties if you cash them in before then. They can be cashed in on demand or held until your death, at which point the value of your policy will be paid into your estate.

A few insurance companies offer guaranteed income or guaranteed growth bonds which offer a fixed return over a set period. But don't confuse these with guaranteed insurance funds which you can often invest in through a unit-linked bond – these funds may offer a money-back guarantee, for example, not necessarily a guaranteed return. (See page 172 for more on guaranteed stockmarket bonds.)

Investment bonds for income?

Investment bonds are often marketed as a way of producing a potentially higher income than ordinary savings accounts. This is partly because of the special tax treatment of single-premium insurance bonds, which means that many people can withdraw a limited amount each year without having an immediate tax bill. Most companies allow you to set up automatic withdrawal options, of either a certain amount each quarter, say, or a certain percentage of your investment.

But unless you buy a guaranteed income bond, don't count on being able to withdraw income:

■ Investment bonds are usually invested in things like stocks and shares and commercial property. Their value could indeed grow by more than a savings account, but they can also fall in value. (A with-profits bond does not, strictly speaking, fall in value, but a market value reduction may mean that you get out less than you paid in.)

The insurance bond family tree

Insurance bond   Any insurance policy into which you pay a single lump-sum premium.

Investment bond

A lump sum investment into a unit-linked or with-profits life insurance fund (see page 198 for more on how these funds work). The return depends on the performance of your chosen fund.

Most bonds offer a choice of funds within the same policy. You can invest in more than one and switch between funds (though there may be a switching fee).

You can cash in all or part of your investment at any time, but you may get back less than you invested, depending on investment performance and any charge the company applies.

Guaranteed income or growth bond

The return does not depend on investment performance - instead you get a fixed return. But you have to invest for a set period, anything from six months to five years. Rates vary frequently, depending on economic conditions at the time you buy, but once you have bought the rate is fixed throughout the lifetime of the bond. You can choose whether you want to draw income.

Unit-linked bond

Your premium buys units in the fund which rise and fall in value in line with the value of the investments in the fund. There's often a wide choice of fund (see page 100), and some companies allow you to invest in funds managed by other companies.

With-profits bond

Your money is invested in the insurance company's with-profits fund. The return depends on investment performance, and comes in the form of bonuses. Once added, bonuses cannot be taken away, but there may be a market value reduction (see page 201) if you withdraw money.

Income bond

The interest rate is paid out as regular income (annually or monthly, say) over the lifetime of the bond. When the bond matures, you get back the amount you originally invested.

Because you get some benefit (i.e. income) earlier than on a growth bond, the rates are generally a bit lower.

Growth bond

You get no income during the lifetime of the bond. Instead the whole of the promised return, plus the amount originally invested, is paid out when the bond matures.

Property bond, distribution bond

Sometimes companies market a bond invested in just one type of fund, such as commercial property, or a distribution fund (designed to pay out regular income).

Smoothed fund

A new type of with-profits fund. Your money buys units which rise and fall in value roughly in line with investment performance. But in order to smooth out fluctuations in the value of your investment, unit prices do not rise by quite as much as investment growth, nor do they fall quite as far (normally).

Stockmarket bond

The return depends on the performance of a particular stockmarket index. (See page 172 for more on these products.)

- If you withdraw income when the bond is falling in value, or the amount of income is more than any growth in value, you are eating into your capital (see page 30).
- If you want to draw money from a with-profits bond or a smoothed investment fund at a bad time for the fund (e.g. when stockmarkets are falling and lots of people want to withdraw money), you may be hit with a market value reduction. These penalties are explained on page 201.
- Unit-linked funds may have penalties if you withdraw money in the first five years (except for regular, planned withdrawals).

There are also tax implications to be aware of (see Tax treatment opposite).

Jargon alert

Clusters and segments

A financial adviser may recommend that your money is split into a number of identical policies, which are called cluster policies. Sometimes this is called segmentation. This makes it easier to cash in part of your policy.

Rates and charges

How much the policy pays out depends on the investment performance of the insurance fund in which your money is invested. But policy charges, which can be high, will reduce your return. See page 204 for how the different types of insurance fund charge you for these costs. According to the FSA's comparative tables, in August 2005 charges could amount to between £500 and £1,850 over a ten-year period for a £5,000 investment, depending on the company.

Also watch out for penalties if you cash in all or part of your policy in the first five years (see above). For example, there might be a 10% surrender charge on withdrawals in the first year after taking out the bond, 8% in the second year, 6% in the third year and so on.

How to buy

Insurance bonds are sold by insurance companies and some friendly societies. You can find out which companies offer them, and their charges, from the comparative tables on the Financial Services Authority website. Some companies allow you to buy direct from them, but others will sell only through a financial adviser. If you use an adviser, you can negotiate for a commission rebate, which increases the amount that is invested on your behalf.

Tax treatment

- If your bond is worth more when you cash it in than what you paid for it, the extra is a taxable gain. This is potentially liable to income tax (not capital gains tax). But because the insurance company fund in which your money is invested is regarded as already having paid basic-rate tax, you have tax to pay only if any of the gain, when added to the rest of your income, falls within the higher-rate tax band. If so, the amount in the higher-rate band is taxed at 20% (the higher rate of tax minus the basic-rate tax you are treated as having already paid, i.e. 40 − 20 = 20%). However, you may qualify for top-slicing relief (see the example on page 212).
- A gain may also increase your tax bill if you are receiving the higher tax allowance for people aged 65 or over, and the gain pushes you over the limit at which the extra allowance starts to be whittled away (£19,500 in the 2005–06 tax year). You lose £1 of allowance for each £2 of income over the limit. Top-slicing relief does not apply in this case. (See Example 4.5 on page 69.)
- If you are drawing income from a bond, you will not have any tax to pay at the time if, each year, you draw less than 5% of the original investment (so if you invested £5,000, you can draw £250 a year for 20 years). You can draw more, but it may affect your tax bill in the year of the withdrawal if it pushes you into the higher-rate tax band or reduces your age allowance.
- Even if you have no tax to pay, you must declare any gain you make to HM Revenue & Customs. The insurance company will send you a 'chargeable gain certificate' for any gain you need to declare.
- A taxable gain could also reduce your eligibility for tax credits.

Trade secret

Putting off a tax bill

You can put off paying tax on the gain from an insurance bond if, in any one year, you withdraw less than 5% of the amount you paid in to the policy plus any unused 5%s from previous years. So if you make no withdrawals in one year, you can withdraw 10% in the second year. The maximum you can withdraw without triggering a taxable gain is 100% (i.e. the amount you put in).

However, this only puts off the taxable gain: it is not a tax-free allowance. When the policy comes to an end – either because you finally cash it in, or on your death – the overall gain from the policy still counts as taxable income (minus any taxable gains so far, i.e. withdrawals above your accumulated 5%s). Deferring your gains in this way can be useful if you are a higher-rate taxpayer now but expect your taxable income to fall. But it might not be such a good thing if you are 65 or over and your other income is close to the age allowance limit. In this case it might be better to draw more than 5% over a number of years rather than risk one big gain at the end of the policy (see below).

Example: Higher-rate tax on an insurance bond

In the 2005–06 tax year Patrick cashed in his investment bond for £20,000, £6,000 more than he paid for it – a taxable gain of £6,000. Patrick has other taxable income of £31,255 (after deducting his personal tax allowance). He is normally a basic-rate taxpayer but the gain will push him over the £32,400 basic-rate limit. His income liable to higher-rate tax is £31,255 + £6,000 − £32,400 = £4,855. The extra tax on this would be £971.

Top-slicing relief may help. First divide the total gain by the number of complete years you have had the policy (five, in Patrick's case) to find the average annual gain: £6,000/5 = £1,200. If the average annual gain, when added to the rest of your income:

- *falls within the basic-rate tax band*, there is no tax to pay
- *falls partly in the basic-rate band, partly in the higher-rate band*, you do not pay the full top rate of tax on your insurance gain. Your tax office or insurance company can tell you how much the tax would be. In Patrick's case, it reduces the tax he has to pay from £971 to £55.

Alternatives to consider

- The main alternatives are unit trusts, open-ended investment companies and investment trusts, held in a stocks and shares ISA if you are a taxpayer.
- If you are not prepared to take some risk, see page 172 for more on guaranteed products.
- If your main concern is to provide income, see page 114.

Life insurance endowment policies

Life insurance policies for regular saving, designed to run for at least ten years. ❶

Good for
- Forcing you to save regularly over a long period.
- Getting exposure to the stockmarket, and other investments offering the chance of capital growth, for modest amounts.

Bad for
- Inflexibility – only buy one if you are sure you can keep the policy going until maturity. If you cash in a policy early, you may get a very poor return.
- Charges – insurance company charges can be high.

Risk factors
- The value of the policy depends on how the insurance fund in which your money is invested performs (see page 198 for more on insurance funds in general).
- Insurance funds are linked to the stockmarket. If a unit-linked policy matures at a time when stockmarkets happen to be at a low level, your return could be low. (See Jargon alert: Lifestyling on page 54 for how to reduce this risk.)
- If you are a policyholder in an insolvent life insurance company you are covered by the Financial Services Compensation Scheme (within limits – see Chapter 2).
- You can usually complain to the Financial Ombudsman Service if you were advised to buy an endowment policy that was unsuitable for you.

Timescale
To comply with tax rules, endowment policies are designed to run for at least ten years, but they can usually be bought to run for up to 25 years. You can cash them in early, but if so you may get back very little – possibly less than the amount you put in – because companies deduct the costs of selling the policy up-front.

> ## Trade secret

Protection or investment?
It may seem a good idea to combine life insurance with investment by buying a life insurance policy, such as an endowment, which will pay out at a set maturity date as well as if you die beforehand. But investment-type policies are much more expensive than protection-only policies, and you risk losing your life cover if you cannot afford to keep your policy up. It's best to keep your protection and investment separate.

How they work

Endowment policies, or savings plans as they may also be called, are life insurance policies designed to provide a lump sum at the end of the policy term, or if you die during the policy. You pay regular premiums into the plan, usually monthly.

Part of your premiums is used to pay for the life insurance and to cover the company's charges. The rest is invested on your behalf in one of the insurance company's funds, either a with-profits fund or a unit-linked fund. Insurance funds are explained more fully on page 198, but depending on how well the investments owned by the fund do, you may get bonuses (on a with-profits policy). With a unit-linked policy, you are allocated units that rise and fall in value throughout the term of the policy.

The amount of life cover depends on the company. With some policies you get a fixed amount, depending on your age and the premium you pay. However, some policies allow you to choose the amount of life insurance, within a minimum and maximum amount, and you may be able to vary the amount at set dates (after ten years, say). It is also possible to buy policies jointly with another person. These may pay out either on the first death or only when both of you die.

These days fewer insurance companies offer endowment policies. They have fallen out of favour after low-cost policies (see Jargon alert overleaf) were widely sold in the 1980s and 1990s as a way of repaying a mortgage, only for the projected value of many of them to fall short of the required amount. See Chapter 1 for what you can do if this has affected you.

Jargon alert

Low-cost endowment policies

These policies were designed to pay off a mortgage and only guaranteed to pay out enough to cover the mortgage if you died. Unfortunately, to keep them low-cost, they did not guarantee enough to repay the mortgage on maturity. Insurance companies set the premiums assuming that policies would continue to provide returns at not much less than existing rates. But this backfired in the 1990s, when returns fell sharply in line with falls in inflation and interest rates.

If you already have an endowment policy

Many endowment policies are cashed in long before they mature – around one in four endowment policies have lapsed within the first four years. But if you cash in your policy this early, the cash-in value will almost certainly be less than the premiums paid to date. However, if the cash-in value is more than the amount paid in premiums, it may trigger a tax bill if you are a higher-rate taxpayer or if you receive the age-related tax allowance (see Chapter 4).

So before you cash in a policy early, ask the insurance company:

- what the surrender value would be, and whether it would be taxable
- whether the policy has a guaranteed minimum value if you carry on paying to maturity. If it has, and the guaranteed amount (minus further premiums you'd have to pay if you kept the policy up until maturity) is higher than the surrender value, you would do better to keep the policy going if you can
- whether you can make the policy paid up, and if so, how this would affect your benefits. This means that you don't surrender the policy but you stop paying the premiums in return for reduced benefits.

You should also investigate the insurance fund's future prospects and, if the company is mutual (see page 170), whether you are in line for a payout should it demutualise.

> Trade secret

An alternative to surrendering your policy
As an alternative to surrendering, you may be able to trade in some types of policy. This means that you sell the policy to someone else who takes over paying the premiums but gets the money when the policy matures (or you die). You may get more than the surrender value, but many policies are not suitable (for example, most unit-linked policies) and you may not find a buyer. You can sell through a traded endowment company, sometimes called a market-maker – contact the Association of Policy Market Makers (see the Fact file).

Rates and charges

How much the policy pays out on maturity depends mainly on the company's investment performance. But policy charges, which can be high, will reduce your return (see page 204). According to the FSA's comparative tables, in August 2005 charges could amount to between £500 and £1,500 over a ten-year period for a £50-a-month policy for a 40-year-old man, depending on the company.

How to buy

Endowment policies are sold by insurance companies or friendly societies. You can find out which companies offer endowment policies, and their charges, from the Financial Services Authority's comparative tables (on their website). Some companies allow you to buy direct from them, but others sell only through financial advisers. If you use an adviser, ask about commission rebates, which increase the amount that is invested on your behalf (see Chapter 5).

Tax treatment

The life insurance fund in which your money is invested is taxed, but there is no personal tax to pay on the proceeds of an endowment policy provided that you keep it to maturity. However, there will be tax to pay if all three of the following apply:

■ You stop paying into the policy, sell it or receive benefits from it within

the first ten years (or, if the policy is intended to last less than 13.4 years, within the first three-quarters of the intended term, for example 7.5 years for a ten-year policy).
- The proceeds from the policy are more than the total premiums paid (the excess is a taxable gain).
- You are a higher-rate taxpayer (or the taxable gain pushes you into the higher-rate tax band).

The tax on the gain is worked out in the same way as a gain from a life insurance bond, explained on page 211.

Alternatives to consider
- If you want the discipline of regular saving, you can set up a regular standing order into a savings account, or a cash ISA if you are a taxpayer.
- If you want some exposure to the stockmarket, consider a stocks and shares ISA (see page 183).
- For the pros and cons of tax-exempt friendly society plans, see page 169.

National Savings & Investments

A government agency that raises money for public spending by providing a range of savings and investments products backed by the government.

Good for
- Offering a range of tax-free investments – useful for higher-rate taxpayers and parents giving larger amounts of money to their own children.
- Non-taxpayers – interest on taxable accounts is usually paid out before tax.
- Index-linked savings certificates guarantee that your money will grow by more than the rate of inflation.
- Security – all products are backed by the UK treasury.

Bad for
- Interest rates – they do not usually offer top rates.
- Accessibility – only the easy access account is suitable for short-term savings.

Risk factors
- National Savings & Investments (NS&I) offer probably the most secure home for your money. With all the products, including premium bonds and guaranteed equity bonds, the amount you originally deposited will always be returned in full.
- If you buy a fixed-term, fixed-interest product, you are taking a bet that interest rates will not rise. You could lose out if they do.
- Even though you can cash in NS&I certificates and bonds early (excluding the guaranteed equity bond), you will get a lower interest rate than if you had chosen a shorter term to start with.
- If you have a complaint about NS&I that you have been unable to resolve, you can complain to the Financial Ombudsman Service.

Timescale
Accounts range from instant access through to five-year bonds. However, many of the NS&I bonds are designed to run for fixed terms and there are

A quick guide to National Savings & Investments

	Type of investment	Interest	Access	Minimum investment	Tax treatment
Tax-free	Cash mini ISA	Variable	No notice required	£10	Tax-free
	Tessa-only ISA	Variable	No notice required	£10	Tax-free
	Fixed-interest savings certificates	Fixed interest added to certificate	Choice of terms (currently 2 or 5 years)	£100	Tax-free
	Index-linked savings certificates	Index-linking plus fixed interest added to certificate	Choice of terms (currently 3 or 5 years)	£100	Tax-free
	Children's bonus bonds	Fixed interest plus bonus added to certificate	5 years	£25	Tax-free
	Premium bonds	None, but may win prizes	No notice required	£100	Tax-free
Growth	Fixed-rate savings bonds	Fixed, can be added to bond or paid out as monthly income	Choice of terms (currently 1, 3 or 5 years); loss of 90 days' interest if repaid early	£500	Taxable but paid with 20% tax deducted
	Capital bonds	Fixed interest added to bond	5 years	£100	Taxable but credited without tax deducted
	Guaranteed equity bond	Linked to performance of FTSE share price index	5 years	£1,000	Taxable but paid without tax deducted

	Type of investment	Interest	Access	Minimum investment	Tax treatment
Monthly income	Pensioners' guaranteed income bonds (for ages 60 and over)	Fixed, paid out monthly	Choice of terms (1, 2 or 5 years); notice period or loss of interest if repaid early	£500	Taxable but paid before tax
	Income bonds	Variable, paid out monthly	No notice required	£500	Taxable but paid before tax
Savings accounts	Investment account	Variable	1 month's notice or no notice and 1 month's loss of interest	£20	Taxable but paid before tax
	Easy access savings account	Variable	Instant access up to £300 a day	£100	Taxable but paid before tax

penalties or notice requirements if you want to get at your money earlier (it is not possible to withdraw money early from a guaranteed equity bond, except on the death of the bondholder).

How they work

National Savings & Investments (previously known as National Savings) offers a range of accounts, certificates and bonds. The table above will help you narrow down your choice, but as a rule, the longer you agree to keep your money tied up for, and the more money you have to invest, the better is the interest on offer. (ISAs are covered on page 183 and guaranteed equity bonds on page 172.)

Jargon alert

Issues and series

Most NS&I certificates and bonds have fixed returns over fixed periods. They are sold in issues or series. NS&I brings out a new issue or starts a new series whenever the fixed interest rates on offer change. This doesn't affect the interest rates on any fixed-rate bonds or certificates you already have, which continue at the fixed rate. But it does mean you can also invest in the new issue at the new rates. This can be useful, as the maximum investment in each issue of the tax-free products is quite small: £15,000 per issue for savings certificates (excluding reinvestments), and £3,000 for children's bonus bonds. The maximum overall holding for other NS&I bonds, by contrast, is £1 million.

Fixed-interest savings certificates

You invest for a fixed period of time (two or five years), and in return you get a fixed rate of tax-free interest added to the certificate. The minimum investment in each issue is £100.

You can cash certificates in early, but this isn't advisable. If you cash them in during the first year, you won't earn any interest at all (except on reinvestments; see Trade secret). If you cash in after the first year but before your certificate matures, you'll earn interest for each complete period of three months, but the interest rate rises each year you hold your certificates, so to get the full return you need to keep them for the full term. For example, this is how interest is earned on the five-year 79th issue:

Year 1	2.65%
Year 2	2.75%
Year 3	2.95%
Year 4	3.25%
Year 5	3.66%

This works out at an average rate of 3.05% if you invest over the full five years. But if you cash in at the end of year 2 you will get only 2.65% + 2.75% = 5.40%/2 = 2.7%. You would have done better to choose the two-year certificate available at the same time, which paid 3% over two years.

Index-linked savings certificates

Chapter 2 explained the risk of inflation eating into your savings. Index-linked savings certificates are designed to inflation-proof your savings by increasing the amount of your investment in line with the retail prices index (RPI) over the term of the certificate (three- and five-year terms are currently available). You also get a fixed rate of interest on top, guaranteeing that your return, though possibly not the highest available, will always beat inflation.

Assume, for example, that you invested £10,000 in the three-year 10th issue of index-linked certificates, which offered index-linking plus an interest rate of 0.95% over the three years. If inflation averages 3% a year, you will get a return of 3% + 0.95% = 3.95% a year. However, if inflation averages 2% a year, your return will be 2% + 0.95% = 2.95%. Note that if the RPI falls (i.e. prices have fallen), the value of your certificates will not be reduced and you will still get the interest.

As with fixed-rate certificates, you lose out if you cash in your index-linked certificates early, because the interest rate rises over the term. If you cash them in during the first year, you won't earn any interest or index-linking. If you cash in after the first year, you'll earn interest and index-linking for each complete month they are held.

Trade secret

Act quickly when a bond or certificate matures

When a fixed-rate bond or certificate matures, NS&I will write to you to explain the options you have. You can carry on for another term, cash in and take the money or reinvest in another NS&I product. Usually, if you do not do anything, your money will automatically be reinvested in the next series or issue of the same product so that it continues to earn interest. However, a new rate of interest and bonus will usually apply, and if you don't want to reinvest you normally have only a few weeks to choose a different option.

In particular, if you have savings certificates or a yearly plan account that matured before 8 October 2001, you should find a more suitable home for your money. If these were not cashed or reinvested, they moved on to a rather low rate of interest called the 'general extension rate', and some matured index-linked certificates earn index-linking only.

Children's bonus bonds

These bonds can be bought in units of £25 for anybody under 16, by anybody aged over 16. The interest is tax-free (which has advantages for parents who want to give them to their children, see page 110), but the maximum investment is £3,000 per issue.

Bonds earn a fixed rate of interest for five years, and on the fifth anniversary a bonus is added. The bonus is fixed when you take out the bond. At the end of each term, you can leave the bond earning a new rate of tax-free interest for a further five years, or until the child is 21, when a final bonus is added.

Bonds can be cashed in by the parent or guardian of a child under 16, and by the child himself or herself from the age of 16. But if you cash in before one of the five-year anniversaries, or before the child is 21, you will lose the bonus. There is no interest at all if you cash in a bond during the first year.

Fixed-rate savings bonds

Like savings certificates, these offer a fixed rate of interest, but they differ in that the interest is taxable, with 20% tax deducted at source. This makes them directly comparable with a fixed-rate bond from a bank or building society, and you should check what rates are available elsewhere.

Interest rates are tiered, which means that if you invest £20,000 or more you will get a better rate. You can either leave the interest to grow in the bond or have it paid out to your bank or building society account (you get a slightly lower interest rate if you do this). But if you want to draw income, you should also check whether either NS&I income bonds or pensioners' bonds might suit you better.

You can choose what period you want to invest for (currently one, three or five years). You can cash a bond in early, but you will lose 90 days' interest (so if you cash in within the first 90 days you will get back less than you invested).

> ## Trade secret

Drawing an income

The NS&I products that can be used to provide an income are pensioners' bonds, income bonds, and fixed-rate savings bonds (with the monthly interest option). Alternatively, buying a five-year savings certificate each year for five years would provide you with a stream of tax-free income in the following five years. This is useful if, for example, you want to top up your income in retirement without affecting your higher age-related tax allowance.

Capital bonds

These are five-year bonds with fixed rates of interest. As with savings certificates, the rate of interest rises each year, so you lose out if you cash in early, and no interest is earned on bonds repaid in the first year. The major difference is that the income is taxable, and you are taxed on it each year, even though it is credited to your account rather than being paid out (there is no monthly income option). Again, you should compare the interest rates with those available on other fixed-rate bonds.

Pensioners' guaranteed income bonds

These bonds are only available to people aged 60 or over. They pay out a fixed rate of interest every month. So, for example, an investment of £10,000 in the five-year Series 43, paying 4.25%, would provide you with a monthly income of £425/12 = £35, paid directly into your bank or building society account on the 19th of each month.

The interest is taxable – which means that these bonds should be approached with caution by people aged over 65 who are at risk of losing their higher age-related tax allowance – but it is paid out with no tax deducted, which makes them particularly convenient for people who pay little or no tax.

Pensioners' bonds are available for a choice of terms (currently one, two or five years). You can cash them in early, but you should avoid doing this because the penalty is steep – a loss of 90 days' interest. You can reduce this to 60 days' loss of interest if you give 60 days' notice of your intention to cash in.

Income bonds

These pay a regular monthly income, but unlike the income from most other NS&I bonds, the interest is variable and fluctuates in line with interest rates in general. It is important to watch the rates and act swiftly if better rates are available elsewhere. You can withdraw your money on demand, without penalty, although it will take a few days for the money to reach you.

The minimum investment is £500, but you get a slightly better rate if you can invest more than £25,000. As with pensioners' bonds, the income is taxable but paid out before tax.

Investment account

This long-running NS&I account is similar to a bank or building society notice account (see page 264). It pays variable interest, with a higher rate the more you invest. The interest is taxable, and you must give one month's notice to draw your money out (although you can get it immediately at a cost of 30 days' interest). It is therefore important to check what banks and building societies are offering before you invest.

The investment account does have two things in its favour: although it is taxable, the interest is paid out with no tax deducted; and you get a passbook for the account, which some people find convenient for keeping track of their savings.

Easy access savings account

This account was introduced in 2004 as a replacement for the old ordinary account (see Trade secret). The main new feature is that it has a cash card, which allows you to draw up to £300 a day on demand at any cash machine with the LINK logo, as well as over the counter at Post Office branches. However, the card is purely a cash card – you cannot use it to pay for goods in shops or to get credit.

You can also register to operate the account by phone. If you want to withdraw more than £300, you can then apply by phone, as well as by post, to have the money paid into your bank or building society account. However, note that if you are making deposits by cheque or debit card, you cannot withdraw the money deposited for 14 days.

Unfortunately, you must keep at least £100 in the account, which makes it unsuitable for small savers, such as children. Another disadvantage is that, unlike the ordinary account, the interest is taxable, although it is paid out before deduction of tax. An advantage is that it offers better interest rates than the old account (with higher rates for savings above £1,000). Interest rates are variable.

> ## Trade secret

Did you have an ordinary account?

The old ordinary account was the Post Office account that introduced so many people to saving. Unfortunately, the interest rates were extremely ordinary as well, even though the first £70 of interest each year was tax-free. The account was closed to new customers in 2004. If you have an ordinary account and have not already closed it or transferred the money to another account, you should do so as soon as possible. Your money will be earning a measly rate of interest.

Premium bonds

These are not strictly an investment, but they may suit you if want a tax-free home for your money and are willing to give up regular interest in the hope of winning a prize in the monthly draw (there are two £1 million jackpot prizes and over 1 million other prizes). The size of the prize fund depends on interest rates, but at the time of writing the odds of winning a prize were 24,000 to 1, and you can always cash in your bonds and get your original stake back.

The minimum purchase is £100, which will buy you 100 bonds, and each bond has an equal chance of winning. However, they are only eligible for the draw once they have been held for one complete calendar month following the month of purchase.

Currently, £23 million lies unclaimed in premium bond prizes. You can check whether you have an unclaimed prize on the NS&I website if you have got your 'Holder's number'; if you haven't got this number, contact the Premium Bonds department at NS&I (see the Fact file).

Rates and charges

NS&I's interest rates reflect those generally available, but they can be slow to change and are rarely the best available. You should also check the details of any current issues before buying. The terms and conditions (such as the length of investment), as well as the interest rates, may change between issues.

How to buy (and sell)

You can buy most NS&I accounts over the phone, from Post Offices or by post. You can also apply for most accounts over the internet, paying with a debit card. Note that advice on NS&I accounts can be hard to come by. NS&I does not pay commission to financial advisers and in the past advisers generally did not cover them.

When it comes to cashing in your money, remember that even if you do not have to give notice, NS&I is run mainly by post or over the phone, so you should allow seven working days.

Trade secret

Looking behind the headline rate

The rates for tax-free NS&I accounts often don't appear competitive. Non-taxpayers should look for better rates elsewhere. But remember that a tax-free interest rate of 3.45% is worth the same to a basic-rate taxpayer as 4.31% from a taxable account, and the same as a taxable 5.75% to higher-rate taxpayers. Tax-free accounts really come into their own for:

- higher-rate taxpayers
- people aged 65 or over whose taxable income is near the level above which they start to lose the higher age-related personal tax allowance (£19,500 in the 2005–06 tax year)
- parents who want to give money to their children. If parents give money to a child that produces income of more than £100 per child per year, that income is taxed as the parents', unless the income comes from a tax-free investment, like children's bonus bonds or savings certificates.

Tax treatment

■ The interest from some NS&I products is free of tax, so the higher your top rate of tax, the better the effective rate of return is for you. Tax-free NS&I products are ISAs, premium bonds, savings certificates and children's bonus bonds.

■ The taxable products fall into two groups:

– *Investment account, easy access savings account, income bonds, capital bonds, pensioners' guaranteed income bonds and guaranteed equity bonds.* Income from all these products is paid out before tax. The income is still taxable, but any tax due is collected either by adjusting your PAYE code or through your tax return.

– *Fixed-rate savings bonds.* 20% tax is always deducted from the income paid out by these bonds. You can reclaim overpaid tax, but non-taxpayers should pick more suitable products. Higher-rate taxpayers will have further tax to pay, either through PAYE or a tax return.

■ Savings certificates have a special feature that can be very valuable. On the death of the holder, they count (like other investments) as part of the deceased person's estate for inheritance tax, but they can be inherited and still remain free of income tax in the hands of the new owners.

Alternatives to consider

■ Banks and building society accounts (see page 264); credit unions (see page 160); British Government stocks (see page 136).

■ If you are willing to take some risk, see page 133 for different types of bond.

■ If your main concern is to draw an income from your money, see Chapter 7. Also see Chapter 7 if you want to give money to children.

Pensions from an employer

If your employer contributes to an occupational pension scheme for you, this effectively gives you extra pay. ❗ (some types)

Good for

- Boosting your retirement income – 44% of recently retired pensioners get more income from employers' pensions than they do from the state.
- Taxpayers – there is full tax relief on contributions and usually a tax-free lump sum on retirement.
- A relatively painless and disciplined way to save, with help from your employer.

Bad for

- Inaccessibility – you can only get back your contributions to an occupational pension scheme if you leave the employer in the first two years.
- Many employers have made their pension schemes less generous in recent years.
- People who change jobs frequently, who may not do so well out of salary-related schemes.

Risk factors

- If your employer has promised you a pension related to your salary, the promise is only as good as the employer (company) that stands behind it. Poor investment returns in recent years mean that many employers' pension funds are short of cash. A few companies have collapsed, leaving pension funds short of funds to meet their promises. If this happens after 5 April 2005, the new Pension Protection Fund will pay 100% of any pensions already being drawn, and 90% for workers not yet retired (up to a limit of £25,000 on retirement at age 65). A limited Financial Assistance Fund may help some people in schemes that collapsed before then.
- If your pension is not related to your salary, but your employer just pays in a set amount, what you get back depends on how investments

perform. You take the risk that they may perform poorly.

■ Employers occasionally defraud pension schemes, for example by failing to pay contributions. If you suspect dodgy practices, contact the Pensions Advisory Service (known as TPAS) or the Pensions Regulator. The Pension Protection Fund can compensate schemes in the event of fraud.

■ If you have a problem or complaint about your pension that you cannot resolve, contact TPAS. They will try to negotiate a solution, but if this does not work you might be able to take your case to the Pensions Ombudsman.

Timescale

Normally, your money is tied up until you draw your pension, although from April 2006 you will not have to stop work to do so. Most schemes have a normal pension age of 60 or 65, and although you can draw a pension early, the minimum age is usually 50, increasing to 55 by 2010 (unless you are retiring through ill-health).

Trade secret

Using new tax rules to your advantage

Because of the generous tax treatment, there are rules for how pension schemes are run and the benefits you can draw. New, more flexible tax rules from April 2006 should make life simpler for most people. However, you should seek advice urgently from an adviser with specialist pensions qualifications if:

■ you are planning to retire before April 2006 – the new rules may change your options and you should get advice on the timing of your retirement

■ you hope to retire at age 50 but won't reach this age until after 2006, when schemes are allowed to increase the normal minimum retirement age to 55

■ you have already built up a large pension pot or are entitled to a higher than normal tax-free lump sum under rules that applied up until 1987. Under the new rules your maximum tax-allowable pension savings will be capped (see page 233), but there are ways of protecting yourself from extra tax if you act immediately.

Jargon alert

Unlocking your pension

Some financial advisers offer to help you 'unlock' money tied up in your pension by transferring your pension assets to another pension arrangement. Beware: this will eat into your retirement savings and advisers may charge large fees. See the Financial Services Authority leaflet *Unlocking pensions – make sure you understand the risks.*

How they work

If you are an employee, you may be offered:

- *An occupational pension* set up for your employer's staff. Statutory schemes are established by Act of Parliament for various groups of public-sector workers, whereas private-sector schemes are usually set up as special trust funds. The employer must pay contributions into the fund.
- *A group personal pension.* These are just a collection of individual personal pension plans run by a pension company. Your employer chooses the company, deducts contributions from your salary and pays them over, but doesn't necessarily contribute itself. When you stop working for the employer, your pension is detached from the group and continues as an individual plan.
- *Access to a stakeholder pension* (a type of personal pension plan). If your employer has more than five employees, it must normally offer you this if it does not have an occupational pension scheme, or a group personal pension to which it pays at least 3% of your earnings. 'Access' simply means that your employer deducts the contributions from your salary and pays them to the pension company – it doesn't have to make any contributions itself.

What all these types of scheme have in common is generous tax treatment. You and your employer both get full tax relief on contributions, and the money grows largely tax-free – although the tax advantages have been reduced because pension funds can no longer reclaim the tax deducted from share dividends.

The main features of occupational schemes are described below. Group personal pensions and stakeholder pensions are personal pensions, covered on page 250.

What you get

Although there are some non-contributory schemes, you are usually required to pay in a percentage of your salary. What you get in return depends on the type of scheme:

■ *Final salary schemes* promise to pay you a proportion of your final salary (often averaged over the final three years) as a pension when you retire. You get a set percentage of your salary for each year you belong to the scheme, usually 1/60th or (less generously) 1/80th. So if you are in a 1/60th scheme for 20 years, you will get a pension that is 20/60th – or one-third – of your final salary.

■ *Money purchase schemes* make no promises as to what pension you will get. Instead, fixed contributions are paid into a pension fund on your behalf. What you get out depends on two factors: how well the investments grow, and annuity rates when you retire (see page 129). This is because your pension fund must usually be used to buy an annuity, which pays your pension income. (A few money purchase schemes may allow income withdrawal, rather than requiring you to buy an annuity – see page 254.)

When you come to retire, you can draw some of your pension fund as cash, but most has to be drawn out as a pension. The tax rules currently allow you to take a tax-free lump sum of up to one-and-a-half times your final salary, with a maximum of £158,400 if you joined the scheme after 16 March 1987. From April 2006, the tax rules will allow you to take a tax-free lump sum of up to 25% of your pension fund, up to a maximum of £375,000, and you won't have to retire to draw your benefits.

Your pension scheme may also pay a range of benefits if you die.

Trade secret

Making the most of a money purchase scheme

These days many final salary schemes are being closed to new members, and money purchase schemes are being offered in their place. This is largely because with a final salary scheme the employer is committed to paying set pensions however badly the investments in the fund are doing. With a money purchase scheme you, the employee, take on this investment risk. The other problem with money purchase schemes is that employers usually contribute less – 7% on average, compared with 16% for final salary schemes.

But money purchase schemes are not necessarily a bad thing – people who don't anticipate staying with the employer until retirement may do better with one. And in practice you rarely have a choice. To make the best of it:

- Take an interest. Some money purchase schemes allow you to choose what sort of pension fund you want your money to be in. See page 198 for more about life insurance funds (a pension fund is a special sort of life insurance fund).
- Negotiate – through a trade union or staff association if not directly – for the highest possible employer's contributions.
- Shop around to buy an annuity when you retire. This can give you as much as 25% more pension income. Your pension scheme may also permit income withdrawal (see page 254), or you may be able to transfer to a self-invested personal pension (SIPP – see page 276) if the circumstances are right for you.

Jargon alert

Defined benefit or defined contribution?

A final salary scheme is often called a defined benefit or DB scheme, because you know what you will get out of it. And because you know only what goes into it, not what will come out, a money purchase scheme is often called a defined contribution or DC scheme.

If you die

If you die before retirement, the pension scheme may pay out a lump sum, usually calculated as a multiple of your salary. Your contributions may be returned as well. Your partner and dependants may also get a pension. If you no longer work for that employer, the scheme is likely to be less generous – you may only get a refund of your contributions.

If you die after retirement, the scheme may pay a pension to your partner and any dependants. Alternatively, it may guarantee to carry on paying your pension for a set period.

If you are not married to your partner, it is particularly important to check the pension scheme's rules to see whether your partner is eligible for a pension.

Trade secret

Express your wishes

The pension fund trustees decide who should receive any payout on your death. They may not recognise unmarried partners, but some schemes allow you to complete an 'expression of wishes' form to tell them who you want to have the money, and they will normally respect your wishes. However, be sure to let the trustees know if you change your mind over who you want to benefit, particularly if you are not married, or if you split up. The tax rules don't require you to be married to any beneficiary. The only condition for receiving a pension is that they are dependent on you, financially or because of disability, or you are financially interdependent.

One advantage is that money paid out directly from a pension scheme does not form part of your estate for inheritance tax purposes.

Leaving your job

You will no longer be able to contribute to your employer's scheme after you leave your job. If you leave within two years of joining the pension scheme, you can get back your own contributions (which may have increased or fallen in value, if it is a money purchase scheme) less a tax charge. Alternatively, from 6 April 2006, if you are in the scheme for at least three months, you can if you wish transfer the value of your pension (including your employer's contributions) to a new pension scheme.

After two years, you cannot get your contributions back. Instead, you have a right to a pension from the scheme worked out as follows:

- *Final salary scheme.* Your pension will be based on your salary when you leave and the number of years of service. The value of your pension must be increased in line with inflation up a maximum of 2.5% a year.
- *Money purchase scheme.* Your and your employer's contributions to date continue to be invested on your behalf as if you were still employed.

Instead of leaving your pension where it is, you can transfer it to your new employer's scheme, to your own personal or stakeholder pension, or to a special plan sometimes called a buy-out bond. Whether it is right for you depends on your circumstances and the comparative benefits of the pension schemes. In the late 1980s, a lot of people were advised to transfer out of good occupational schemes into personal pensions. If in doubt, don't transfer out. Get advice from a financial adviser with the special pension transfer qualification. Also see FSA booklet *FSA Guide to the risks of occupational pension transfers*.

It is easy to lose track of your pension if you change jobs frequently. The Pension Tracing Service may be able to help (see the Fact file).

Getting divorced

If either of you has built up a pension, it should be taken into account when splitting up your assets between you. The divorce courts can earmark part of one spouse's pension to be paid to the other on retirement. Or they can issue a pension-sharing order, which means that the ex-spouse becomes a member of the pension scheme in his or her own right, or, if the scheme rules do not allow this, part of the pension can be transferred into a separate pension for the other spouse. It is important to get specialist pensions advice on what is best for you.

Either way, one partner has lost part of his or her own pension, and will have less income in retirement unless extra savings are built up.

Rates and charges

Most schemes require you to pay in a set percentage of your earnings, say 5%. With a money purchase scheme, your employer also pays a set percentage; with a final salary scheme, your employer pays however much it costs to meet the pension you have been promised. Some schemes are non-contributory and the employer picks up the whole cost. With other schemes, the employer's contribution may vary.

You can boost your pension by contributing more, provided you stay within certain limits (see below). If you want to contribute more, you can:

■ pay additional voluntary contributions, or AVCs, to your occupational scheme, or buy added years of membership if your scheme allows it

■ contribute to a separate personal pension or stakeholder pension (before April 2006, you cannot do this if you are earning £30,000 or more, or if you are a director who owns more than 20% of the company that employs you)

■ buy a free-standing additional voluntary contribution (FSAVC) plan from a pension company – but this may have higher charges than AVCs to your employer's scheme, and if you don't want to invest through your employer, the new rules for pensions, starting in April 2006, mean that you can just buy a separate personal or stakeholder pension

■ choose a non-pension investment such as an ISA (see page 183).

How to buy

The first place to go for information is your employer's pensions administrator. A trade union or staff association representative may be able to help if you have difficulties, and the FSA, the Pensions Advisory Service and the TUC all have useful leaflets (see the Fact file).

If you want independent advice about occupational pensions, you will need a financial adviser with a specialist pensions qualification. You are likely to have to pay a fee.

You may have to wait for a period before you are eligible to join your employer's pension scheme.

Tax treatment

- Your contributions to an occupational pension qualify for full tax relief. This is achieved by deducting the contributions from your pay before the tax on it is worked out. (See below for restrictions on the amount you can contribute.)
- You get tax relief on contributions below a certain limit. From 6 April 2006, you will be able to pay the whole of your earnings into pensions (or up to £3,600 before tax relief if your earnings are less than this), provided that both of the following conditions apply:
  – the value of all your contributions to any type of pension, plus your increased benefits, is not more than £215,000 in the 2006–07 tax year
  – the amount of total pension savings over your whole lifetime does not exceed the lifetime allowance, set at £1.5 million for the 2006–07 tax year. With a money purchase fund, you should get regular statements of what your fund is worth. With a final salary scheme, the value of your pension savings is worked out on the assumption that £1 of pension will cost £20 of capital to buy (in practice it may cost more or less than this). So, broadly, a £75,000 pension is the maximum pension you can have and still stay within the lifetime allowance (£75,000 × £20 = £1.5 million)
- You can contribute more than these limits, but you will get no tax relief on any excess contributions, and there will be tax to pay on any surplus fund above the lifetime limit when you retire.
- Depending on the rules of the scheme, you can take part of your pension in the form of a tax-free lump sum (see page 233).
- The rest of your pension from an occupational pension scheme is taxable in the same way as your earnings before you retire. Tax will usually be deducted under PAYE, and this will include tax on your state pension (see page 248).

Alternatives to consider

- You do not have to join your company's pension scheme. But if you do not, you will not benefit from the contributions the employer must pay into the scheme on your behalf, unless you have enough bargaining power to persuade your employer to increase your pay instead.
- If you are trying to decide whether to pay in extra to your employer's

pension scheme, you need to take into account the possible effect on means-tested state benefits in retirement, in particular the pension credit (see page 243).

■ If you are currently a member of a final salary scheme, you should not leave it without careful thought. Even if your employer closes the scheme to further contributions, your existing rights in the scheme remain.

Pensions from the state

Before you can decide how to save for your retirement, you need to know what you will get from the state.

Good for
- A secure foundation for your retirement income.

Bad for
- An adequate income in retirement – the basic state pension on its own is unlikely to provide this.
- Unmarried couples, who cannot inherit their partner's state pension.

Risk factors
- If your earnings are too low to pay National Insurance Contributions this will reduce your pension entitlement.
- There is no knowing what changes any future government might make to the state pension before you retire.
- Failing to claim your full entitlement. Under the current rules, an increasing proportion of your minimum pension entitlement will be made up of the means-tested pension credit. If in doubt whether you qualify, contact the Pension Credit helpline (see the Fact file).

Timescale
You won't become entitled to draw your state pension until state pension age (see Jargon alert), although you don't have to stop work to do so. But you should check how much state pension you are entitled to well in advance of state pension age, as this will affect how much you decide to save for retirement.

Jargon alert

State pension age

The age at which you become entitled to draw the basic state pension. This is:

- for all men, and women born after 5 April 1955 – age 65
- for women born before 6 April 1950 – age 60
- for women born between 6 April 1950 and 5 April 1955 – age 60 plus one month for every month (or part month) that their birthday falls after 5 April 1950. So if you were born on 10 November 1952, say, you become eligible for state pension when you are 62 and 8 months old.

Note, though, that both men and women can claim the pension credit (guarantee element) at the women's state pension age (currently 60, rising to 65 after 2010).

How they work

You don't get much choice about investing in a state pension. It is funded by your National Insurance Contributions, and you have to pay those if you earn more than a certain amount and are under state pension age. The table overleaf is a guide to the main types of state pension. You can obtain a state pension forecast from the Pension Service (see the Fact file).

Once you have this information, you need to check the following:

- Will your state pension be enough? Use the financial stock-take in Chapter 1 to help you work it out.
- Will the pension credit, a means-tested top-up to the state pension, mean that you are better off not saving?
- Should you pay extra National Insurance to boost your state pension?
- If you are 'contracted-out' of the additional state pension, should you contract back in?
- When will you need a retirement income? Many people stop work before state pension age. If so, will you need your savings to top up your income before you can draw a state pension? Or will your income be high enough to allow you to defer your state pension?

What types of state pension might you get?

Basic state retirement pension	Your entitlement depends on the number of years in which you pay standard rate National Insurance Contributions (NICs) (employed or self-employed). Years in which you were not working still count if you received certain state benefits (including child benefit), or if you are recognised by the Pension Service as a carer, or if you paid voluntary contributions. Broadly, you need to have an entitlement for every year since you were 21 to get a full basic state pension. But if you are getting no pension, or only a small amount: ■ you may be able to claim a pension based on your husband's (and sometimes your wife's) contributions, if you are married, divorced, or widowed ■ you get a limited non-contributory pension once you are over 80.	Full pension is £82.05 a week (£4,266 a year) for single people, £131.20 (£6,822) for couples
Additional state pension	An earnings-related pension built up under: ■ the state earnings-related pension scheme (SERPS) that ran from 1978 to 2002; for employees paying standard rate NICs only ■ the state second pension that started on 6 April 2002; for employees, plus some carers and people with long-term illnesses or disabilities. However, you can contract-out (see Jargon alert opposite).	Depends on earnings, but current average is just over £20 a week

Pension credit – guarantee credit	A means-tested top-up to your state pension, designed to bring your income up to a guaranteed minimum. The guaranteed minimum is increased if you are severely disabled, or caring for someone who is, or have some types of housing cost.	Enough to bring weekly income up to £109.45 (single people), £167.05 (couples)
Pension credit – savings credit	A means-tested top-up if your weekly income is: ■ single people – more than £82.05, but less than about £150 ■ couples – more than £131.20 but less than about £220. If your income is more than the upper limit you may still qualify, but it depends on your circumstances.	Up to £16.44 a week for single people, £21.51 for couples

Jargon alert

Contracting-out

Contracting-out means that you give up your right to all or part of the earnings-related additional state pension (SERPS and the state second pension) and build up a replacement for it in your own pension instead. Note that you do not build up any right to an additional state pension during periods in which you are self-employed – you only build up rights to the basic state pension. This means that contracting-out is not relevant to you, if you are self-employed.

The pension credit and your savings

The pension credit is made up of two elements: the guarantee element tops up the income of everybody aged at least 60 to a guaranteed minimum amount. In the 2005–06 tax year, the guaranteed minimum pension is

£109.45 for single people, £167.05 for couples, but you may get more if, for example, you are disabled.

The savings credit element is an extra payment designed to give people an incentive to save for retirement. You get it only if you have income above the level of the basic state pension (in the 2005–06 tax year, £82.05 a week or £131.20 for couples). A couple's income is assessed jointly. If your income is:

- *above the basic state pension but below the guaranteed minimum pension,* you get a savings credit of 60p for each £ of income above the basic state pension; the maximum credit (in 2005–06) is £16.44 a week for single people, £21.51 for couples
- *above the guaranteed minimum pension,* the maximum savings credit is reduced by 40p for each £ of income above your guaranteed minimum pension.

Income for this purpose includes state and private pensions (even if you have delayed drawing them), earnings and some state benefits. It also includes an amount to reflect your income from savings and investments, property and land (excluding the home you live in, but including tax-free investments such as ISAs and PEPs). You are treated as receiving income of £1 a week for each £500 (or part £500) of any such assets you own above a total of £6,000, or £10,000 if you live permanently in a care home. So if you have investments of £20,000, you are treated as receiving income from them of £20,000 – £6,000 = £14,000/500 = £28 a week. The amount you actually get is ignored.

The savings credit means that most people will get some benefit from saving for retirement. However, this applies only if you can save enough to take your retirement income over the threshold of £82.05 a week, or £131.20 for couples. This may not be possible if you are close to retirement, with small savings, and your ability to save is limited. Saving might not benefit you if you are in this situation.

There are rules to stop you artificially boosting your right to credit, for example by giving a second home to your children. Further information is available from the government's Pension Service, Age Concern and Help the Aged (see the Fact file).

> Trade secret

Protecting your right to a state pension
People who run their own small businesses often employ family members, paying them less than the threshold at which National Insurance has to be paid (£4,895 in 2005–06). But a wage of at least £82 a week (£4,264) will mean that the employment counts towards the employee's National Insurance record – even if it is below the threshold for paying contributions – and so protects their right to a state pension.

Boosting your state pension

If you will not be entitled to a full state pension on retirement, you may be able to boost it by making a voluntary National Insurance Contribution. Whether this is worthwhile depends on your entitlement to pension credit. If your retirement income is very low, the guarantee element will bring your income up to a minimum, even if you take no action. Boosting your state pension is worthwhile only if it takes your income above the threshold for the savings credit element (£82.05 a week for single people).

The following people should consider paying extra contributions:

- people who work abroad, but are hoping to draw a UK state pension
- self-employed people who are claiming an exemption from Class 2 National Insurance Contributions because they have small earnings
- women who married before 6 April 1977 and chose to pay a reduced rate of Class 1 National Insurance Contributions.

Before you decide, obtain a state pension forecast (see above) and see HMRC leaflet CA08 *Voluntary National Insurance Contributions*.

Deferring your state pension

You don't have to draw your pension at stage pension age – you can defer it in return for a higher pension. From April 2005 you can defer your state pension indefinitely. In return, you can choose:

- a larger pension when you do start to draw it – currently you get roughly 10% extra for each year you delay your pension, or
- your normal pension, plus a lump sum consisting of the pension you deferred and interest to compensate you for the delay in getting it. However, to choose this option, you have to defer for at least a year.

Both options give you a good return on your money. And if you were to die before receiving your pension, your husband or wife (but not other partners or relatives) would inherit your extra pension (either as extra pension or a lump sum).

If you are already drawing your state pension, you can decide to stop claiming it in order to receive an increased pension later on.

Before deciding to defer, you need to think about the effect on your tax and benefits, as well as your income needs, marital status and life expectancy. And you cannot earn extra pension if you claim certain benefits, such as incapacity benefit, during the deferral period. See Pension Service leaflet SPD1 *Your state pension choice: pension now or extra pension later*.

Example: **Deferring your pension**

Edgar has a state pension of £90 a week (£4,680 a year). If he defers his state pension for five years, he has the choice of:

- an increased state pension, when he does draw it, of £136.80 a week, or
- a state pension of £90 plus a lump sum of £27,691.

All the figures above are based on 2005–06 figures. In practice, he will get more because of the annual cost-of-living increases.

Should you contract out?

If you are in the additional state pension scheme, you can contract-out of it and build up your own private pension instead. You can do this by:

- joining a contracted-out employer's pension scheme; if so, you pay a lower rate of National Insurance
- making your own decision to contract out through a stakeholder pension or personal pension; in return, a rebate of part of your National Insurance Contributions is paid into your pension.

Opting out looks less attractive these days, and if you are contracted-out you should consider opting back in for the future (this is possible only if you are still eligible for the additional pension scheme, i.e. you are not self-employed). But you cannot 'buy back' any past years in the state scheme. Ultimately, your decision depends on whether you prefer to depend on the security of the state scheme or the possibility of higher future investment returns from a private scheme.

You also need to take your personal circumstances into account, particularly if you have a partner. A contracted-out pension must provide a widow's or widower's pension for your spouse (including a registered civil partner, for same-sex couples), but you can waive this if you are unmarried. Similarly, if you are contracted in, your spouse may qualify for half of your additional state pension. However, neither of these benefits applies to unmarried partners.

If you die before you retire and you have contracted-out through a money purchase scheme, your contracted-out pension fund will pass to your estate to be distributed in accordance with the terms of your will.

A state pension forecast will give you information about your entitlement to additional pension. A financial adviser may be able to give you an illustration of how much private pension you would end up with, under various investment scenarios. See the FSA factsheet *Contracting out of the state second pension* and the Pension Service leaflet PM7 *Contracted-out pensions. Your guide.*

Rates

See the table on page 242 for rates that apply in the 2005–06 tax year. The basic and additional state pension are increased each April in line with rising prices. The pension credit is also increased, but, to date, in line with the increase in earnings (which generally increase faster than prices). The different methods of increasing the state pension and the pension credit mean that over time, more and more people will be eligible to claim the pension credit.

How to buy

The Pension Service has a network of local pension centres that should be your first port of call for help and information about your state pension. Look in your local phone book under 'Pension Service' for your nearest centre.

Tax treatment

- There is no tax relief on National Insurance Contributions to a state pension, unlike contributions to a private pension scheme.
- The basic state retirement pension and the additional state pension are both taxable. The only state pensions that are tax-free are the pension credit, the pensioners' £10 Christmas bonus, any winter fuel allowance, war widows' pensions, and any wound or disability pensions paid to members of the forces.
- State pensions are always paid out before tax, even when they are taxable, and so are most other state benefits. If the basic state pension is your only source of income, you are unlikely to be a taxpayer, but if tax is due on your state pension, HM Revenue & Custom prefers to collect it by adjusting your tax code for any other source of income which is taxed under PAYE, such as a private pension. This may mean that quite a high proportion of your private pension goes in tax.
- A pension is taxed as your income if it is paid out to you, even if you are claiming a pension based on your husband or wife's National Insurance Contributions.
- If you choose to defer your state pension in return for a lump sum, the lump sum will be taxable in the year you receive it, but it is proposed that it will not affect your age allowances or push you into a higher-rate tax band.

Alternatives to consider

- See pensions from an employer on page 230, and other pensions on page 250.
- You may also want to consider ISAs as a form of long-term saving (see page 183).

Personal pensions and stakeholder pensions

A way of building up your own pension pot, where the pension you get depends on the growth of your investments. ❗

Good for
- Tax relief – everybody gets basic-rate tax relief added automatically, even if they are not a taxpayer. Higher-rate taxpayers get extra tax relief.
- Tax-free lump sums, which can be taken when you draw your pension.
- People who do not have access to a good-quality employer's pension scheme.

Bad for
- Inaccessibility – see Timescale opposite.
- Wide variety of charges – so shop around.
- Most of the money has to be used to provide an income on retirement.

Risk factors
- Your money is invested in a range of investments, usually including stocks and shares. What you get back depends on how these investments perform. You take the risk that they may perform poorly.
- If a unit-linked pension matures at a time when stockmarkets happen to be at a low level, your return could be low. (See Jargon alert: Lifestyling on page 54 for how to reduce this risk.)
- You cannot tell in advance how much pension you will get as this depends on economic conditions and annuity rates when you retire.
- A personal pension may mean you lose part of any means-tested state benefits in retirement. See page 244 for the effect of saving on the pension credit.
- If you have a problem or complaint about your pension that you cannot resolve, contact the Pensions Advisory Service (see the Fact file). They will advise you on whether you can take your case to the Pensions Ombudsman or the Financial Ombudsman Service.
- If you have money invested in an insolvent pension company, the Financial Services Compensation Scheme will pay limited

compensation (see Chapter 2). However, it can take years for an insolvency to be resolved and it is more likely that the pension fund will close to new policyholders first (see page 202 for more on closed funds).

Timescale

Pensions are long-term investments. Normally, your money is tied up until you draw your pension, although you can transfer your money to another pension company. The tax rules set a minimum age of 50 in most cases, increasing to 55 by 2010 (unless you are retiring through ill-health). However, the minimum age for policies sold before 1 July 1988 was usually 60. With some policies, you can choose when you draw your pension (within the tax rules); with others, you may be required to choose a pension age, and penalised if you draw your pension earlier.

Trade secret

Using new tax rules to your advantage

New, more flexible tax rules for pensions are being introduced in April 2006. These should make life simpler for most people. However, the following should seek advice urgently from an adviser with specialist pensions qualifications:

- anybody planning to retire before April 2006 – the new rules may change your options and you should get advice on the timing of your retirement
- anybody hoping to retire at age 50 but who doesn't reach this age until after 2010, when the normal minimum retirement age rises to 55
- people who have already built up large pension pots. Under the new rules the maximum pension savings on which you get tax relief will be capped (see page 258), but there are ways of saving extra tax if you act immediately.

Trade secret

Virtually anyone can have one

Even if you have no income, you can contribute to a personal or stakeholder pension, provided that you are aged between 16 and 75. You can also pay into one for someone else (including a child, though they won't get the benefits until they are 55). You can have as many different policies as you want, provided you don't pay more than the maximum contributions. However, until 6 April 2006, you cannot usually pay into one as well as an occupational scheme if you are a director with a controlling stake in your company, or if you earn more than £30,000.

How they work

You pay contributions to a pension company, which is almost always a life insurance company (although the policies may be sold under the brand name of a bank or other such organisation). Part of your contribution is deducted to pay the cost of selling and administering your plan, and the rest goes into a pension fund, which pools your money with that of other investors. You also get a helping hand from the government, in the form of tax relief (see page 257).

How well the pension fund's investments grow will determine the amount that builds up in your personal pension pot. When you decide to draw your pension, up to a quarter of your pension pot can be taken out as a tax-free lump sum, but the rest has to be used to provide you with an income (see page 254 for the different ways this can be done).

If you die before you draw your pension, your pension pot is paid out as a tax-free lump sum. When you take out a plan, you will normally be asked to nominate someone to receive the money. However, if you have used the plan to contract-out of the additional state pension (see page 247), the contracted-out part of your pension pot must be used to provide a pension for your widow or widower.

A pension fund will usually be either unit-linked or with-profits, and works in the same way as a life insurance fund of the same type, but it has more favourable tax treatment. Life insurance funds are explained on page 198 and you should read that section to find out more about them. If you choose a self-invested personal pension (SIPP – see page 276), you will have a wider choice of investments.

Jargon alert

Money purchase pensions

Any pension where the amount you get is not guaranteed, and depends on the amount you invest and how your investment grows, is known as a money purchase pension. Money purchase pensions include personal and stakeholder pensions, group personal pensions and any employer's pension scheme with defined contributions (see page 234). All these schemes work in a similar way. Tax changes from 6 April 2006 will mean that broadly the same tax rules will apply to all money purchase schemes.

Stakeholder pensions

A stakeholder pension is just a personal pension that meets the following minimum standards:

- *Capped charges.* The charge for managing your fund cannot be more than 1.5% a year for the first ten years, and 1% after that.
- *Low minimums.* You must be allowed to pay in amounts as low as £20.
- *Flexible contributions.* Regular or one-off payments must be allowed, and there are no penalties if you miss a payment.
- *Transfers without penalty,* so that you can transfer your pension pot to another company if you want.

This means that stakeholder pensions are generally of reasonable value, although competition from them has encouraged companies to introduce better terms on their personal pensions. The disadvantage is that the choice of funds may be more restricted than for personal pensions, although this is unlikely to be a problem for most people. A useful feature is that stakeholder pensions must offer a 'lifestyling' option (see Jargon alert on page 54) from 6 April 2006 at the latest.

Drawing your pension benefits

You don't have to stop work to draw your benefits, provided you have reached the minimum age (see Timescale). But you do need to time things carefully in order to get the best value. This is because you have to use at least three-quarters of your pension to buy a pension income, and there are various ways of doing this:

- The least risky option is to buy a pension annuity (explained on page 129). The annuity pays out an income guaranteed for your life, and your partner's life if you wish, but it's a once-and-for-all decision – you cannot get your money back after you've bought. However, from 6 April 2006 you may be able to buy just a short-term annuity (lasting up to five years), leaving the rest of your money invested, or a 'value protected' annuity (this will return the cost of your annuity, minus tax and minus any income already received, if you die before age 75).
- Alternatively, you can withdraw income directly from your pension fund, leaving the rest of your fund invested (if your pension company doesn't offer this option, you may be able to transfer your fund to a company that does). But with this option you could run out of money if the investments in your fund fall in value or you live longer than expected. Because of this, the tax rules set a limit on the maximum you can withdraw each year, which is related to the amount you would have had from an annuity, and require you to have a regular review of your fund, which also puts the costs up.
- Some plans permit you to phase your retirement. They do this by splitting up your pension pot and putting it into a number of identical policies, so that you can draw your benefits over a number of years.

Until 6 April 2006, you must buy an annuity once you reach age 75. If you reach 75 after that date, and have put off buying an annuity, you will be able to withdraw income instead of buying an annuity (this is called an alternatively secured pension). But the maximum you can withdraw will fall to only 70% of what you could have had with an annuity.

The cost of an annuity has increased greatly in recent years, partly because of improvements in life expectancy. You may want to delay buying an annuity in the hope that the cost will fall, but you could be caught out if life expectancy continues to improve. A further consideration is your family. You cannot inherit an annuity, although you can buy guaranteed annuities that return part of your fund if you die early. If you have not bought an annuity, and instead are withdrawing income, your family can inherit the rest of your fund (minus tax) and carry on drawing an income from it.

It depends on the size of your pension pot and whether you have other sources of retirement income. You should consider income withdrawal only if your fund is large (over £100,000, say) or if you have other sources of retirement income. See the leaflets available from the Financial Services Authority and take advice from a specialist pensions adviser.

Trade secret

Increasing the value of your pension

Any income from a pension is taxable, whether you take it in the form of an annuity or income withdrawal. This means that you should check if you could get a better overall income by taking the maximum tax-free lump sum from your pension pot, even if you just invest it in a non-pension annuity. Part of the income from a non-pension annuity is tax-free. You can also boost your retirement income by shopping around for your annuity – you do not have to buy it from the pension company. Current rates for pension annuities are shown in the comparative tables on the FSA website.

Trade secret

Very small pension funds

If you have a very small pension fund, you can take it all as a lump sum. Currently 'small' means that it would buy you benefits of less than £260 a year, but from 6 April 2006 if your total pension fund, from all schemes, is less than £15,000, and you are aged at least 60, you can take it all in cash. One-quarter of the cash is tax-free, and the rest is taxed as income.

Rates and charges

You can make regular monthly or annual contributions, or pay lump sums whenever you want. The minimum contribution can vary from £10 for some stakeholder plans up to several hundred pounds, or £1,000 upwards for non-stakeholder lump-sum plans. However, you need to pay in a reasonable amount to get a reasonable income in retirement (see Chapter 7).

With older plans, you may be charged if you have agreed to pay regular contributions and want to vary the amount. Such charges are not common with plans on the market now. However, unless you need the discipline of regular saving, there is nothing to be lost by only committing yourself to paying irregular lump sums. If you do choose a regular premium policy, you can pay extra for a waiver of premium option, which means that the insurer will keep the plan going in certain circumstances, such as disability.

Also bear in mind the charges for administering the pension and investing your money. The same sorts of charges are made as for life insurance policies (see page 204). Charges vary widely. According to the FSA's comparative tables in August 2005, the charges deducted from a policy for a 45-year-old, investing £100 a month for 20 years, could amount to between £5,000 and £13,000 over the whole period, depending on the company and assuming the investment grows by 7% a year.

Jargon alert

Retirement annuity contracts

These were the forerunner of personal pensions, which were available until 1 July 1988. They work in the same way as personal pensions, but the tax rules are slightly different (although the differences will disappear from April 2006). The minimum age at which you can draw a pension is usually 60, and you get tax relief only if you are a taxpayer.

How to buy

You do not have to buy from just one company – you can spread your money among several. You can find companies that offer personal or stakeholder pensions, and details of their schemes, in the FSA's comparative tables.

Also a few industries and the TUC have collective stakeholder schemes that anybody in that industry or union can join.

Pension companies may not be prepared to provide more than basic advice on stakeholder pensions. To help you decide whether this sort of pension is suitable for you, the FSA has a stakeholder pension 'decision tree', available either on its website or its consumer helpline. If you decide that you need advice, consider paying a fee for independent advice (see Chapter 5) and check that the adviser has specialist qualifications such as the G60 pensions exam.

Tax treatment

- Basic-rate tax relief of 22% is paid into your plan by the government. This works out at a further 28 pence for each £1 that you contribute (£1.28 × 22% = 28p). You get this whether or not you are a taxpayer and the pension company claims it for you automatically.

- If you pay higher-rate tax (set at 40% in 2005–06), you can also claim further tax relief of 40% − 22% = 18%, either on your tax return or by contacting your tax office. The tax relief will be given either through your tax code (if you have income from a job or pension) or by adjusting your tax payments.

- In the 2005–06 tax year, the overall maximum you can pay into personal and stakeholder pensions is the higher of:
  - £2,808 (the government adds tax relief that brings this up to £3,600);
  - a percentage of your taxable earnings, provided that you are not also in an employer's pension scheme. The percentage is before tax relief, so you would actually hand over a bit less. The maximum earnings that can be taken into account are £105,600, but you can base your contributions on earnings of any of the previous five tax years if this would allow you to pay more. The percentage is:

Age on 6 April 2005	% of earnings
35 or less	17.5
36–45	20
46–50	25
51–55	30
56–60	35
61–74	40

- From 6 April 2006, you will be able to pay the whole of your earnings into pensions (or up to £2,808 if your earnings are less than this) and still get tax relief on your contributions, provided that:
  - the value of all your contributions to any type of pension, plus your increased benefits, is not more than £215,000 in the 2006–07 tax year, and
  - the amount of total pension savings over your whole lifetime (including personal and employers' pensions) does not exceed the lifetime allowance, set at £1.5 million for the 2006–07 tax year. You should get regular statements of what your pension fund is worth.
- You can contribute more, but you will not get tax relief on any contributions over these limits.
- If you pay into a plan for someone else, the contributions count against their contributions limit not yours, so you can pay the maximum into your own plan and still make contributions to theirs.
- You can take up to a quarter of your pension in the form of a tax-free lump sum (up to a maximum of £375,000 from 6 April 2006).
- The rest of any income, whether it is taken in the form of an annuity or as income withdrawals, is taxable in the same way as income from a job. Tax will usually be deducted under PAYE.

Alternatives to consider

- Before you take out a personal pension, check whether your employer has a scheme into which it pays contributions. If so, you should usually join it (see page 230).
- If you are worried about committing yourself to a pension, consider an investment like an ISA. But you won't get tax relief on the money you pay into an ISA.

Property

Property you invest in can be either commercial – shops, offices and factories – or residential, such as your own home or one you let out. ❗

Good for
■ Diversifying your risk away from stockmarket-linked investments, by having some money in property.

Bad for
■ Small investors – it is not easy to buy into property in a low-risk and low-cost way.

Risk factors
■ Direct investment in property is not regulated. Property funds run by a UK life insurance company, unit trust or OEIC are regulated by the Financial Services Authority (FSA), but there is no compensation if you lose money because your investment falls in value, unless you were advised to invest and the advice was unsuitable.
■ Property values are vulnerable to an economic turndown.
■ Property may not be readily saleable. Property funds may also have restrictions on when you can get at your money. You may have to wait for a set period (with unit trusts, up to six months) to cash in your investment.
■ If you borrow to buy, changes in interest rates will affect your return. You are also exposed to gearing, which means that any potential increases or falls in the value of your property are magnified (see page 147). The same applies if you invest through a property fund that has large borrowings.
■ Investing through a property fund is less risky than direct investment, but funds may still be medium to high risk, depending on what they invest in, the spread of companies or properties in the funds and whether they are permitted to borrow.
■ Some equity release schemes that allow you to raise cash from your home are regulated by the FSA, and the rest will be, but from a date yet to be decided.

Timescale

Property is a long-term investment. If the housing market slumps, you may only be able to sell at a loss, if at all. When the housing market fell in 1989, the average house price fell by one-fifth and did not get back to earlier levels until 1998. Similarly, the commercial property market slumped in the early 1990s and did not recover until the mid-1990s.

How it works

Property is an attractive investment to investors, because it provides a useful counterbalance to share-based investment. For example, since the stockmarket fell in 2000, commercial property has risen at an average rate of about 10% a year. However, this is an average: some types of property, such as offices, rose by much less. A big problem is the amount of money needed to buy property, whether commercial or residential, and the relatively high costs of buying and selling. This makes it difficult to spread your risk across more than one property.

The main routes for the private investor into property are:

- buy to let (see page 144)
- bonds that don't invest directly in property, but tie your return to the growth in a property index – these are only occasionally available (see page 174)
- buying shares in a property company listed on the stock exchange – but shares in these generally move in line with the stockmarket rather than with property prices (see page 279 for more on share investment)
- pooling your money with other people by investing through a property fund, or through a private company, partnership or syndicate formed specially to buy commercial property
- buying your own home.

> ## Trade secret

Beware the property scammers
Property training courses are a common con. Would-be investors attend a free presentation and are persuaded to join an expensive course. They are then encouraged to pay thousands of pounds to join a property investment service of dubious value run by the scammers. A variation is a buy-to-let scheme where companies offer to source, renovate and manage properties, claiming good returns from rental income. In practice, the properties are near-derelict – if they exist at all – and the tenants are non-existent.

Pooling your money

A property fund may be set up as an insurance policy (see page 196), a unit trust, an OEIC or an investment trust (see pages 287 and 189). Private companies, partnerships and syndicates are not available off-the-shelf but may be put together by specialist financial advisers for wealthy investors. The government is also considering the introduction of a new form of Real Estate Investment Trust (REIT) that it hopes will make it easier for private individuals to invest in property.

Property funds do not avoid all the problems, and the managers of smaller funds have similar difficulties to private investors in spreading their risk across lots of properties. The fund may buy properties directly, or buy shares in property companies, or put part of the money into shares or bonds in other companies. You need to check exactly what you are buying into and whether there is an appropriate spread of investments.

Property companies, partnerships and investment trusts are allowed to borrow to buy property, which increases the risk.

Your home as an investment

A lot of people have all their wealth tied up in their homes and the problem is then getting it out without having to move. Options are:

- letting part of your home – the income can be tax-free, within limits
- developing or selling off part of your property – it's important to get

professional advice on how to do this, and you may have to pay capital gains tax on the gain
- trading down to a cheaper property in order to release cash
- equity release schemes, where you either sell or mortgage part of your home in return for a lump sum or income. You have the right to remain in the property for the rest of your life.

Equity release is a useful last resort, but tread carefully. It can be expensive and you may lose part or all of any rise in the value of your home. Once you are in a scheme you cannot easily get out of it, if at all. There are other drawbacks – for example, extra income may mean that you lose means-tested state benefits. Age Concern and the FSA both have useful leaflets.

Jargon alert

Equity and equities
Equity can mean several things, but in financial circles it is usually taken to mean your share of the ownership of a particular asset. So your equity in your home is the amount of the value that belongs to you, after deducting any mortgage. An equity is also often used to mean a share in a company, so shares are often called equities.

Rates and charges
If you invest through a property fund, you will have to pay the manager's fees, usually consisting of an initial fee and an annual charge. Charges are usually more expensive than for some less specialised funds. The minimum investment in a property fund is anything from £500 upwards, but it will cost £10,000 or more to buy into a partnership investing directly in commercial property.

How to buy
The simplest ways to invest in commercial property are to buy property unit trusts (or OEICs) or life insurance unit-linked bonds. Once your money is in an insurance bond, you can choose from a range of funds, and most

companies have a property fund. Details of property unit trusts are available from the Investment Management Association, but currently there are only a few available.

If you want to invest in anything other than a unit trust or insurance bond, you will need to have large sums at your disposal and a good appetite for risk. You should seek advice from one of the specialist independent financial advisers dealing in this area. Remember to check their expertise, such as any relevant qualifications.

Tax treatment

- With direct investment in property, as well as the normal property taxes you may be liable to income tax on the rents and capital gains tax on any profits when you sell (see page 64). However, capital gains tax is only payable if your total profits from all assets exceed a certain limit (£8,500 in 2005–06), and profits on your main home are usually exempt.
- With property funds, it depends on how the fund is structured. See Table 6.1 on page 99 for the major differences in tax treatment between the different types.
- If you invest by buying shares in a property company, you are liable to income tax on the dividends and capital gains tax on any profit when you sell the shares. Income from a property partnership is taxed as business income.
- You can hold commercial property in your own self-invested personal pension (SIPP), and from April 2006 it will be possible to hold residential property in a SIPP (see page 276).

Alternatives to consider

- See Buy to let on page 144.
- There is no true equivalent to property as a class of investment, but if you are willing to take a risk in the hope of capital gain, you should consider stockmarket-linked investments.

Savings accounts

In return for depositing your money with a bank, building society, or other account-provider, you will be paid interest, with minimal risk to the amount you deposited.

Good for
■ An essential starting point for your savings.
■ Easy access accounts or interest-paying current accounts are a convenient way to accumulate enough spare cash to transfer to a longer-term home for your money.
■ Safety – you should always get your money back unless the organisation goes bust.

Bad for
■ If the interest rate is lower than the rate of inflation, the purchasing power of your savings will not keep up with rising prices. You must be prepared to keep an eye on interest rates and move to a better account if necessary.
■ Easy access accounts require some discipline to encourage you not to spend your savings.

Risk factors
■ Savers are entitled to fair and reasonable treatment under the Banking Code, but this is a voluntary code and not all banks and building societies subscribe.
■ Accounts may tempt punters in with high interest rates (so-called honeymoon rates) and later drop them to an uncompetitive level. Under the Banking Code, if you have a variable-rate savings account containing more than £250, the organisation must tell you if the interest rate drops by 0.5% or more during a year, compared with the Bank of England base rate, and give you a chance to move your money without penalty. If you don't feel that these terms have been met, or you have been treated unfairly, complain (see Chapter 2).
■ If a UK-authorised firm with which you have a savings account goes bust, you get full compensation from the Financial Services

Compensation Scheme for only the first £2,000, and 90% compensation for the next £33,000. If you have more savings, you might want to spread them among several firms.

■ If you open a savings account with an overseas firm (including firms in the Channel Islands and Isle of Man), you are not covered by the Financial Services Compensation Scheme or the Financial Ombudsman Service. But it is not always clear where an organisation is based, particularly for internet accounts. Always check the small print to see whether you have rights to a compensation or complaints-handling scheme. Remember that fake websites do exist – the FSA website has a section on how to spot them.

■ To stop cheque fraud, if you are depositing money by post, write on the cheque the name of the person whose account you want it to go into, for example XYZ Building Society, J. Smith.

Timescale

Savings accounts range from instant access to a five-year term.

How they work

A bank or building society may have as many 20 different accounts to choose from, and to make it more difficult they do not necessarily categorise their accounts under similar names. Also the distinctions between some categories are breaking down – for example, there may be restrictions on withdrawals even from a no-notice account. So too are the distinctions between the sorts of organisations that offer interest-paying deposit accounts, with life insurance companies, mortgage brokers and even supermarkets now muscling in on the territory traditionally occupied only by banks and building societies.

To help you make sense of the choices open to you, the table overleaf provides a spotter's guide to the sorts of accounts available, with the accounts that are easiest to get your money out of listed at the top. (See also Chapter 6 for guidance on choosing a savings account.)

Typical features of bank and building society accounts

Type of account	Typical names	Opening restrictions	Withdrawals	Interest
Interest-paying current account	High-interest cheque account; internet account	No minimum deposit for some accounts, otherwise a minimum such as £1,000 a month, or a minimum salary	May be through a chequebook, debit card or by transfer to another account; usually no restrictions, but may not offer full range of services, e.g. no automatic overdraft facility	Variable; taxable
No-notice account	Instant access; easy access; deposit; share account	Minimum deposit of £1 to several thousand pounds	None, but may be a limited number of withdrawals	Variable; taxable
Cash ISA (see page 183)	Mini cash ISA	Minimum deposit often £1, but may be up to £3,000	May be on demand or notice account; may be charges if transferred	Fixed or variable; tax-free
Notice account	60 day; 90 day	Minimum deposit £100 to several thousand pounds	Need to give notice to get your money back, usually 30–120 days; can withdraw earlier with a penalty of the equivalent number of days	Usually variable; taxable

Type of account	Typical names	Opening restrictions	Withdrawals	Interest
Term account	Bond	Minimum deposit anything from £1 to several thousand pounds	Account lasts for set term (6 months–5 years) or until a set date; early withdrawals may not be possible; if permitted, penalties are steep	Usually fixed; taxable
Deposit-based stockmarket bond (see page 172)	Guaranteed, investment-linked	Minimum usually several thousand pounds	Usually a 5-year term; penalties for early withdrawal or may not be possible	Depends on performance of linked investment; taxable
Child Trust Fund (see page 150)	–	Only for children born after 31 August 2002, but other people can contribute (minimum £10)	Only child can withdraw money, and only when reaches age 18	Usually variable; tax-free

Jargon alert

Base rate

The base rate is the minimum rate at which a bank will lend money. The Bank of England is responsible for setting its own base rate at the level it thinks necessary to meet the government's economic aims. Other banks take this as a cue for changing their own rates, including the rate payable on savings accounts.

Jargon alert

Stakeholder accounts

Stakeholder accounts must meet certain minimum standards, laid down by the government, which are designed to make them reasonable value. They replace the CAT-mark standards that worked in a similar way up to April 2005. Stakeholder accounts must:

- pay interest at a rate not more than 1% below the Bank of England base rate (explained on page 267)
- accept minimum payments of no more than £10
- pay out your money within seven days, if you want to withdraw or transfer it.

Running your account

Before you can choose an account, you will need to decide how you want to run it: in a branch, using a passbook or card, or by phone, post or internet. Several banks also have current accounts that pay better interest than run-of-the-mill savings accounts. These used to be called high-interest cheque accounts (HICAs) and have a chequebook, but these are being superseded by other accounts, particularly internet-based accounts, which may offer a debit card but not a cheque book.

Non-branch-based accounts generally pay the best interest rates, but with an internet or telephone account you will need to be either computer-literate or comfortable using telephone keypads, and, above all, capable of remembering security questions and personal identification numbers (PINs). If you find this difficult, but don't need access to a branch, a postal account may suit you better, although security checks will still be necessary if you need to phone for any reason. Alternatively, a few organisations have now reintroduced passbook accounts with high interest for some types of customer (such as pensioners).

If your account is not branch-based, you need some way of withdrawing cash. If a cash withdrawal card is not offered (and some accounts pay more if you are happy not to have one), you will have to request a cheque. Alternatively, some non-branch-based accounts ask you to set up a direct debit between the account and a current account – this does not mean a regular transfer of money (as it would if you were paying a electricity bill), but that money can be transferred between accounts on your instructions.

Another option is to link your current account with your mortgage, through an offset mortgage. This way any spare cash automatically reduces your mortgage balance, effectively earning you interest at the mortgage interest rate (see page 31).

Restrictions on withdrawals

The general rule used to be that the more restricted your access, the better was the interest rate. However, these days notice accounts rarely offer a better interest rate than the best no-notice accounts. But some restrictions on withdrawals are creeping into no-notice accounts, in particular limits on the number of withdrawals in a year. There are other restrictions to watch out for:

- No notice does not necessarily mean instant access. Even with a branch-based account, it can take as much as 14 days after paying in a cheque before it is cleared so that you can withdraw money against it. There may also be restrictions on the amount of cash you can withdraw, or the size of cheque, without prior notice, so check first if you want (say) a cheque to buy a car.
- With a notice account, check whether you have to give notice to close the account. Sometimes the requirement to give notice applies for only a fixed period, after which you can get your money on demand, but otherwise you may have to give notice to close the account without penalty.
- Act promptly at the end of a term or notice account. There may be a narrow window of time during which you can get your money out without penalty, after which your money is automatically reinvested in another notice or term account.

Fixed-rate deals

In return for agreeing to tie your money up for a set term – anything from six months to five years, or until a set date – you may get a higher interest rate which is usually fixed.

Fixed rates are attractive if you think that interest rates are on their way down, but if you get it wrong you could find that you are trapped in the account, because you may not be able to get your money out until maturity. Even if some withdrawals are allowed, there are usually steep penalties – for example, a loss of interest which would cancel out the advantage of the high interest rate. Some accounts require you to give notice and pay a penalty.

Fixed rate deals are often available for only a short period, so you need to act quickly if you see a good deal. But given the penalties on withdrawal, it is best not to tie your money up for more than three years.

Monthly income

A few accounts are marketed as monthly income accounts, but many other types of account have a monthly interest option. The interest is automatically paid out to a nominated bank or building society account. However, because you get the benefit of the interest earlier than if it were paid annually (see Jargon alert), the interest rate is usually a bit lower than for annual interest. There may also be a higher minimum deposit.

Jargon alert

The annual equivalent rate or AER

You may notice an 'AER' shown in ads for savings accounts. This refers to the annual equivalent rate, which takes into account not only the interest rate but also how often it is paid (the compounding; see page 23). Normally, bank and building society accounts pay interest annually. This means that you get interest for each day the money is in the account, and at the end of the year the interest is added to the amount on which interest is calculated. So after a year, you get interest on the interest.

If the interest is paid just once a year, the AER will be the same as the gross (before-tax) rate. If the same interest rate is paid more frequently (e.g. monthly), the AER will be higher – for example, an interest rate of 4.65% paid monthly has an AER of 4.75%.

Regular savings

A few accounts are marketed as specifically for regular savings, and recently some have been launched with excellent interest rates. However, you may have to commit yourself to making a set number of deposits each year (usually by standing order), there may be restrictions on withdrawals and one-off deposits may not be permitted. You will be less restricted if you simply set up a standing order into a best-buy savings account. If you really need discipline to save, choose an account that doesn't let you take your money out too easily.

Children's accounts

Your choice of account will depend on whether you are seeking to:

- build up long-term savings for a child
- open a 'pocket money' account for the child's own savings (although you will have to sign for a child who is below a certain age, which depends on the organisation but is usually seven or ten in England and Wales).

For a child's own savings, many banks and building societies offer special accounts with low minimum investments and, sometimes, incentives such as magazines and free offers. Alternatively, some organisations simply offer higher rates on their standard range of accounts. Your choice may be dictated by how near a branch is, but beware: although some accounts offer excellent interest rates for children, other branch-based accounts have shockingly low rates. Some accounts offer a cash card for older children (which cannot be used to overdraw).

Whichever account you choose, make sure you complete form R85 so that interest is paid out before tax (see page 274).

If you are interested in saving for a child, see Chapter 7 for various options. See also Child Trust Funds on page 150, and for children aged at least 16, ISAs on page 183.

Joint accounts

If you want to open a joint account, you will need to tell the organisation, on the application form, whether just one or both of you needs to sign for withdrawals. Some accounts, however, can be opened only on the basis that just one of you needs to sign. If the account is not branch-based, ask how the security checks will be set up, for example whether you will each need separate passwords.

For income tax purposes (but not inheritance tax), the money is jointly owned by you, regardless of who actually supplied the funds. If the account is set up so that only one person's signature is needed for withdrawals, and one of you dies, the account will stay open and all the money in it automatically passes to the survivor. Similarly, if you fall out with the other account holder, you cannot prevent them from drawing all the cash from the account. Get in touch with the account provider quickly, as they may be able to change it so that both of you need to sign for withdrawals. Alternatively, they may freeze the account.

Note that the rules in Scotland will depend on how the account is set up and may differ from those described here. For more information about this, and joint accounts in general, see the British Bankers' Association leaflet *You and your joint account*. Also see Chapter 7 for more on investing as a couple.

Jargon alert

Carpetbagging

This is the rather dismissive name given to people who join a mutual institution such as a building society in the hope of a payout if the organisation is floated on the stockmarket, taken over or merged. Considerable amounts were paid out in this way in the past, but these days most institutions have effectively put a stop to the practice by changing their rules for new members so that, for example, any payouts will go to charity. This does not affect the rights of long-term members, so if you have an account with full membership rights think twice before closing it.

Rates and charges

The interest you get on your account will depend on bank base rates (see Jargon alert on page 267). For fixed-rate deals, the rates also depend on how financial organisations expect rates to move in future. So if they expect base rates to rise, you are likely to get a better deal than if they expect rates to fall. However, rates also depend on the competition and the tactics the organisation is pursuing (see Trade secret on page 93).

Always check the AER (see Jargon alert on page 270), which tells you the true rate of return on your investment. If the AER is lower than the headline interest rates, for example, it suggests that a short-term bonus is being used to make the rate look better than it really is.

How to buy

It is straightforward to buy a savings account direct from your chosen bank or building society. Savings accounts are also covered in the comparative tables on the Financial Services Authority's website. For tips on choosing a savings account, see Chapter 6.

If you decide that you have made a mistake in opening a particular account, the Banking Code gives you a 14-day cooling off period, during which you can withdraw without penalty. Note that this does not apply to fixed-rate accounts.

Jargon alert

Money laundering checks

Financial organisations have a legal requirement to check a customer's identity to protect against criminal and terrorist activity, such as money laundering (recycling money received from the proceeds of crime so that the criminal can safely use it later). However, the law does not set down a rigid list of what you must provide. Each organisation will have its own list, but industry guidelines suggest a wide range of documents that could be accepted as evidence of your identity and address. Organisations should be flexible. If you are having difficulties, ask if a letter from someone like a teacher, doctor or religious leader will be acceptable, and if you feel that the person you are speaking to is being unreasonable, ask to speak to someone higher up the organisation.

Tax treatment

- Savings accounts within an ISA or Child Trust Fund pay tax-free interest. Other savings accounts pay out interest which has normally had tax deducted at 20%. If you are a basic-rate taxpayer, you will have no further tax to pay. If you are a higher-rate taxpayer, you will have a further 20% tax to pay (either through PAYE on your earnings or through your tax return), which will bring the total tax up to 40%. After the end of the tax year, you may receive a statement of interest received which you can use to fill in your tax return; otherwise you will need to consult your statements.

- If you are a non-taxpayer you can claim to have the interest paid out before tax, or claim a rebate if tax has already been deducted. Ask the bank or building society for form R85. You are a non-taxpayer if the savings interest plus all your other taxable income comes to less than £4,895 in the tax year (£7,090 if you are aged 65 or more, £7,220 if you are aged 75 or more). Note, though, that if you have a joint account, the other person must also be a non-taxpayer for interest to be paid out before tax, unless the bank or building society agrees to pay half the interest before tax.

- You can also claim tax back if you should pay some tax but not as much as has been deducted, for example if your top rate of tax is only 10% (the starting rate). Ask your tax office or phone the Revenue's Taxback helpline.

- If you save in an offshore savings account (including one in the Channel Islands or Isle of Man), UK tax will not be deducted. But the income is still taxable in the UK and must be declared to HM Revenue & Customs. However, you can get a credit against your UK tax for any overseas tax paid.

- Savings accounts are not liable to capital gains tax (unless, in some circumstances, you received a lump sum when the organisation was taken over or floated on the stock exchange).

Alternatives to consider

- The main alternatives are offered by National Savings & Investments (see page 219) but you could also consider a credit union (covered on page 160) if you are eligible to join one, or are interested in setting one up.

- If your main need is for income, see Chapter 7.
- When interest rates are low, some investment-linked products may be marketed as alternatives to savings accounts, for example corporate bonds and guaranteed stockmarket bonds (see pages 154 and 172). However, some of these can be risky and you must be sure what you are getting into before buying.

Self-invested personal pensions (SIPPs)

A personal pension wrapper which allows you to hold and control a wide range of investments within your pension plan. ❶

Good for
- People who are sure that they need and will use the investment freedom offered by a SIPP.
- People who are interested in making income withdrawals from a substantial pension fund, rather than buying an annuity.
- Families – any funds left in your SIPP when you die can be used by other family members who belong to the SIPP, although there may be a tax charge.

Bad for
- Cost – this can be higher than for an off-the-shelf stakeholder pension or personal pension plan, although cut-price on-line deals are available.
- People with small pension funds – you need to be sure that the costs don't outweigh the benefits.
- Anybody who isn't fully confident that they know what they're doing.

Risk factors
- You can hold a wide range of investments in your SIPP. If you choose the wrong investments – or your investment manager or adviser does – you could lose your retirement savings. If you decide to take decisions without advice, you have no comeback for poor decisions.
- If you borrow to buy something you hold in your SIPP, your investment is geared. See page 147 for how this can increase your risk.
- Forthcoming tax changes mean that the SIPPs market is changing rapidly. Further tax changes cannot be ruled out, so make sure you have up-to-date information.
- Everyone now appears to be jumping on the SIPPs bandwagon. Make sure that any adviser you use really knows their stuff – look for specialist pensions qualifications.
- The service you are buying may or may not be regulated by the Financial

Services Authority, depending on whether you are paying for regulated investment advice or just the administration of your SIPP. Check the legal position carefully, and in particular whether you will have access to a compensation scheme or the Financial Ombudsman Service.

Timescale

This is a long-term investment. You cannot get your money out until you draw your pension benefits, and then there are limitations on how you can draw them. The rules are the same as for personal pensions (see page 257).

How they work

A SIPP is just a personal pension. But instead of having to invest through the pension fund of a life insurance company, you can choose a wide range of investments to sit inside your SIPP wrapper. As well as investments such as stocks and shares and unit trusts, you can buy commercial property such as farmland or business premises. From 6 April 2006, the investment choice will be widened still further, and you will also be able to buy residential property through your SIPP.

The ability to include property makes SIPPs particularly interesting to small businesses and, from April 2006, buy-to-let landlords (see page 144). Another important feature of SIPPs is that they are allowed to borrow to buy property (within limits).

Other people can be members of your SIPP (your children, say). If you die without having spent all the money in your fund, any remaining funds can be used to benefit them, although there may be a tax charge.

Rates

A SIPP may cost more than a standard personal pension. You have to pay someone to set up and administer your SIPP wrapper – this might cost a few hundred pounds each year. Once your SIPP is set up, you have to pay the administrator to buy and sell the investments and property held in it. Check how these transaction costs compare and whether you qualify for any discounts – for example, a reduction in the initial charge on investment funds. Cut-price deals are available, often online, but again you should check exactly what the service covers.

Unless you are confident of being able to take your own decisions, you also need to take the cost of advice into account (see Chapter 5).

How to buy

SIPPs are offered by some insurance companies, financial advisers, firms of actuaries and stockbrokers. There is a SIPP Providers Group (see the Fact file), but this does not include financial advisers.

Tax treatment

■ This is the same as for personal pensions (see page 257).

Alternatives to consider

■ A personal or stakeholder pension.

Shares

Investing directly in company shares, rather than through an investment fund. ❗

Good for
- The chance of a capital gain. If you strike lucky, you could make a lot of money. You also get income in the form of dividends.
- People who are interested in investing as a hobby, particularly if they are happy to use the internet.

Bad for
- People with only small amounts of money to invest. Because of the costs of buying and selling, it is not economic to invest less than about £1,000 or £1,500 in each company, and you should invest in a spread of companies to reduce the risks.
- Novice investors. Only venture into shares when you have the rest of your finances sorted out and a sound basis of less risky investments.

Risk factors
- The performance of your shares cannot be predicted. You may get back less than you put in or even end up with worthless shares.
- There is a huge range of companies to invest in. You need to do enough research to find sound companies, or use an investment manager (see Chapter 5).
- If you invest in an overseas company or a UK company with overseas interests, the value of your shares may be affected by changes in exchange rates.
- Shares owned directly are not regulated in the same way as most other investments. Unless you invest on the recommendation of an authorised financial adviser, you are not covered by the Financial Services Compensation Scheme if the company goes out of business or the Financial Ombudsman Service if you have a complaint. But companies quoted on the Stock Exchange must comply with listing rules that require them to meet certain standards, such as making accurate information accessible to all investors.

Timescale

You should be prepared to keep your investment for a minimum of 5–10 years. In theory, you can sell shares at any time, but if you are forced to sell at a bad time you may make a loss. The ability to sell may also be suspended at certain points, for example during takeover bids. Active traders may buy and sell much more frequently, but remember that every time you sell you incur costs.

How they work

So far this book has focused on investing in the stockmarket through an investment fund, but you can of course buy shares in a company directly. As a shareholder, you become a part-owner of the company. You get a share in the company's earnings, paid out as dividends (usually twice a year), and if you are lucky, you will be able to sell your shares for more than you paid for them, producing a capital gain. Unless your shares are in a nominee account (see Jargon alert on page 282), you also have the right to attend and vote at the company's annual general meeting.

You can buy shares in individual companies through a wrapper, such as a self-select stocks and shares ISA (see page 183), a SIPP (see page 276) or an investment trust savings scheme (see page 189).

Choosing a company

There are three types of company in which an investor might consider buying shares:

- *Private companies.* These cannot offer their shares to the general public, but some entrepreneurial investors (known as business angels) actively seek out private companies with strong growth prospects, and there are tax incentives for doing so (see the Enterprise Investment Scheme on page 163). You may also be given shares in a private company that employs you. In either case, it may not be easy to sell your shares – it's up to you to find a buyer.
- *Public companies.* Certain minimum conditions must be met before these companies can offer their shares to the public. The problem of matching people who want to sell their shares with willing buyers is

solved by 'listing' or 'quoting' the company on a stock exchange. This means that share prices are published and you can easily buy and sell through a stockbroker. The main exchange is the London Stock Exchange, which also runs the Alternative Investment Market (AIM) for smaller, growing companies. You can also buy shares listed on overseas stockmarkets, although many major foreign companies are listed on the London Stock Exchange.

■ *Investment companies*. Quoted companies that are set up to buy and sell the shares of other companies – a type of investment fund. (See Investment trusts on page 189.)

In most cases companies issue ordinary shares, but there are other types – for example, preference shares normally pay fixed interest and have preferential rights to payment of dividends and capital, but limited voting rights. Shares are issued at a nominal value – 10p per share, for example – and that is the price you will see on the share certificate, but once the shares are issued the price will float up and down in line with demand.

Quoted companies are divided into a number of sectors, including construction, retailing, software, small companies or large blue-chip companies. You should aim to invest in a number of companies in a number of sectors, in case one does badly. Investors use various different methods for picking individual companies, none of which is foolproof. Some look at the fundamentals of the business, as revealed by the company accounts, others look at charts of a company's share price to see if any patterns emerge. But all methods depend on getting accurate and up-to-date information.

Newspapers cover financial stories and give share prices, but if you are serious about share investment it is worth getting on the internet. Do be careful to check the source of any information, though – right from the birth of stock exchanges people have tried to rig the market by planting misleading rumours (see Trade secret on page 39). ifsProShare, an organisation that supports wider share ownership, has many useful factsheets, including one listing reputable websites.

Owning shares

In the past, once you bought shares you received a share certificate and your name was listed on the company's share register. However, following the introduction of the London Stock Exchange's electronic dealing service, CREST, you have three options. You can:

- hold on to your certificates
- hold your shares in paperless form, in a nominee account (see Jargon alert)
- become a personal member of CREST (which costs £10 a year). Your name appears on the register, and you continue to receive documentation from the company. Some stockbrokers can organise this for you, but shares held like this cannot be kept in an ISA.

Jargon alert

Nominee accounts

Firms that offer a share-dealing service also usually offer a nominee account. A nominee is a specialist company that holds stocks and shares on your behalf. You still own the shares, but you don't get a share certificate and the nominee's name is on the share register, not yours. This means that you lose the right to vote at company meetings and you do not get the company's annual report and accounts (although some nominees will supply them, and in practice they are easy to get hold of through free annual report services offered by financial publications and the London Stock Exchange). You may not get the perks that some companies offer their shareholders (such as discounts on the company's products) – it depends on the company.

However, there are advantages to using a nominee. If you lose a share certificate, you have to get a replacement from the share registrar (for which there is a charge) before you can sell the shares. Without a certificate, it is much quicker to transfer the shares, and it is also cheaper. Most of the cheap share-dealing services require you to open a nominee account with them before you can trade.

For a small fee, you can transfer shares you already own into a nominee account, so you have them all in one place. You will get regular statements of your account.

Check whether there are any extra charges for the service. Some are free, but others charge a regular fee (£12 a quarter, say), which may come to more than the money saved in cheaper dealing fees. Also check how often dividends will be sent and what insurance is in place to cover any losses (nominees are regulated by the Financial Services Authority).

Jargon alert

The spread

Stockbrokers quote two prices for the same share. The price you pay to buy a share is called the offer price; the price you get when you sell is called the bid price. The bid price is always lower than the offer price, and the difference is called the spread. Before you can make any profit, your share has to grow by more than the spread plus other costs (see below), so it is more difficult to make a profit from a share with a wide spread.

The spread is kept by the market-maker – the wholesaler to whom stockbrokers pass on their orders for execution and who sets the price. When a share is popular, the spread may be small, because the market-maker's costs are low; when demand falls, the spread widens. Other factors may also affect the spread.

Note that just one price, a mid-price, is quoted in newspapers.

Share clubs

You can invest in a wider range of companies if you pool your resources with friends and family and start up a share club. Members pay in, say, £25 a month each and have regular meetings to decide where to invest. You do need to set up a club properly, and ProShare Investment Clubs has a special support service. It sells a manual with draft documentation for £25 plus postage.

Rates and charges

Before you can make any profit from your shares, the price has to rise by enough to cover:

- the spread (see Jargon alert)
- dealing charges – these vary significantly, and don't forget that you pay twice, when you buy and when you sell. The smaller the value of the 'trade', the higher the fee, with traditional stockbrokers charging, say, 1.65% of the value of the deal for deals up to £2,500, and 1.25% for deals up to £5,000, and there will be a minimum fee of, say, £25. Online services are much cheaper (the table overleaf shows typical costs)

- possible administration charges – for example, £50 a year to have your shares held in a nominee account. There may also be one-off charges for things like transferring your shares
- stamp duty, currently 0.5%, payable by the purchaser only
- on deals over £10,000 (currently), a £1 levy for the Panel on Takeovers and Mergers

Typical prices for share-dealing

Value of deal (£)	Online (£)[a]	Telephone (£)[a]	Share certificate sales (£)
Up to 2,500	11.95	£15	£30
2,501–5,000	11.95	£30	£50
5,001–10,000	11.95	£40	£75
Over 10,000	11.95	£60	£100

a Assumes shares are held in a nominee account.

How to buy and sell

You need to buy and sell through a stockbroker. The Association of Private Client Investment Managers has a directory of members (see the Fact file) but most high-street financial organisations also have share-dealing services. You can deal by post or over the telephone, but there are many cut-price internet trading services as well.

The cheapest share-dealing services are execution-only and do not give advice on which shares to buy or sell. If you want advice, you will need an advisory service; and if you want to delegate all the decision-making, a discretionary service allows your stockbroker to buy and sell on your behalf without consulting you. See Chapter 5 for more information on the types of investment management services available.

Generally, shares must be paid for within three days of the deal, and stockbrokers (including internet services) may require you to open an account and deposit some money before you can buy through them. Give yourself time to set up an account and prove your identity (this may be required to deter money-laundering; see Jargon alert on page 273). The minimum deposit ranges from £100 to £1,000; it earns interest, but you should check how much. If you just want to sell a few shares for which you have share certificates, a telephone or postal service should allow you to do so straightaway without opening an account, but payment may take ten days (see Trade secret).

Some internet share-dealing services offer real-time trading while the stockmarket is open, so that you can buy and sell at the actual price you see on the screen. Otherwise the price quoted for the shares is only a guide: the actual transaction will go through at the price applying at the time. Some stockbrokers may allow you to set a limit on the price, requiring them to buy, say, only if the price is below a figure set by you. Otherwise, once you have confirmed your acceptance of the price, you are bound to buy or sell, and you cannot change your mind.

After the transaction has gone through, you will receive a contract note setting out the details – it is important to keep this for tax purposes. If you are selling shares for which you have a certificate, you must get this to the stockbroker within the time stated on the contract note, usually three days but sometimes ten days.

Trade secret

How to get rid of unwanted shares

Many people don't actively seek to become shareholders. Shares may be acquired through an employee share scheme, privatisation, demutualisation (see page 170) or inheritance. The problem is that you can end up with an unbalanced set of shares. If you decide that they are not a suitable long-term investment for you, then look for a good time to sell (and get ready to do so by setting up a share-dealing account).

If you have shares that you no longer want, whatever their value, you can donate them to charity. Many charities will accept shares and make no charge for selling them, for example Sharegift (see the Fact file). Your gift will qualify for tax relief (see HM Revenue & Customs leaflet IR178 *Giving land, buildings, shares and securities to charity*).

Alternatively, if you decide that direct ownership of shares is not for you but you still want a stockmarket-linked investment, many fund management companies offer share exchange schemes where you can swap your shares for an investment in their fund, on preferential terms.

Tax treatment

- Dividends are paid with a tax credit of 10%. You cannot reclaim this, even if you are a non-taxpayer and even if the shares are held in an ISA. There is no further tax to pay if you are a basic-rate taxpayer. Higher-rate taxpayers will have to pay extra tax unless the shares are held in an ISA (see page 183).
- Any gain you make when you sell your shares is liable to capital gains tax if your total gains for the year exceed the tax-free amount (£8,500 in the 2005–06 tax year). But there is no capital gains tax if the shares are held in an ISA.
- If you sell your shares at a loss, you can use the loss to reduce your taxable capital gains (see page 68), provided you tell the Revenue about the loss within five years and ten months of the end of the tax year in which it arose. But you cannot use losses in this way if they arise from shares held in an ISA.
- You must declare any taxable dividends or gains in your tax return. If you do not get a return, you must tell the Revenue that you have taxable amounts by 5 October after the end of the relevant tax year.

Alternatives to consider

- If you are interested in stockmarket investment but direct share ownership is impractical, consider an investment fund such as a unit trust or OEIC, or an investment trust.

Unit trusts and Open-ended Investment Companies (OEICs)

A way of pooling your money with other people to invest in stocks, shares and other investments. ❗

Good for

- Putting your money in a broad spread of investments with a possibility of capital growth, even if you have only modest amounts to invest.
- The value of your investment always reflects the value of the underlying investments held by the fund.
- Ease of purchase – you can buy and sell direct from the manager, or through a fund supermarket or other wrapper (see page 125).

Bad for

- Risk of high charges – so choose your fund with care. A high-charging fund has to perform very well in order to cover its costs.

Risk factors

- Like all stockmarket investments, the performance of unit trusts and OEICs cannot be predicted. You may get back less than you put in.
- If a fund is invested overseas, its value may be affected by changes in exchange rates.
- If you have money in an insolvent UK unit trust or OEIC, you get limited protection from the Financial Services Compensation Scheme (see Chapter 2).
- You can usually complain to the Financial Ombudsman Service if you were advised to buy a unit trust or OEIC that was unsuitable for you.

Timescale

You should be prepared to keep your investment for a minimum of 5–10 years. In theory, you can cash in your units at any time, but if you are forced to do so at a bad time you may make a loss. However, guaranteed and protected trusts restrict your ability to cash in, and property funds may reserve the right to do so if the fund is doing exceptionally badly.

How they work

Unit trusts are a type of investment fund where you pool your money with other investors. The unit trust fund manager then invests in shares, corporate bonds, British Government stock and other stockmarket-linked investments. A few funds also invest in property.

The fund is divided up into units. Your money buys you a certain number of units, which then rise or fall in value in line with the value of the investments in the fund. You can usually cash in your investment at any time, by selling your units back to the fund manager. You can opt to get an income from the fund, called a distribution — how often this is paid out depends on the fund.

Open-ended investment companies, or OEICs, work in a similar way except that they are technically companies and you buy shares in them, not units. Whereas each unit trust fund is separate, OEICs have several sub-funds within the one company. OEICs, which are relatively new, were introduced because investment companies in Europe are structured this way. Some unit trusts have been converted into OEICs, so the information about unit trusts applies equally to OEICs. (See Jargon alert for a definition of open-ended.)

You have a wide choice of funds to invest in, and you can switch between funds. There is more about investment funds in Chapter 6.

You can hold unit trusts and OEICs in an ISA (see page 183) or SIPP (page 276).

Jargon alert

Hedge funds

Hedge funds are private investment funds, usually set up overseas, that aim to exploit ups and downs in various stockmarkets in order to produce a high overall return. However, there is no guarantee that the fund managers will be able to achieve their aims. Other disadvantages are high charges, and the fact that they are complex and largely unregulated. 'Funds of hedge funds' have been introduced, but these may be even more expensive.

Jargon alert

Open-ended or closed-end?

A closed-end fund, such as an investment trust (see page 189), has a fixed number of shares in issue at any one time. If you want to invest, you have to buy a share from another investor. This means that the share price reflects the shares' popularity, not just the value of the underlying investments.

With an open-ended fund, such as a unit trust fund or OEIC, the fund manager can create more units to reflect investor demand. The fund is valued on a daily basis, and the price of the new units is the value of the investments in the fund divided by the number of units in existence. If you want to sell, you do not have to find a buyer. The manager must buy the units from you, even if this means selling some of the fund's investments. And whatever the fund's popularity, the unit price always reflects the value of the underlying investments.

Jargon alert

Exchange Traded Funds (ETFs)

These are open-ended funds, quoted on the London Stock Exchange, that track the performance of a particular stockmarket index. As such they are alternatives to an index-tracking unit trust. The great attraction is the cost: there is no initial charge and the annual management fee ranges from 0.2% to 0.75%. However, because they are shares their price changes throughout the day and you have to buy them through a stockbroker (although they can be bought cheaply through an investment trust savings scheme and some fund supermarkets). These are early days for ETFs in this country, but they are very popular in the USA.

Jargon alert

Single-pricing

Traditionally, unit trusts and unit-linked insurance funds are dual-priced. They have separate prices for buying and selling – you pay more when you buy (the offer price) than you get when you sell (the bid price). The difference between the two is called the spread, which includes the initial charge. OEICs, however, have a single price, and you pay the initial charge on top (so-called single-pricing). These days, single-pricing is regarded as being clearer; some unit trusts have already moved over to the new system.

Rates and charges

Before you can make any profit from your investment, it has to rise in value by enough to cover:

- the initial charge (which covers the cost of setting up your investment and an adviser's commission), say 5%, although it can be more or less. This may be included in the price you pay, or charged on top of the price, depending on whether the fund is single-priced or not (see Jargon alert). A few fund management companies have low initial charges, and instead make an exit or redemption charge when you cash in your investment. The charge reduces the longer you hold your investment, and is usually nil after five years
- the annual management charge, deducted from the value of your investment, normally 1–1.5% (but occasionally more), of which part usually goes to your adviser as 'trail' commission. The total expense ratio (TER) is a measure of a fund's annual costs (see page 106)
- other costs deducted from the value of the fund, such as auditors' fees and the cost of buying and selling the fund's investments. You won't be told what these amount to, but some are reflected in the TER
- any separate charges for advice or portfolio management.

Specialist funds, such as those investing in less accessible overseas markets or property funds, are likely to have the highest charges. However, managers of popular funds may also put their charges up. Their argument is that high charges may be outweighed by good performance. But there is a great deal of research to suggest that good performance in the past is not necessarily repeated.

Conversely, fund managers may offer a discount to push new funds.

> Trade secret

Beware of performance fees

A few funds base their annual charges on the performance of their fund – for example, a fund may raise its fee to 2% if it is in the top 25% of funds in its sector for 12 months, but otherwise charge 1.25%. Take all such offers with a big pinch of salt, as they may cream off some of the extra performance when things are going well, without really costing the manager much when things go badly. After all, 1.25% is not cheap.

How to buy

You can buy direct from the fund manager. However, it is usually cheaper to buy from a discount broker (see Chapter 5) or fund supermarket (see page 125) that will waive part or all of the initial charge.

You can invest lump sums of a few hundred pounds (different funds have different minimum contribution levels), but many fund management companies offer regular savings schemes with monthly subscriptions as low as £20, though £50 is more typical.

To help you choose a fund, the Investment Management Association has a free directory of funds and a useful 'Find a fund' service on its website. But there are many internet sites that give information about investment funds, including analysts' ratings (see Chapter 6).

Note that the unit price is worked out by valuing the fund each day, and with most funds your sale or purchase will go through at the price applying at the next valuation point. This means that you cannot be sure of the amount you will get when you sell. Most unit trust prices are published in newspapers and are widely available on the internet, but you can also ask the fund management company for the current value of your investment.

Tax treatment

- Funds that are invested in shares pay income in the form of dividend distributions. These are paid with a tax credit of 10%. You cannot reclaim this, even if you are a non-taxpayer and even if the investment is held in an ISA. There is no further tax to pay if you are a basic-rate taxpayer. Higher-rate taxpayers will have to pay extra tax unless the unit trusts are held in an ISA (see page 183).

- Funds that are invested in things that pay interest, such as government stocks or corporate bonds, pay interest distributions. These come with 20% tax deducted. You can claim this back if you are a non-taxpayer or starting-rate taxpayer, but higher-rate taxpayers have a further 20% to pay. However, if the unit trusts are held in an ISA, there is no tax to pay, and the ISA manager will claim the tax back on your behalf.

- Any gain you make when you sell is liable to capital gains tax if your total gains for the year exceed the tax-free amount (£8,500 in the 2005–06 tax year). But there is no capital gains tax if the investment is held in an ISA.

- If you sell for a loss, you can use the loss to reduce your taxable capital gains (see page 68), provided you tell the Revenue about the loss within five years and ten months of the end of the tax year in which it arose. But you cannot use losses in this way if they arise from unit trusts held in an ISA.

- You must declare any taxable income or gains in your tax return. If you do not get a return, you must tell the Revenue that you have taxable amounts by 5 October after the end of the relevant tax year.

Alternatives to consider

- If you are interested in stockmarket investments, insurance bonds, investment trusts and Exchange Traded Funds (see page 289) are the major alternatives.

- If you are nervous about investing in the stockmarket, stockmarket-linked bonds or protected funds may be offered as an alternative (but see page 172 for why these may not be such a good deal).

Fact file

How will your savings grow?

Table 1 shows how much an initial deposit of £100 will be worth after each year if you receive interest at various rates. Remember that this assumes you pay no tax on the interest – a 5% rate of interest would be worth only 4% to you if you were a basic-rate taxpayer, 3% if you were a higher-rate taxpayer.

Table 1: How a deposit of £100 might grow[a]

| Value of £100 after year | Annual rate of interest (%) | | | | | |
	2.5	5	7.5	10	12.5	15
1	102.50	105.00	107.50	110.00	112.50	115.00
2	105.06	110.25	115.56	121.00	126.56	132.25
3	107.69	115.76	124.23	133.10	142.38	152.09
4	110	122	134	146	160	175
5	113	128	144	161	180	201
6	116	134	154	177	203	231
7	119	141	166	195	228	266
8	122	148	178	214	257	306
9	125	155	192	236	289	352
10	128	163	206	259	325	405
11	131	171	222	285	365	465
12	134	180	238	314	411	535
13	138	189	256	345	462	615
14	141	198	275	380	520	708
15	145	208	296	418	585	814
16	148	218	318	459	658	936
17	152	229	342	505	741	1,076
18	156	241	368	556	833	1,238
19	160	253	395	612	937	1,423
20	164	265	425	673	1,055	1,637
21	168	279	457	740	1,186	1,882
22	172	293	491	814	1,335	2,164
23	176	307	528	895	1,501	2,489
24	181	323	567	985	1,689	2,863
25	185	339	610	1,083	1,900	3,292

a Rounded to whole numbers from year 4.

The effect of inflation

Table 2 shows how much £100 will be worth, in terms of its purchasing power, at the end of each year if inflation runs at various rates. You can also use Table 1 to find how much £100 needs to grow in order to match inflation – £100 will need to grow to £163 to match ten years of inflation at 5%.

Table 2: Purchasing power of £100

Value of £100 after year	Annual rate of inflation (%)					
	2.5	5	7.5	10	12.5	15
1	97.56	95.24	93.02	90.91	88.89	86.96
2	95.18	90.70	86.53	82.64	79.01	75.61
3	92.86	86.38	80.50	75.13	70.23	65.75
4	90.60	82.27	74.88	68.30	62.43	57.18
5	88.39	78.35	69.66	62.09	55.49	49.72
6	86.23	74.62	64.80	56.45	49.33	43.23
7	84.13	71.07	60.28	51.32	43.85	37.59
8	82.07	67.68	56.07	46.65	38.97	32.69
9	80.07	64.46	52.16	42.41	34.64	28.43
10	78.12	61.39	48.52	38.55	30.79	24.72
11	76.21	58.47	45.13	35.05	27.37	21.49
12	74.36	55.68	41.99	31.86	24.33	18.69
13	72.54	53.03	39.06	28.97	21.63	16.25
14	70.77	50.51	36.33	26.33	19.22	14.13
15	69.05	48.10	33.80	23.94	17.09	12.29
16	67.36	45.81	31.44	21.76	15.19	10.69
17	65.72	43.63	29.25	19.78	13.50	9.29
18	64.12	41.55	27.20	17.99	12.00	8.08
19	62.55	39.57	25.31	16.35	10.67	7.03
20	61.03	37.69	23.54	14.86	9.48	6.11
21	59.54	35.89	21.90	13.51	8.43	5.31
22	58.09	34.18	20.37	12.28	7.49	4.62
23	56.67	32.56	18.95	11.17	6.66	4.02
24	55.29	31.01	17.63	10.15	5.92	3.49
25	53.94	29.53	16.40	9.23	5.26	3.04

Useful addresses

Age Concern England
Astral House
1268 London Road
London SW16 4ER
Tel: 0800 009966
www.ace.org.uk

Age Concern Scotland
Causewayside House
160 Causewayside
Edinburgh EH9 1PR
Tel: 0845 8330200
www.ageconcernscotland.org.uk

Age Concern Northern Ireland
3 Lower Crescent
Belfast BT7 1NR
Tel: 028 9024 5729
www.ageconcernni.org

Age Concern Cymru (Wales)
13–14 Neptune Court
Vanguard Way
Cardiff CF24 5PJ
Tel: 029 2043 1555
www.accymru.org.uk

**Association of British Credit
   Unions Ltd (ABCUL)**
Holyoake House
Hanover Street
Manchester M60 0AS
Tel: 0161 832 3694
www.abcul.coop

Association of British Insurers
51 Gresham Street
London EC2V 7HQ
Tel: 020 7600 3333
www.abi.org.uk
www.pensioncalculator.org.uk

**Association of Consulting
   Actuaries**
Warnford Court
29 Throgmorton Street
London EC2N 2AT
Tel: 020 7382 4594
www.aca.org.uk

**Association of Investment
   Trust Companies**
9th Floor, 24 Chiswell Street
London EC1Y 4YY
Tel: 020 7282 5555
www.aitc.co.uk

**Association of Policy Market
   Makers**
The Holywell Centre
1 Phipp Street
London EC2A 4PS
Tel: 020 7739 3949
www.apmm.org

**Association of Private Client
   Investment Managers and
   Stockbrokers (APCIMS)**
114 Middlesex Street
London E1 7JH
Tel: 020 7247 7080
www.apcims.co.uk

**The Association of Residential
   Letting Agents (ARLA)**
Maple House
53–55 Woodside Road
Amersham
Bucks HP6 6AA
Tel: 0845 3455752
www.arla.co.uk

**Association of Solicitors and
   Investment Managers**
Riverside House
River Lawn Road
Tonbridge
Kent TN9 1EP
Tel: 01732 783548
www.asim.org.uk

**The Banking Code Standards
   Board**
6 Frederick's Place
London EC2R 8BT
Tel: 0845 2309694
www.bankingcode.org.uk

British Bankers Association
Pinners Hall
105–108 Old Broad Street
London EC2N 1EX
Tel: 020 7216 8909
www.bba.org.uk

Building Societies Association
3 Savile Row
London W1S 3PB
Tel: 020 7437 0655
www.bsa.org.uk

Computershare
PO Box 2411
The Pavilions
Bridgwater Road
Bristol BS3 9WX
Tel: 0870 7030143
www.computershare.com/uk/
   investor/gilts

**Consumer Credit Counselling
   Service**
Wade House
Merrion Centre
Leeds LS2 8NG
Tel: 0800 1381111
www.cccs.co.uk

Council of Mortgage Lenders
3 Savile Row,
London W1S 3PB
Tel: 020 7437 0075
www.cml.org.uk

Ethical Investment Association
c/o UKSIF (see below)
www.ethicalinvestment.org.uk

**Ethical Investment Research
Service (EIRIS)**
80–84 Bondway
London SW8 1SF
Tel: 020 7840 5700
www.eiris.org.uk

Financial Services Authority
The Financial Services Authority
25 The North Colonnade
Canary Wharf
London E14 5HS
Tel: 020 7066 1000
www.fsa.gov.uk/consumerhelp
www.pensioncalculator.org.uk
Consumer helpline: 0845 6061234
Endowment mortgage
    publications: 0845 4561555
Firm Check service: phone
    the FSA consumer helpline
    or see www.fsa.gov.uk/
    firmcheckservice/index.html
Misleading ads hotline:
    0845 7300168

**Financial Services
    Compensation Scheme**
7th Floor, Lloyds Chambers
1 Portsoken Street
London E1 8BN
Tel: 020 7892 7300
www.fscs.org.uk

Financial Ombudsman Service
South Quay Plaza
183 Marsh Wall
London E14 9SR
Consumer helpline: 0845 0801800
www.financial-ombudsman.org.uk

Help the Aged
207–221 Pentonville Road
London N1 9UZ
Tel: 020 7278 1114
Seniorline: 0808 800 6565
www.helptheaged.org.uk

Help the Aged Cymru (Wales)
12 Cathedral Road
Cardiff CF11 9LJ
Tel: 029 2034 6550
Email:
    infocymru@helptheaged.org.uk

Help the Aged Scotland
11 Granton Square
Edinburgh EH5 1HX
Tel: 0131 5516331
Email:
    infoscot@helptheaged.org.uk

**Help the Aged Northern
    Ireland**
Ascot House
Shaftesbury Square
Belfast BT2 7DB
Tel: 028 9023 0666
Email: infoni@helptheaged.org.uk

HM Revenue & Customs (HMRC)
(formerly **Inland Revenue**)
Child Trust Fund helpline: 0845 3021470
Taxback helpline: 0845 0776543

IFACare
37–38 The Old Woodyard
Hagley Hall
Hagley DY9 9LQ
Tel: 01562 881888
www.ifacare.co.uk

IFA Promotion
Tel: 0800 0853250
www.unbiased.co.uk

ifsProShare
6th Floor
100 Cannon Street
London EC4N 6EU
Tel: 020 7444 7101
www.ifsproshare.org

Institute of Financial Planning
Whitefriars Centre
Lewins Mead
Bristol BS1 2NT
Tel: 0117 945 2470
www.financialplanning.org.uk

Institute of Islamic Banking and Insurance
16 Grosvenor Crescent
London SW1X 7EP
Tel: 020 7245 0404
www.islamic-banking.com

Investment Management Association
65 Kingsway
London WC2B 6TD
Tel: 0207 269 4639
www.investmentfunds.org.uk

London Stock Exchange
10 Paternoster Square
London EC4M 7LS
Tel: 020 7797 1000
www.londonstockexchange.com

Money Advice Trust
Bridge House
181 Queen Victoria Street
London EC4V 4DZ
Tel: 020 7489 7796
www.moneyadvicetrust.org

The National Approved Letting Scheme
Tavistock House
5 Rodney Road
Cheltenham GL50 1HX
Tel: 01242 581712
www.nalscheme.co.uk

The National Association of Estate Agents
Arbon House
21 Jury Street
Warwick CV34 4EH
Tel: 01926 496800
www.naea.co.uk

National Debtline
The Arch
48–52 Floodgate Street
Birmingham B5 5SL
Tel: 0808 8084000
www.nationaldebtline.co.uk

National Savings & Investments
Tel: 0845 9645000
www.nationalsavings.org.uk

One Plus One Marriage and Partnership Research
The Wells
7–15 Rosebery Avenue
London EC1R 4SP
Tel: 020 7841 3660
Information line: 020 7841 3672
www.oneplusone.org.uk

The Pensions Advisory Service (TPAS)
11 Belgrave Road
London SW1V 1RB
Tel: 0845 6012923
www.pensionsadvisoryservice.org.
uk

Pension Protection Fund
Knollys House
17 Addiscombe Road
Croydon CR0 6SR
Tel: 0845 6002541
www.pensionprotectionfund.org.
uk

The Pensions Ombudsman
11 Belgrave Road
London SW1V 1RB
Telephone: 020 7834 9144
www.pensions-ombudsman.org.uk

The Pensions Regulator
Napier House
Trafalgar Place
Brighton BN1 4DW
Tel: 0870 6063636
www.thepensionsregulator.gov.uk

The Pension Service
There is a nationwide network of
pension centres. Look under
Pension Service in the phone
book (or the Social Security
Agency in Northern Ireland).
Pension Credit: 0800 991234
www.thepensionservice.gov.uk
Pension Credit NI: 0808 1006165
www.dsdni.gov.uk

State Pension Forecasting Team
Future Pension Centre
The Pension Service
Tyneview Park
Whitley Road
Newcastle upon Tyne NE98 1BA
Tel: 0845 3000168
www.thepensionservice.gov.uk/
    atoz/atozdetailed/forecast.asp

Pension Tracing Service
The Pension Service
Tyneview Park
Whitley Road
Newcastle upon Tyne NE98 1BA
Tel: 0845 6002537
www.thepensionservice.
    gov.uk/atoz/atozdetailed/
    pensiontracing.asp

The Personal Finance Society
20 Aldermanbury
London EC2V 7HY
Tel: 020 8530 0852
www.thepfs.org.uk

ProShare Investment Clubs
3rd Floor, 8–11 Lime Street
London EC3M 7AA
www.proshareclubs.co.uk

**Royal Institution of Chartered
  Surveyors**
RICS Contact Centre
Surveyor Court
Westwood Way
Coventry CV4 8JE
Tel: 0870 333 1600
www.rics.org

ShareGift
5 Lower Grosvenor Place
London SW1W 0EJ
Tel: 020 7337 0501
www.sharegift.org.uk

TUC
Congress House
Great Russell Street
London WC1B 3LS
Tel: 020 7636 4030
www.tuc.org.uk
For TUC guides to your rights at
  work:
www.worksmart.org.uk

**The United Kingdom Debt
  Management Office**
Eastcheap Court
11 Philpot Lane
London EC3M 8UD
Tel: 020 7862 6500
www.dmo.gov.uk

UK Social Investment Forum
Unit 203
Hatton Square Business Centre
16 Baldwins Gardens
London EC1N 7RJ
Tel: 020 7405 0040
www.investability.org

The Unclaimed Assets Register
Bain House
16 Connaught Place
London W2 2ES
Tel: 0870 2411713
www.uar.co.uk

Which?
2 Marylebone Road
London NW1 4DF
Tel: 0845 3074000
www.which.net/endowmentaction

Index